*Women's Intercultural Performance* explores contemporary feminist performance in the contexts of current intercultural practices, theories, and debates. It is the first in-depth examination of contemporary intercultural performance by women around the world.

In this study, Holledge and Tompkins raise major questions about the relationship between politics and aesthetics, the transmission of culturally specific identity spaces, the sexually and culturally differentiated female body in performance, and the commodification of this body within the global marketplace. In analysing these questions the book draws on material from the early years of the twentieth century to the 1990s and from the work of artists in many countries – Ghana, South Africa, Algeria, Iran, Great Britain, Argentina, Canada, Australia, China, Japan, and Korea.

While this study is still predicated on the existence of cultural and sexual borders, it acknowledges that these borders are constantly shifting. *Women's Intercultural Performance* is a fascinating analysis of cultural production and exchange and is essential reading for anyone studying or interested in women's performance.

**Julie Holledge** is Professor of Drama and Director of the Drama Centre at the Flinders University of South Australia. She is the author of *Innocent Flowers: Women in Edwardian Theatre* and has worked in the theatre as a director, actor, and dramaturg.

**Joanne Tompkins** teaches at the University of Queensland. She is a co-editor of *Modern Drama* and has published on postcolonial, multicultural, and intercultural theatre. She is the co-author of *Post-colonial Drama* with Helen Gilbert.

University of Chester, Seaborne Library

Title: Women's intercultural performance /
Julie Holledge.
ID: 01140275
Due: 26-02-16

Title: Contemporary feminist theatres : to
each her own / Lizbeth Goodman
ID: 01015590
Due: 26-02-16

Total items: 2
05/02/2016 11:34

Renew online at:
http://libcat.chester.ac.uk/patroninfo

Thank you for using Self Check

3

# Women's Intercultural Performance

Julie Holledge and
Joanne Tompkins

London and New York

First published 2000
by Routledge
11 New Fetter Lane, London EC4P 4EE

Simultaneously published in the USA and Canada
by Routledge
29 West 35th Street, New York, NY 10001

*Routledge is an imprint of the Taylor & Francis Group*

Typeset in Bembo by Florence Production Ltd, Stoodleigh, Devon
Printed and bound in Great Britain by T.J. International Ltd, Padstow, Cornwall

*British Library Cataloguing in Publication Data*
A catalogue record for this book is available from the British Library

*Library of Congress Cataloguing in Publication Data*
Holledge, Julie
Women's intercultural performance / Julie Holledge and Joanne Tompkins.
p. cm.
Includes bibliographical references and index.
1. Women in the performing arts. 2. Rites and ceremonies.
3. Intercultural communication. I. Tompkins, Joanne. II. Title.

PN1590.W64 H65 2000
791'.082–dc21
                                        99–089005

ISBN 0–415–17378–7 (hbk)
ISBN 0–415–17379–5 (pbk)

# Contents

# Plates

# Acknowledgements

Various funding bodies have provided us with the means to complete this project. We are indebted to the Australian Research Council, University of Queensland New Staff Grant fund, and the Research Committee of the Faculty of Education, Humanities, Theology and Law at Flinders University. We would also like to acknowledge the colleagues in our respective departments for their support throughout the project.

We have been particularly fortunate to have had such a talented and culturally diverse group of research assistants, including Monica Farias, Marilie Fernandez, Mary Ann Hunter, Rebecca Lawson, Li Jiaojiao, Jane McGrory, Yoko Nemoto, Anne Thompson, and Christine Watson. Particularly warm thanks go to Tseen Khoo, Adele Chynoweth, Alice Parkinson, and Anna Johnston.

A project as broad as this inevitably requires assistance with translation from a variety of languages, namely Japanese, Mandarin, Spanish, Korean, Warlpiri, Tagalog, and French. In addition to the research assistants who worked on this project, we would like to thank the following professional translators: Sabina Chang, Emiko Mayer, Jennifer Hargreaves Nampijinpa, Kay Ross Napaljarri, and Elizabeth Ross Nungarrayi.

Others who provided various types of adminstrative help include Kate Ferry, Noel Ferry, Michael Harries of the Yuendumu School, Jackie Hayvice, Annette Henderson, Li Ying Ning, and Carmel O'Shannessey of the Lajamanu School.

We would like to thank the following people for providing us with feedback and/or assistance at various points in the project: Frances Bonner, Lynne Bradley, Rustom Bharucha, Lee Cataldi, Hyun Chang, Catherine Fenn, John Frow, Miriam Lo, Sue Magarey, Nima Naghibi, Paul Newman, Dimitri

Poulos, Suh Kwang Seok, Sue Sheridan, Peta Tait, and Chong Zhou.

Practitioners, artists, and arts administrators who have assisted us include: Michiko Aoki, Robyn Archer, Australian Performing Arts (APA), Rob Brookman, Venetia Gillot, Nicholas Heyward, Kim Kum hwa, Mary Moore, Ian Scobie, and Tomiko Takai.

Finally, we would like to thank Talia Rodgers for being a marvellously supportive and insightful editor, and Mary Moore and Alan Lawson for catering and comic relief.

The authors and publishers would like to thank the following for permission to reproduce copyright material: Waseda University Theatre Library for Plates 1 and 2; Ross Terrill for Plate 3; Dariush Mehrjui and Hashem Seifi for Plate 4; Lucila Quieto for Plate 5; Clara Rosson for Plate 6; Lisa Tomasetti and the Third International Women Playwrights' Conference for Plate 7; Kate Ferry and Dolly Daniels Nampijinpa for Plate 8; Venetia Gillot for Plate 9; Mary Moore for Plate 10; Takarazuka Revue for Plate 11; David Wilson for Plate 12; Fabienne Sallin for Plate 13; and the Adelaide Festival for Plate 14.

# Introduction
## Culture, feminism, theatre

Culture as product, thing, substance is culture disembodied from experience. It is culture neutralized and turned into objects of consumption.

(Friedman 1994a: vi)

Interculturalism could be viewed as a 'two-way street', based on a mutual reciprocity of needs. But in actuality, where it is the West that extends its domination to cultural matters, this 'two-way street' could be more accurately described as a 'dead-end'.

(Bharucha 1993: 2)

It is not a matter of finding common elements among the texts written or produced by women and defining them in terms of a presumed femaleness or femininity, which, to my mind, is highly suspect of sexual metaphysics; rather, it is our task to envision a feminist theory of the process of textual production and consumption, which is of course inseparable from a theory of culture.

(de Lauretis 1987: 92)

Intercultural theatre projects that originate in the west tend to focus on aesthetics first and politics second, almost as an afterthought or superficially. Interculturalism all too frequently is perceived to become 'political' only when a critic complains about (mis)representations of otherness or appropriations of culture. Feminist theatre, meanwhile, usually operates in reverse: the political imperative that underpins feminism – women's equality to men – is the starting point for feminist performance. When women produce intercultural theatre, they frequently begin from the point where cultures meet to speak about women. In the following pages we explore numerous examples in which intercultural performance by women is refracted through culture and gender, or how the self meets the other (in terms of both gender and culture) in theatre.

The ways in which interculturalism assumes a significant role in both local and global cultural interactions are frequently paradoxical. In fact, paradoxes and oppositions abound in interculturalism. We begin our analysis by locating ourselves among these sometimes oppositional terms. Our own positions as two women living in Australia mirror the global/local paradox: any sense of an unproblematic cultural connection to Australia, the country in which we live, is impossible for both of us, living and working in a culture that is comparable to our birth cultures, but not quite our own: we share a language, dominant race, and basic understanding of feminism with the culture in which we live, but our work finds us interacting more and more with people from other cultures. Our access to any fixed sense of identity is compromised by the actuality of our migrations to Australia. Our western backgrounds (English and Canadian, respectively) fix us as economically privileged, relative to many non-western cultures. Our heritages have been variously inflected by the latent effects of imperialism. Yet our impulse is to find intersecting points within the national identities which we can claim – even tangentially – rather than assuming an overarching globalist position which risks accepting automatic membership to numerous cultures at the expense of acknowledging cultural difference.

In its current form in the late twentieth century, intercultural performance has emerged principally from the practice of western artists, in particular the practice of performing well beyond the borders of their own countries. It is complicit with a postmodern licence to borrow theatrical techniques from different cultures (both in the west and beyond) within a western defined global and theatre practice. We find ourselves able to engage with the underpinnings to these practices *and* able to deploy some of the very cogent arguments that critics of these practices have developed from outside the west. Rather than an attempt to sit on both sides of the metaphorical fence, this insider/outsider position reflects the multi-dimensional locations that culture, interculturalism, gender, identity, and performance now inhabit.

This study introduces many of the important debates in the development and consumption of women's intercultural performance work, a subject that has been sadly neglected in critical work on interculturalism and performance generally. We do not provide a singular definitive model of interculturalism or of women's intercultural performance because such a model would risk assuming too many similarities among cultures and theatrical practices, and ignoring too many of the crucial local differences. Instead, we provide ways of thinking about and analysing contemporary performance and, particularly, representations of the performing, female, culturally marked body. While our principal focus is on intercultural performance, we are also aware that contemporary theatre tends to deploy various postcolonial, intercultural, and feminist performance theories, and that critics and audiences alike are seeking more politically astute ways to read contemporary theatre. This book aims to produce politically and culturally inflected reading strategies for contemporary performance.

Given the multiplicitous influences on theatre and culture generally, we find it useful to unravel some of the specific theoretical strands and the political/cultural considerations that shape contemporary performance: culture, feminism, and theatre all operate as mechanisms that define and contest (often simultaneously) self, identity, representation, and context. Among its functions, theatre in the west helps to make culture intelligible. Phillip Zarrilli explains that 'performance as a mode of cultural action is not a simple reflection of some essentialized, fixed attributes of a static monolithic culture but an arena for the constant process of renegotiating experiences and meanings that constitute culture' (Zarrilli 1992: 16). In western societies, theatre can be defined as that practice which removes culture from its flow, isolates an aspect of it, packages it, and sells it back to the community. Just as theatre acts as a mechanism for making culture intelligible in the west, each culture has a mechanism for making *another* culture intelligible. This intelligibility is frequently achieved by consuming the 'other' as an attempt to understand it, own it, and/or control it. Theatre artists frequently try to represent or configure on stage what is outside their own identity space (the global) not in terms of homogeneity but in terms of a *clashing* of ethnoscapes and the global/local relationship. The *specificity* of both one's own perception of the 'local' and the other's 'local' becomes important in this context. There are very few critical mechanisms for analysing this representation of the other's culture on stage. To that end, we apply Zarrilli's dynamic model of culture and cultural performance, enabling us to analyse the constant renegotiation of the shifting definitions of culture.

## CULTURE

Culture is frequently associated with nationalism, yet efforts to configure the world in terms of a *global* culture continue to dominate western discourses. Postmodernism often tends to draw on cultures and histories without concern for previously demarcated boundaries. Many companies advertise their products as bringing the world together or making the world smaller in a contemporary adaptation of Marshall McLuhan's global village. The success of this discourse is compromised, however, by the continued influence of ethnic imperatives or 'ethnoscapes' – to employ Arjun Appadurai's expression in a more specific context (Appadurai 1990: 296). Partly in an attempt to bridge the divide that has emerged in the latter half of the twentieth century between globalism and nationalism,[1] Appadurai developed five 'scapes' – ethnoscapes, mediascapes, technoscapes, finanscapes, and ideoscapes (ibid.: 296) – which act as formative social, cultural, and political structures. The importance of ethnoscapes points to the continuing significance of culture, even in a global climate that frequently purports to have transcended any need for cultural difference.

Of course, culture is not an isolated concept or an empty sign waiting to be filled by that which we deem 'intelligible'. Culture has a context as well, which Clifford Geertz's 'thick description' makes clear.[2] Culture is located in the construction of the self (or the subject position) and in the context for that self. Culture is, of course, always more than just the national cuisine and costumed folk dance that are frequently used to represent it: culture is the way in which we understand our own identities and the means through which we encounter other cultures. Any understanding of culture is inevitably refracted through one's own experiences, or 'identity spaces', to use Jonathan Friedman's phrase. For Friedman,

> culture is about the products of a more complex and specific substrate of cathected identity spaces embedded in hierarchical processes of socialization. Identity spaces . . . are about the construction of selfhood and worldhood. The two are aspects of the same process.
>
> (Friedman 1994a: 76)

One of the major unifying strands of our argument in this study is the complex and shifting nature of identity spaces accessed through performance.

Part of the complexity associated with identity spaces results from the fact that identity formation does not remain fixed: as Stuart Hall explains, 'identities are never completed, never finished; . . . they are always as subjectivity itself is, in process' (Hall 1991b: 47). This constant re-negotiation of identity and identity spaces is central to this study. One of the basic and formative components of identity space for the performers in this study is, of course, gender.

## FEMINISM

Like culture, feminism as a discourse is based on and in western experience and makes our world intelligible to us as western women; this feminist methodology – or ideology – is not necessarily transferable to other cultures, but most other cultures have ways of categorising according to sex.

Western feminist critique is, as Janelle Reinelt metaphorically explains, as integral to one's subject position as culture:

> since it is political and also deeply personal, it cannot be put on and taken off again like a critical coat every time the scholar goes calling on a new topic; it is rather more like a second skin, which goes everywhere.
>
> (Reinelt 1992: 227)

Paradoxically, this second skin has not been adequately considered in intercultural work, because intercultural performance's prestigious international profile has ensured that interculturalism has been a male-dominated field.

It is a truism in feminist theory now that there are many feminisms; but many women in non-western countries refuse the word altogether because of a perception that feminism is based on western women's activism and its tendency to essentialise women's experiences, forgetting the specific importance and place of history, culture, race, class, and politics. Chandra Mohanty (1991a: 7) claims that 'third world women have always engaged with feminism, even if the label has been rejected in a number of instances', and Rajeswari Sunder Rajan provides an example of such feminist work in India:

> The resistance of oppressed groups, including women, takes place on several levels of response, ranging from non-violent collective struggle, as in anti-dam and ecology struggles, to armed insurgency, as in several secessionist movements. The subjectivities of women, as victims of violence and agents of resistance, are constituted through the negotiations of these situations.
>
> (Sunder Rajan 1993: 6)

Both critics maintain the importance of specificity when referring to women from non-western regions, so as to avoid creating monolithic categories of a particular, culturally or geographically defined 'Woman'. As Mohanty explains,

> Western feminist discourse, by assuming women as a coherent, already constituted group which is placed in kinship, legal, and other structures, defines third world women as subjects *outside* social relations, instead of looking at the way women are constituted *through* these very structures.
>
> (Mohanty 1991b: 72)

The definition of feminism presents another problem for the texts that we address: not all the work that we discuss in this text is feminist according to understandings of western feminism. For instance, the theatre of the Japanese women's troupe, Takarazuka, which we discuss in Chapter 4, cannot be described as implicitly feminist in its politics and execution, even though it is created for the almost exclusive enjoyment of female audiences. Most of the companies or practitioners that we consider foreground women, even if the political underpinnings are not necessarily theoretically feminist according to the western definitional models. In order to address both the political problems of general terms like feminism and to acknowledge the variety of performance traditions in which women engage, we have adopted the use of 'women's intercultural performance' instead of 'feminist intercultural performance' as we analyse the ways in which women work *across* cultural boundaries.

## INTERCULTURALISM

[Interculturalism is characterised by] the tension between common goals and clashing cultures.

(Lampe 1993: 153)

Interculturalism is the meeting in the moment of performance of two or more cultural traditions, a temporary fusing of styles and/or techniques and/or cultures. Interculturalism is sometimes confused with theatre anthropology which analyses another culture's 'theatre' – or events which the anthropologist considers to be theatrical – without a sharing of traditions.[3] If every theatre collaboration can be fraught with difficulties (including personal interactions and production problems), intercultural collaboration also brings with it different expectations regarding culturally determined processes and the additional problems of working in translation (both the translation of different languages and theatre 'languages'). It is impossible to provide an elaborate 'recipe' of or for interculturalism because the nature of the interrelationship between cultures and between artists depends heavily on the individuals and the individual cultures concerned. It also depends on the encounter, the exchange, any financial contributions, and the complexities of mixing certain cultures. Some collaborations will work well, as Eelka Lampe documents regarding the intercultural collaboration between Anne Bogart and Tadashi Suzuki across American and Japanese cultures: the two practitioners 'plainly accept and respect their differences; they do not attempt to artificially merge their culturally and individually acquired styles and ethics, but have allowed themselves to take a risk and open up to a creative coexistence and learning experience' (Lampe 1993: 156). Much like a chemical explosion generated by two otherwise non-reactive substances, the nature of interculturalism is such that collaborations may not work despite all best intentions and good planning.

Interculturalism is, of course, hardly a recent phenomenon. It could be said to be inevitable as cultures attempt to define themselves by exploring their boundaries: once cultures push that exploration beyond their borders, they intersect and/or clash with other cultures. Antonin Artaud's use of Balinese techniques and Bertolt Brecht's forays into Chinese theatre traditions (to choose just two early examples) illustrate the ways in which elements of non-European theatre represented exotic devices for western stages.[4] The motivation of early interculturalists tended to vary greatly from those artists crossing cultures today: neither Artaud nor Brecht endeavoured to bring two (or more) types of theatre together. Rather, as modernists, they were interested in uncovering new traditions and theatrical languages to make artistic and/or political statements in the western theatre.

## Three intercultural models

We reiterate at this point that our aim in this study is not to provide a model of women's intercultural performance. We must, however, outline examples of existing models. The most general is Marvin Carlson's model, to which we broadly subscribe. Endeavouring to itemise the gradations of interculturalism, Carlson has developed a seven-step model of the 'possible relationships between the culturally familiar and the culturally foreign':[5]

1   The totally familiar tradition of regular performance.
2   Foreign elements assimilated into the tradition and absorbed by it. The audience can be interested, entertained, stimulated, but they are not challenged by the foreign material.
3   Entire foreign structures are made familiar instead of isolated elements. The Oriental *Macbeth* would be an example of this.
4   The foreign and familiar create a new blend, which then is assimilated into the tradition, becoming familiar.
5   The foreign itself becomes assimilated as a whole, becoming familiar. Examples would be *commedia dell'arte* in France or Italian opera in England.
6   Foreign elements remain foreign, used within familiar structures for *Verfremdung*, for shock value, or for exotic quotation. An example would be the Oriental dance sequences in the current [1990] production of *M. Butterfly* in New York.
7   An entire performance from another culture is imported or recreated, with no attempt to accommodate it with the familiar.

(Carlson 1990: 50)

Carlson's model acknowledges that there is a great deal of variance among intercultural activities. A successful intercultural project in which both cultures engage in an equitable exchange does not necessarily have to coincide with Carlson's fourth step.

If Carlson's definition of interculturalism is deliberately wide-ranging, Bonnie Marranca's formula for interculturalism is based on social commitment. She distinguishes between geo-political engagement: '[t]hose artists inclined toward formal experimentation and abstraction as a performance mode will draw closer to Japanese aesthetics. Others who declare themselves for a politically engaged, popular theater will emphasize Latin American, Indian, Southeast Asian, and African affiliations' (Marranca 1996: 213). While many projects are not as easily categorised as Marranca suggests, the 'aesthetic' opposition to the 'popular' theatre can provide one generic frame.

Patrice Pavis has pioneered a more extensive intercultural theory with his hourglass model of intercultural exchange:

(1) cultural modeling (*modélisations*), sociological, anthropological codification, etc.
(2) artistic modeling
(3) perspective of the adapters
(4) work of adaptation
(5) preparatory work by the actors, etc.
(6) choice of theatrical form
(7) theatrical representation/performance of culture
(8) reception-adapters
(9) readability
(10) reception in the target culture
   A. artistic modeling
   B. sociological and anthropological codification
   C. cultural modeling
(11) given and anticipated consequences

(Pavis 1992: 185)

Since the direction of this model pertains to only one of the collaborating cultures, the hourglass must be turned upside down, each of the two cultures taking a turn at being 'source' and 'target'. Pavis explains:

It is turned upside-down as soon as the users of a foreign culture ask themselves how they can communicate their own culture to another target culture . . . [and such turning enables cultures to] question once again every sedimentation, to flow indefinitely from one culture to the other.

(ibid.: 5)

He acknowledges the risks inherent in the hourglass:

> If it is only a mill, it will blend the source culture, destroy its every specificity and drop into the lower bowl an inert and deformed substance which will have lost its original modeling without being molded into that of the target culture. If it is only a funnel, it will indiscriminately absorb the initial substance without reshaping it through the series of filters or leaving any trace of the original matter.
>
> (ibid.: 5)[6]

Pavis's hourglass model accounts for most of the factors involved in the research, production, performance, and critical reception of intercultural theatre work, but, as he himself is all too aware, the use of the model is not foolproof.

## Chief criticisms of interculturalism

Interculturalism in the late twentieth century continues to be a theoretical, theatrical, and cultural minefield. The most celebrated theatre event which exemplifies this minefield, Peter Brook's marathon performance, *The Mahabharata* (1985), based on the Hindu epic, has been heavily documented.[7] The most notable critic of *The Mahabharata* has been Rustom Bharucha, for whom Brook's version represents a cultural theft perpetrated on India by western theatre practitioners: 'borrowing, stealing, and exchanging from other cultures is not necessarily an "enriching" experience for the cultures themselves' (Bharucha 1993: 14). More specifically, Bharucha finds in the Brook version of *The Mahabharata* a potent example of other ways in which many western intercultural events manipulate their non-western 'partners':

> the implications of interculturalism are very different for people in impoverished, 'developing' countries like India, and for their counterparts in technologically advanced, capitalist societies like America, where interculturalism has been more strongly promoted both as a philosophy and a business.
>
> (ibid.: 1)

Brook's production and Bharucha's critique have been the most public and visible discussions in intercultural theatre, raising a completely new ethical debate for theatre artists working in an increasingly global arts market. This global market in theatre has provided artists with increased access to the performance techniques and theatrical signs and symbols of other cultures. In most western cultures, this market opened up in the 1970s, when large numbers of artists began to travel (often with the assistance of government arts grants) and study the traditional performance techniques of other cultures. Trained to value the uniqueness of their artistic voice above other aesthetic considerations, they viewed all the artefacts available in the intersecting flows of the new global culture as accessible building blocks for their original performance texts. The right of western artists to draw freely on the signs and symbols circulating within their social worlds has hardly been questioned. In contrast, many of the cultures they were studying had rigid mechanisms for determining the right of artists to practise performance techniques. For example, the Japanese traditional forms of Kabuki, Noh, and Kyogen,[8] which have a magnetic attraction for western artists, are practised through rights of inheritance by the natural or adopted male heir.

The increasing number of commercially and critically successful western intercultural productions which employed techniques from the theatre of east and South-east Asia prompted further accusations of appropriation echoing Bharucha's. At gatherings of Asian artists, western theatre practitioners were frequently accused of building their international reputations by bastardising 'oriental' performance techniques. Inevitably such claims of appropriation and exploitation were vigorously denied by western theatre practitioners, the majority of whom identified with oppositional elements in their own cultures and found it difficult to see any parallels between their fascination with world theatre and facets of neo-imperialism. As Una Chaudhuri notes, however, 'well-meaning intercultural projects can unwittingly perpetuate a neo-colonialism in which the cultural clichés which underwrote imperialism survive more or less intact' (Chaudhuri 1991: 196).[9] With the intercultural theatre debate, new questions arose about cultural production and the nature of the theatrical process. The use of the modernist perception of an artist, free to borrow at will from various cultures to depict their artistic vision, has continued in intercultural practice at the end of the century where postmodernism appears to approve of cultural 'patchwork' activities. What impressions and influences did artists have a right to use? Could artists draw on cultural traditions and symbolic forms that originated outside of their immediate cultural context?

Interculturalism also risks fixing on easy cultural markers or signs of cultural difference as a shorthand that precludes research or cultural understanding and reduces culture to a stageable sign. Chaudhuri calls this 'museum interculturalism' which 'literalizes difference itself, reducing it to the grossest and most material of conceptions' (ibid.: 196). Daryl Chin reads this type of interculturalism as 'a form of connoisseurship, a new form of worldliness' (Chin 1991: 94). The overwhelming criticism of the intercultural practice of western artists leaves little space for artists to negotiate the paradox of their experiences as both local and global practitioners. Despite all the admonitions from critics and theorists, they work in an increasingly global environment with colleagues from other cultures.

## Commodification and interculturalism

While many right-wing politicians and commentators cling to fixed, outmoded signifiers of culture and identity, culture constantly evolves. Just as culture changes and mutates, it also has the capacity to be bought and sold when culture turns from a way of reading the self in the context of the world to a commodity that is for sale to the world. The global environment is, as the advertising for multinational corporations constantly reminds us, predicated on convincing consumers to desire and purchase products. Theatre is no exception to such laws of supply and demand: certainly theatre companies' subscription series are carefully designed to maximise financial returns in this product-oriented way. This is hardly new, although, as Lukács outlines, we frequently tend to assume that 'art' is somehow exempt from market forces. McClintock (1995: 212) explains that for Lukács, 'the commodity lies on the threshold of culture and commerce, confusing the supposedly sacrosanct boundaries between aesthetics and economy, money and art'. The potential is even greater for intercultural performance than for other performance modes to be circumscribed in a world of commodification, particularly when the economics of first world/third world intercultural collaborations come into play.[10]

This partly results from intercultural work – even more than other types of performance – frequently seeking cultural difference in the form of 'exoticism', particularly for western audiences.[11] When interculturalism brings at least two cultures to a performance relationship, the audience impulse tends to read the performance in terms of cultural difference only. This is to some extent unsurprising, since, as Barbara Kirshenblatt-Gimblett maintains, such objectification has already occurred when people from other cultures are put on display in ethnographic or festival contexts. She argues that '[e]ven when efforts are made to the contrary, live exhibits tend to make people into artifacts because the ethnographic gaze objectifies' whatever it sees. She cautions that '[w]hether the representation essentializes (one is seeing the quintessence of Balineseness) or totalizes (one is seeing the whole through the part), the ethnographic fragment returns with all the problems of capturing, inferring, constituting, and presenting the whole through parts' (Kirshenblatt-Gimblett 1991: 415, 416). In an effort to recognise culture's relationship with commodification, this study also traces the processes by which cultures – and women – are consumed in performance. The commodification of culture, performance, and women forms one of the major strands of our argument. While commodification helps shape each chapter, it is the major focus of Chapter 5 on the marketing of women's intercultural performance at arts festivals in particular. We now turn to the most specific form of the intercultural relationship that helps generate this heavily commodified equation, the self–other duality.

## The self–other duality

Interculturalism requires a perception of the subject–object or self–other duality.[12] Adorno and Horkheimer term the subject–object duality of western thought 'instrumental rationality' (cited in Gardiner 1996: 125). As our study focuses on women's intercultural performance, it is hardly surprising that we are influenced by feminist theories of alterity, which in the light of Jessica Benjamin's assertion that the 'missing piece in analyzing rationality and individualism is the structure of gender domination' (Benjamin 1986: 81), helps us determine a working relationship for this duality. If we ascribe feminist principles to this construction – specifically if 'instrumental rationality' is predicated on a male subject and a female other – then women artists have a vested interest in creating an aesthetics of intersubjectivity or finding methods of bringing subject and object into a different relational order. The experience of playing the other within their own culture may make them weary of imposing the same role on a cultural other. A formulation of interculturalism as an exploration of intersubjectivity, then, is at the basis of this study. We explore cultural encounters, not only through audience perceptions, but also through the motivations and subjective experience of artists.[13] This is not to imply that the intentions of the artists are synonymous with the reception of their work, but rather that the space between intention and reception provides a rich seam of intercultural enquiry. It is this contested transitional space between cultures, and the ways in which female artists and their audiences negotiate this intersubjective space, that we find particularly intriguing.

## WOMEN'S INTERCULTURAL PERFORMANCE

The field of culture is . . . a constant battlefield where there are no victories to be gained, only strategic positions to be won and lost. Cultural practice then becomes a realm where one engages with and elaborates a politics.

(Niranjana *et al.* 1993: 7)

As will be obvious by now, this study is not a history of interculturalism, but rather an analysis of cultural production and exchange at work in examples of women's intercultural performance. Our definitional approach to intercultural performance remains as broad as Carlson's possibilities for cultural interaction, so that interculturalism can contain both the on-stage interaction between two or more cultures and the culturally homogeneous audience presented with a foreign cultural artefact. The structuring principle for this book comes from the theatre itself. Each group of performance texts is discussed through the framing device of one of the following theatrical tropes: narrative, ritual, theatrical space, the body, and markets. This structure enables us to demonstrate how interculturalism and feminism intersect through space and time in performance to generate a variety of possible identity spaces for women from different cultures. It also enables us to highlight the interaction between theatre and politics.

Chapter 1 concentrates on narrative or theatrical plot, which is generally the first exchange between western and eastern theatre. We trace the cultural exchange of two European plays, Ibsen's *A Doll's House* and Sophocles' *Antigone*, through numerous transformations in Asia, the Middle East, and Latin America to consider how identity spaces can shift. Nora, from *A Doll's House*, has been played by Matsui Sumako, one of the first women to appear on the public stage in Japan, by Jiang Qing (Madame Mao), and by the popular Iranian film actress, Niki Karimi. The different sociopolitical contexts for these narrative transformations create a useful model for understanding how one narrative can provide so many different possible identity space options. Numerous women playwrights have reworked *Antigone* to help counter totalitarian regimes, including Argentina in the 1970s and 1980s. Our example here, Griselda Gambaro's *Antígona Furiosa*, enables us to trace in more depth the effects of the manipulation of identity spaces for women in Argentina. The chapter analyses the ways in which non-western women artists have translated and adapted these narratives to foreground the struggle for women's rights within public and private spheres.

The second chapter concerns ritual: often considered to be theatre's ancestor, ritual continues to be performed around the world, albeit in the different cultural and social circumstances of postmodernity. Rather than analysing ritual *per se*, we focus on the postmodern desire to consume 'authentic' indigenous performance. The first section charts the translocation of a shaman ritual from central Korea to four Australian cities, and analyses the heavily commodified representation of the leading performer and shaman, Kim Kum hwa, in the Australian media; the second section addresses a ritual performance by Warlpiri women from central Australia. In both accounts, we consider the divergent meanings attributed to the ritual performances by the artists and their urban Australian audiences, and assess the impact these intercultural encounters have on the identity spaces occupied by their participants. Chapter 2 acts as a complement to Chapter 1 in its continued exploration of the public and private sphere.

Rather than overtly addressing the public/private sphere, the next chapter concerns public and private space. Chapter 3 analyses the use of theatrical space as a metaphor for colonial (and sociopolitical) displacements, enabling us to reconsider transformations of space in the light of the multiple subject positioning that informs feminist and postcolonial theories. In an endeavour to narrow down the vast topic of theatrical space, we address the postcolonial situation of the return 'home', particularly when that 'home' is multiply articulated in the national imaginary. We focus on three plays from Algeria, South Africa, and Ghana that stage the return 'home': inevitably more intricate than 'just' a conflict between coloniser and colonised subjects, this return triggers a conflict between at least two competing socio-political identity spaces. Theatrical space, then, acts metonymically for a variety of geo-political displacements in order to address multiple subject positioning and the spatialisation of personal and public imaginaries.

While Chapter 3 explores theatrical space and theatre space, Chapter 4 narrows further the theatrical metaphor from space to the acting body in space. The female performing body is the site of the next intercultural encounter. Every performance involves a complex interrelational dynamic between bodies, but in Chapter 4 we confine our attention to three genres of women's performance. The first genre is taxonomic, because it seeks clearly to demarcate the boundaries between cultures; the second is hybrid, because two cultures in some way merge; and the third is nomadic, because cultural and geographical boundaries are transgressed. Our examples include the work of Takarazuka, the all-female Japanese revue company, which has perfected an intercultural, 'inter-gendered' performance style; and an adaptation of *Masterkey*, a thriller by Masako Togawa, involving a cross-cultural female cast and crew presented in 1998 at the Perth Festival and Telstra Adelaide Festival. Finally, we address the work of artists who combine diverse cultural influences in their solo performance work, including the *butoh* performers Tomiko Takai and Yoko Ashikawa from Japan, and Pol Pelletier, a Canadian actor/director who mixes a number of 'oriental' techniques to harness performance energy. From our analysis of these examples we assess the representation of racial and cultural identity via the sexually differentiated performing body.

The final chapter considers the larger market forces which govern the distribution of women and women's performance in the international marketplace. While not a performance trope as such, the marketing of performance can significantly determine its shape, content, and politics. Chapter 5 pursues the image of the female body but in the context of the marketplace where the issue of censorship compromises the nature of the performances.

We explore the dynamic that exists between the voluntary exchange of the female performing body through the international arts market, and the enforced exchange or trafficking of the commodified female body through the international 'black' market. Our analysis, then, draws attention to the many levels of commodification that inevitably underpin any discussion or production of international intercultural women's performance. The analysis in Chapter 5 points to the importance of further situating performance in the context of its socio-political and economic environments.

The materialist approach to women's intercultural performance that is key to Chapter 5 structures the entire study to some considerable extent. The diverse and wide-ranging performance examples demonstrate the struggles women performers encounter in order to establish identity spaces, and to make larger cultural and political statements. Such performance work is often mediated by local and global forces, enabling us to examine the development *and* consumption of women's intercultural work in different locations. *Women's Intercultural Performance* investigates how culture, feminism, and theatre intersect with one another and with globalism, commodification, and consumption to weave together a complex and often paradoxical social and theatrical practice.

# Chapter 1

# Narrative trajectories

## A Doll's House and Antigone

How many other women in this world live a life like Nora's?
Her awakening is the awakening of the women of the world.
Yet awakening is the beginning of a new battle, a battle that
needs a strong will. Women must build their own lives for themselves. We must throw off the bindings that men have placed
on us and cross over the border to freedom.

(*Seito* 1912: 96)

Nobody can pretend not to see them. Here they are in the
bright afternoon light with their white kerchiefs and with the
photographs of their disappeared hanging from ribbons around
their tired necks. They are willing to use women's true and
ineffable recourse in their battle: the body itself as a weapon,
exposed, subjected to hunger strikes, to long marches, to all sorts
of abuse, at times given over to torture.

(Agosin 1987: 433)

We begin this investigation of women's intercultural performance
with the simplest form of cultural exchange in theatre: the
adaptation and translation of dramatic texts. As Rey Chow explains
in a different context, translations are never perfectly 'faithful'
to their 'original' texts (Chow 1995: 176) and adaptations are
even less so. It is for this reason that adaptations are ideal
intercultural texts because they mix (at least) two cultures, two
time periods, and in some cases, two divergent theatrical worlds.
New dramatic narratives emerge from story-lines, plots, and
characters as they travel through time and across cultural
borders; these transformations and mutations are the subject of this
chapter.

In recent intercultural theatre criticism, the two major strands of debate over translation and adaptation have concerned the appropriation of mythic or sacred texts by western practitioners, and the process of assimilation and abrogation of the western canon by postcolonial artists. We shift this focus to consider specifically women-orientated intercultural transmissions, in which European texts from the western canon have served women's political struggles in Japan, China, Iran, and Argentina. These texts are translated, adapted, or completely rewritten by non-western artists for explicitly socio-political as well as aesthetic reasons, and they speak directly to, or about, women. We examine the specific ways in which these texts are reproduced as women-centred narratives, encouraging an interactive engagement with gendered subjects in their new audiences, and assuming a symbolic importance in wider political struggles. Despite the fact that these same texts are frequently refracted or interpreted in contemporary European productions through feminist discourses, we are aware of the universalising tendencies in western feminism and seek to avoid automatic assumptions concerning the meanings these narratives hold in their new contexts.

The dramatic texts that dominate this chapter, Sophocles' *Antigone* and Ibsen's *A Doll's House*, have been linked in twentieth-century dramatic criticism by the perception that they share a common theme: the conflict between the individual (and specifically a female individual) and the state (specifically the patriarchal power invested in that state). *A Doll's House* is seen to raise questions concerning the role of women in the *private* sphere, while *Antigone* fulfils the same role in the *public* sphere. We do not wish to engage in a comparative criticism of these texts, but we shall indulge in some structural paralleling in considering the processes by which they are chosen, adapted, and employed by their new hosts. Barbara Herrnstein Smith provides us with the starting point:

> At a given time and under the contemporary conditions of available materials, technology, and techniques, a particular object – let us say a verbal artefact or text – may perform certain desired/able functions quite well for some set of subjects. It will do so by virtue of certain of its 'properties'.
>
> (Herrnstein Smith 1984: 30)

We begin by attempting to identify the 'contemporary conditions' in host cultures that match 'properties' contained in the imported texts. In the case of *Antigone*, we consider these 'contemporary conditions' to be the political instability induced by totalitarian regimes. Our approach follows Friedrich Hölderlin's suggestion that the play thrives in a context of '"national reversal and revolution", a dramatic revaluation of moral values and political power-relations' (cited in Steiner 1984: 81). In contrast to these volatile power reversals, the 'contemporary conditions' that underpin the adaptations of *A Doll's House* appear to be the social upheavals associated with modernity. Our analysis of *A Doll's House* covers 50 years, beginning in East Asia in the early twentieth century, and takes its cue from Erika Fischer-Lichte's statement that theatrical innovators in Japan and China imported European social realist texts 'to popularize the representation of the individual in society, as well as to introduce rationalism and to demand further modernization' (Fischer-Lichte 1990b: 15).

We are particularly interested in the central protagonists in both plays, Nora and Antigone. There are major dramaturgical differences in the translations and adaptations we consider, but in all these intercultural productions the characters of Nora and Antigone are invested with extraordinary degrees of symbolic significance. They appear to offer women spectators identity spaces, which in Chun's terms act as 'interpretative mechanisms . . . to negotiate a meaningful life space' (Chun 1996: 69). These characters offer up possible identities that are tested out by spectators during the performance, either through analysis and observation, or directly through an empathetic relationship. Outside the theatre – on the streets, in lectures, and in pamphlets – the characters are recreated as icons in a collective struggle. One of the crucial textual 'properties' that facilitates this process is the open-ended structure of the original narrative which allows the artist/adapter the freedom to write alternative endings and dramatic sequels.

*A Doll's House* dominates the first section of this chapter, and in a series of snapshots through time and space, we consider the multiple meanings that have been invested in Nora: as an icon of resistance against feudalism; a comrade involved in a revolutionary struggle; a victim of western decadence; and an advocate for a radical reinterpretation of the Qur'an. In the second part of the chapter we take a detailed look at a recent adaptation of *Antigone* and its place in the 25-year struggle between the Mothers of the Plaza de Mayo and the Argentinian state.

## THE MANY FACES OF NORA

In the first half of the twentieth century, Henrik Ibsen was the most performed dramatist in the world, with *Ghosts, Hedda Gabler*, and *A Doll's House* his most popular plays. Before we can explore *A Doll's House* as an intercultural site, we must first investigate the dynamic new identity space that Nora offered late nineteenth-century Europe.

When the European critics and audiences of the late nineteenth century dubbed Nora and Hedda Gabler 'new' or 'modern' women, they saw them as representatives of the middle-class women who were agitating for financial independence, the vote, equality before the law, access to education, and a place in the workforce. These women were gaining control over their lives in a world where traditional family structures were being disrupted by demographic upheaval and urban growth, and women's labour power was both invisible in the home and undervalued in the marketplace. The critics were not implying that Nora and Hedda were 'modernist' literary heroines, any more than that the texts were 'modernist' plays. The modernity embodied in Ibsen's characters was reflective not of aesthetic modernism (associated in theatre with dramatists such as Pirandello, Wedekind, and Brecht), but of the quality defined by Habermas as the essence of modernity, or subjective freedom: 'the space secured by civil law for the rational pursuit of one's own interests: in the state, as the in-principle equal rights to participation in the formation of political will; in the private sphere, as ethical autonomy and self-realisation' (Habermas 1987: 83). This subjectivity, established through the Reformation, Enlightenment, and French Revolution, had already been claimed by the bourgeois male citizen, but it was not until the late nineteenth century that it became available to the bourgeois female citizen. The historical specificity of this late nineteenth-century struggle by European women for a subjectivity tied to modernity is crucial to an understanding of *A Doll's House*.

The conventions of a social-realist text surround the identity space embodied by Nora. The text conceals its own construction, hides its author and its theatrical tricks, and pretends that it has sprung into existence directly from the lived reality of its audience. It moves through time by means of a narrative structure based on the logic of cause and effect, and it organises space behind a 'fourth wall' to create the illusion of a single perspective that ties the viewer into a unified subject position. Ibsen uses these conventions to work an extraordinary sleight of hand, without disturbing the supposed transparency with which the world of the play reproduces the world of the audience: he shifts the single viewing eye out of the universal male body and into the female body.

The audience views the play through the actions of the female protagonist, which are the logical result of the causal flow of events embedded in the plot. At the opening of the play, the Helmer family is about to celebrate Christmas; Nora has been buying the children presents and is thrilled that her husband has been made the vice-president of the local bank. She is relieved because the additional income from this new position will release her from a secret debt incurred when her husband fell ill in the early years of their marriage. At this time, doctors advised Nora that Helmer would not recover unless he was moved to a warmer climate, and she secured a loan to pay for the journey by forging her dying father's signature. Nora has never told her husband about the debt, and every month for eight years she has repaid the loan with her secret earnings as a seamstress. Krogstad, who works at the bank and negotiated Nora's loan, believes Helmer intends to sack him. In order to secure his job, Krogstad attempts to blackmail Nora; when this fails he tries to blackmail Helmer. Nora is convinced that her husband will defy Krogstad and sacrifice himself rather than allow her to be harmed; but when Helmer reads the blackmail letter it becomes clear that he will neither confront Krogstad, nor risk his reputation to save his wife. He tells her that she is corrupt and unfit to be the mother of his children. The threat of blackmail passes, but Nora can no longer accept her role as Helmer's protected songbird. She decides that she must leave her 'doll's house' and become an independent human being.

If the audience is to believe Nora's decision to leave her children to be logical and causally justified, it must engage empathetically with her character. The success of this psychological stratagem depends on the way Ibsen lures the audience into a powerful sense of identification with Nora. These narrative hooks were designed to connect with the gendered experience of the middle classes in late nineteenth-century Europe. The play opens with an idealised depiction of the happy bourgeois couple in a beautiful home with lovely children. Gradually, Ibsen reveals the power dynamics underlying this image: a dependency that forces women to survive by seducing, amusing, and coaxing their husbands while their labour remains invisible and their bodies are subject to constant surveillance. At the most fragile point in the text, when the whole structure might collapse if the audience fails to sympathise with Nora, ambiguity silences any misgiving. The door may slam shut behind the departing figure of Nora, but the openness of the text leaves her in limbo, subject to endless rewritings, critical speculations, and dramatic sequels. The audience is free to fantasise about the return of Nora to her children, the reconstruction of the marriage, or Nora's new life as an independent woman.

This potential for variations on the text made the play a powerful tool for women struggling with the social changes associated with modernity. By imaginatively inhabiting the role of Nora, women on the cusp of new social identities were able to explore possible futures and the consequences of possible actions. There is ample evidence that this interactive mechanism in the play worked for a large number of the European women who were actively engaged in the first wave of the women's movement. In the accounts of the actresses who played Nora, and the audiences who watched her in late nineteenth-century Europe, the most striking quality is the depth of the empathy felt by these women for this fictional character. They stated repeatedly that Nora was 'them' (Holledge 1981: 24–32). The process of identification was so strong that the character was operating as a conduit through which a new subjectivity was being explored. The impact of the play can be judged, not only through the theoretical writings of women like Eleanor Marx and Alexandra Kollontai[1] who used Nora as a representational paradigm in discourses on women's emancipation, but also in the subsequent attempts by drama critics to save the play from feminist 'contamination' (Templeton 1997: 110–28).

At a specific stage in the history of social modernity, A Doll's House gave European bourgeois women the opportunity to explore subjective freedom through a process of empathy and identification. But if A Doll's House is tied to a subject position defined by European modernity, how does it function as an intercultural text? Does it require certain parallel social structures to thrive? Any attempt to identify parallel social patterns in non-European societies risks falling into the trap of creating a metanarrative of modernity in which the whole world is categorised according to a western definition of development and progress. Such a system of categorisation is based on the colonial assumption that each culture is stationed at a different point on the 'road to progress': the 'west' inhabits the present, while the 'rest' are locked in the past.[2]

Sociologist Goran Therborn's theory of the 'Four Gateways' provides a structural mechanism for analysing global flows of modernity which bypass such western-centred narratives of cultural 'progress' (Therborn 1995: 132). The empirical basis of Therborn's structure is based on democratic voting procedures. He is interested in two social spheres – the economy and the family – and looks at a range of conflicts and confrontations in these spheres through patterns of individualism and association. With its emphasis on voting systems, the family, collective and individual subject positions, Therborn's structure provides a sympathetic framework for examining Nora's travels.

A Doll's House was produced under the sign of Therborn's first gateway to modernity, the European gate of 'revolution or reform' (ibid.: 131). European artists toured the play through his second gateway of 'independence' to the new worlds (ibid.: 132), and through his fourth gateway of 'conquest, subjection, and appropriation' to the colonies (ibid.: 133). It is the journey Nora took through his third gateway, of 'imposed or externally induced modernity' (ibid.: 132), that provides us with the most fascinating translations and adaptations of Ibsen's work. This third gateway involves the selective importation of aspects of modernity: industrialisation, education, scientific knowledge, technology, new bureaucratic structures, including various degrees of enfranchisement. Simultaneously though, this gateway maintains traditional power structures within the host society. Therborn cites Japan as the society that has perfected this delicate balancing act, China as attempting 'a Sino-Communist variant of the same game', and the Shah of Iran as the leader who went through this gateway and hit a cul-de-sac (ibid.: 133). In each of these countries, artists have translated and adapted A Doll's House to fit the specific dynamics of gendered power relations within their culture. We look at the political contexts surrounding some of these productions, and ask whether the play still carries a discourse of European emancipatory feminism.

## Through the third gateway

The cultural transmission of *A Doll's House* from Europe to Japan was comparatively smooth; the play moved from one confident culture to another, and both the Japanese artists who produced it, and the women activists who critiqued it, had a clear understanding of how the text could be made to operate in Japan. Originally translated into Japanese in 1901, *A Doll's House* was first performed in September 1911 by the Association of Literature and Arts at Bungei Kyokai Shenjyo in Waseda, and directed by Shimamura Hogetsu (Sato 1981: 278). Social drama, in the form of realist texts, was one of the many features of European modernity imported into Japan in the early years of the century, and the most popular of these texts prior to 1941 was *A Doll's House*. Writings on women's emancipation in Europe and America, including dramatic texts, started to be available in translation during the period immediately after the Russo-Japanese War in 1904–5, and debates about the relationship between the sexes became popular in intellectual circles. In 1907, the 'new woman' became a popular expression after it appeared in *Quilt*, a novel by Tayama Katai. When Nora walked on to the Tokyo stage four years later, she immediately became the quintessential 'new woman' from the 'west' (ibid.: 278).

Although the Japanese women activists claimed that they were 50 years behind Europe in their struggle for emancipation, they used the play not as a model for action, but as a catalyst for debate about gender relations in their own culture. The heart of this debate appeared in *Seito* [Bluestocking], a magazine that first appeared in the same month as the 1911 production of *A Doll's House*: it was mockingly referred to as 'a nursery for Japanese Noras'.[3] The women associated with *Seito* analysed major differences between traditional family structures in Japan and the west, and made a key distinction between structures that favoured the consolidation of family interests through arranged marriages, and the selection of marriage partners through individual feelings of love and sexual attraction. Traditional family life in Japan was deeply influenced by Buddhist and Confucian thought and in many respects placed women as subservient to men. Women were governed by three obediences: from the daughter to the father, the wife to the husband, and the mother to the son. Seven sins were added to this list: the inability to bear a son and the denying

*Plate 1* The *Seito* Collective, 1912. Photo reproduced with the permission of the Waseda University Theatre Library.

of sexual intercourse to a husband, disobeying parents-in-law, talkativeness, theft, jealousy, stubbornness, and incurable disease. These rules began to break down in the last quarter of the nineteenth century as women were recruited into the industrial workforce, particularly in textile and other light industries. They were further eroded by the growth in educational opportunities for women, regardless of the fact that the stated aim of many of the new girls' schools was the education of 'good wives and wise mothers' (Nolte and Hastings 1991: 158).

'Of course, the success of Nora had no little influence on the world of drama', the critic Akiba Taro wrote in 1937, 'but more than that, it considerably stimulated the world of thought in that age. It was this age when a group of "new women", the Bluestockings, advocated Noraism for the emancipation of women' (cited in Sato 1981: 279). Raicho Hiratsuka, the *Seito* editor, devoted the first issue of 1912 to *A Doll's House*. The female reviewers concentrated almost exclusively on the character of Nora, and they were not entirely sympathetic: 'Nora, Japanese women find it incredible that you could be such a thoroughly instinctive and blind woman' ('H' 1912: 133). Helmer was perceived to be weak and shallow, but not violent, so the relationship was considered unsatisfactory but not irredeemable. Opinion was divided over Nora's decision to leave her children and her husband. This element of the plot, so controversial in Europe, appears to have attracted less debate than the nature of Nora's 'awakening'. 'Under a withered field that has suffered the harshness of winter', wrote 'Midori', 'buds beneath the cold ground await spring. And in Nora's heart the buds of awakening lie' (ibid.: 118). This concept of the 'awakening woman' was prevalent even in the Japanese newspapers. The implication behind the term was that the 'new woman' must awaken, in a Buddhist sense, from the illusions of the visible world if she is to free her inner self. In the introduction to the first edition of *Seito*, Raicho wrote that 'sexual differentiation of man and woman belongs to the middle or the lowest strata [*sic*] of self that is transient, false, and to die and disappear' (cited in Sato 1981: 275). Within this philosophical framework, Nora's claim to an awakening within a period of three days appeared superficial:

> Self-awakening is no simple thing. If you think that a woman can become a human being simply by doing what you did,

you are wrong. One's true self is not something that can be
discovered with such ease.

('H' 1912: 138)

Whereas European audiences concentrated on the social drama of
the play, the Japanese Bluestockings appear to have been looking
for a metaphysical reading of character. This search for a spiritual
dimension within the text resulted in one of the most fascinating
sequels ever written to *A Doll's House*. In 1924 a Buddhist
missionary, Tanaka Chigaku, wrote *Out of a Doll's House*, a play
set in Italy several years after Nora has left home (Nakamura 1985:
166). After seeking spiritual enlightenment in a convent, she travels
to Paris to join an aviator school and train as a pilot. She hears
that an Italian company is planning to promote world peace with
a series of flights to East Asia. She applies for a job only to discover
that Krogstad and Kristine run the company, with Helmer as their
employee. Reunited with her husband, who is filled with remorse
over his past conduct, her marriage is saved through the miracle
of their mutual desire for world peace and harmony.

The male critics who attended the first Tokyo performance
of *A Doll's House* made an interesting conflation between the
'new woman' as represented by Nora, and the 'new woman' as
personified in the actress, Matsui Sumako. As Kusuyama Masao
pointed out:

> Without reservation or exaggeration, I believe that the Nora
> played by this actress Matsui Sumako must be remembered as
> a monument which resolved for the first time problems of
> using actresses in Japan, and which, on stage, emancipated
> women for the first time.
>
> (cited in Sato 1981: 278)[4]

In the two Japanese reinterpretations of *A Doll's House* that
appeared after the 1911 production, this implicit connection
between Nora and performance practices became explicit in the
character's transformation into a professional entertainer. In *Feeble
Husband* (1914) Yukiko is an actress who leaves her husband
to pursue her career (Nakamura 1985: 165), and in *Sunrise, Nora
in Japan* (1912) Hamako is an ex-geisha who commits suicide to
escape her dishonourable past (Nakamura 1985: 163). These
reworkings of the play develop the implication within Ibsen's text

*Plate 2*  Matsui Sumako as Nora in the Shimamura Hogetsu production of *A Doll's House* at Bungei Kyokai Shenjyo in Waseda, Japan, 1911. Photo reproduced with the permission of the Waseda University Theatre Library.

that Nora's role as wife and mother includes the acting out of Helmer's sexual fantasies: she is his personal geisha or actress when she dances the tarantella for him.

Instead of discussing her position as one of the first actresses in Japan, or the conflation between the role of actress and character, Matsui Sumako's published comments on the production focus on the response of the audience:

> Listening to people's reactions after the performance, some expressed their dismay at what a strong and cold woman Nora had become. . . . Perhaps their dismay is due to the fact that it has long been accepted practice for women, even when they have a husband like Helmer, to hide their suffering and

sacrifice themselves unendingly as if this was a woman's virtue.
. . . I believe that the average person, even if derisive of
Helmer's response, was scathing of Nora's actions.

(Matsui Sumako 1912: 163)

Matsui Sumako does not imply that it was her intention to represent a 'cold' Nora: she clearly equates the character's situation with
the plight of sacrificing and suffering wives, but it is still impossible to gauge whether it was her performance or the character's
actions that elicited this reaction in the Tokyo audience. Yet the
actress's comments provide a fascinating insight into the workings
of the production because they indicate that she did not feel an
empathetic connection with the audience in the final scene of the
play. While departing from her doll's house, the actress must have
sensed that the audience was not responding sympathetically to the
character's emotional state. Whereas this absence of empathy in a
European production might have indicated that the performance
was not successful, the records show that in Osaka and Tokyo the
production was extremely popular. This presents us with an interesting intercultural conundrum: if the play was working despite
this empathy, how did the audience read the performance? At
this point we must take a conjectural leap and question whether
a text that is designed as realism in one culture can be consumed
as realism in another. In other words, was it possible for the
character of Nora to work empathetically with an audience
that had no familiarity with the middle-class domestic life of late
nineteenth-century Europe?

The Japanese audiences which watched this first production of
*A Doll's House* were not familiar with the cultural milieu reflected
on the stage. Consequently the basic premise of a realist text could
not function, nor could the acceptance of the inevitability of causal
connections, and the invisibility of theatrical artifice. The Japanese
audiences were watching the representation of a 'foreign' relationship between Nora and Helmer enacted within a 'foreign'
performance convention. It was not just the Japanese audience that
experienced these conventions as strange: according to Matsui
Sumako, the actors found working in European costumes and
constructing an occidental image extremely challenging. 'When
Helmer returns home from the dance, he slings the coat over a
chair and because both sides are black it is difficult for him to
distinguish between the collar and the hem and he often gets into

a muddle' (Matsui Sumako 1912: 162). This lack of familiarity with the European clothing codes indicates the degree of strangeness with which the Tokyo audience viewed the production. Not only the characters, but also their actions were carried out under a sign of racial and cultural difference which inevitably limited the possibility of audience empathy and identification.

Visually, culturally, and theatrically, the audience was distanced from the text, but this distance allowed them to use the play to compare and contrast the potential subjectivities available to the 'new woman' on a global scale. It appears that the audience did explore the identity space provided by Nora, but in a highly selective way. Aspects of traditional culture were assessed in relation to the imported European model and an amalgam of European emancipatory thought and traditional Buddhist beliefs were merged by the *Seito* writers into new identity spaces. This combination of influences is apparent in their 1912 editorial which introduced the issue on *A Doll's House*:

> Men and women must empathise with each other and compromise to find peace between them. Of course a woman must be a 'good wife and wise mother', but to ask her to be obedient compromises a woman's self-respect. This is not to suggest that all women must be wives or mothers. There are many scholastic and artistic ambitions that are not compatible with marriage. In the west the number of single women increases year by year. Many have their own professions and support themselves. Ideally, women, whether they choose to marry or remain single, should be able to stand equal with men. Women should not have to abide by laws created by men. They should have the right to vote.
>
> (*Seito* 1912: 105–6)

The merging of influences reflected in this *Seito* editorial on *A Doll's House* is typical of the delicate balance between traditional thinking and imported elements of social modernity that characterised Japanese society in the early twentieth century. In contrast, it is the turbulence of China's journey through the 'third gateway' of modernity that is reflected in the Chinese production history of *A Doll's House*, the most widely known foreign drama prior to 1949. The Chinese Nora wore an ever-changing face in the 44 years that separate the first performance in Shanghai in 1912 and the 1956 production commemorating the half-century since Ibsen's death. The early history of *A Doll's House* in China was linked to Japan through two students studying in Tokyo in 1911. When they returned home to Shanghai in 1912, they established the New Play Group; two years later they created Chunliu Theatre and presented *Nora* in a theatre on the Nanjing Road.

It is uncertain whether a woman played the first Chinese Nora, because the New Play Movement relied on female impersonators. If Chunliu Theatre was using a translation of the play, it was never published: it is possible that the actors were working from a *mubiao*, or summary, pinned to the back of the stage (Min 1962). It was not until 1918 that the first translation of *A Doll's House* appeared in *New Youth* (Wu 1956), a periodical associated with the May Fourth Movement. This reform movement took its name from the date of the student protest demonstration against the terms of the Treaty of Versailles, which had legitimised Japan's claim to a province in Northern China. Hu Shi, a leader of the May Fourth Movement and an advocate of the total westernisation of China, was one of the translators of the play (Yan 1992: 56).

Over 400 new periodicals appeared in Beijing during this period and a number of them ran special features on Ibsen. The 'women's question' was debated at length in many of the journals, including a number that were written and published exclusively by women. *New Woman*, the most successful of these feminist publications, included in its manifesto the promotion of the 'latest American and European literature on the new woman' (Croll 1978: 85). In the drama clubs based in the Beijing colleges and universities, productions of *A Doll's House* were ubiquitous, but in 1924 the warlords who controlled Beijing banned the play on the grounds that its popularity was undermining the moral integrity of China (Min 1962). A number of Chinese plays based on *A Doll's House* appeared during this period including Hu Shi's *The Great Event of Life*, which is often mistakenly referred to as the first Chinese spoken play.[5] The dramaturgical structure of Hu Shi's play is based on Ibsen, but the plot line revolves around the conflict over an arranged, rather than an unsatisfactory, marriage. The heroine, Tian Yamei, elopes at the end of the play and leaves her parents the following note: 'This is the greatest event in your daughter's life. Your daughter ought to make this decision for herself. She has left in Mr Chen's car. Goodbye for now' (Yan 1992: 56).[6]

Feminist activity reached a height in the early 1920s, but there was a growing impatience with the liberal humanist agenda imported from the west that had characterised Nora's popularity, namely individual rights and liberties for women. Even Hu Shi, the great advocate of individualism, began to question whether capitalism could 'lead human beings to attain their true "freedom, equality, and fraternity"' (ibid.: 60). As the feminist activists drew closer to the anti-imperialist and socialist parties, Ibsen's play no longer appeared relevant. In this new phase of activism, militant women's unions were established, and 'girl agitators' (Croll 1978: 151) took the demands for women's emancipation into the countryside. Their zeal for change was notorious, particularly in rural areas where they claimed divorce rights for wives of labourers and peasants. In 1927, a violent backlash occurred when the coalition between the Guomindang and the Communist Party broke down, and Chiang Kai-Shek began a military offensive against the CCP. The repression against women's activism[7] was eased in 1930, when the Guomindang released their Civil Code in an attempt to balance traditional values with aspects of modernity. The Code improved the legal position of women, but only middle-class urban women benefited. Continued efforts to establish Confucian precepts within the framework of a modern western democracy resulted in the Guomindang launching the New Life Movement in 1934 (Croll 1978: 157). It was within the context of this attempt to reconcile women's emancipation with traditional values of motherhood, sacrifice, loyalty, and honour that the most famous Chinese production of *A Doll's House* appeared in Shanghai.

In the entire global history of *A Doll's House*, the Nora who appeared in the 1935 Shanghai production must be the most infamous. Jiang Qing, known outside China as Madame Mao, played Nora when she was still a relatively unknown actress in her early twenties working under the stage name of Lan Ping. She had arrived in Shanghai two years before, joined a left-wing theatre group giving benefit performances for striking tobacco workers, and became involved in the League of Left-Wing Theatre People. She had no connection with the underground Communist Party in Shanghai, but she was arrested and imprisoned for her propagandist activities. Jiang Qing claimed that she was a fearless prisoner, but there is evidence to suggest that she implicated others during her interrogation and signed a confession that gained her an early release in 1934. A few months after her term in prison, she was cast in *A Doll's House*, and 1935 became known as the 'Year of Nora' in Shanghai theatre. The production ran for two months at the Golden City Theatre. It was directed by the Stanislavskian Zhang Min; he believed that foreign plays should be performed in ways that maximised their positive influence on Chinese society. His production of *A Doll's House* was noted for its emotional intensity and the integrity of the characterisation. Zhao Dan, the prominent actor known for his left-wing affiliations who played Helmer, recalls in his autobiography the director telling the cast that an actor 'must absolutely believe that what his character does is completely right and reasonable. That it is the only way to behave' (Zhao Dan 1980: 136). Jiang Qing claimed that *A Doll's House* had been her favourite play since she had studied Ibsen at the Arts Academy in Jinan (Terrill 1984: 67). Her interpretation of Nora became the subject of numerous reviews and newspaper articles; she felt that she had discovered the 'woman-rebel' in the play and the critics and the audiences concurred (Terrill 1984: 67). Cui Wanqui, a leading Shanghai critic, commented: 'it was breathtaking, she took Nora as such an extreme rebel. And being her, she said this was all very revolutionary' (ibid.: 68). While recalling the performance in an interview with Roxane Witke, Jiang Qing suggested that her connections with the cultural elite in Shanghai may have influenced the critics, but added that the audience enthusiastically applauded her performance, an unusual practice in Shanghai theatre during the 1930s (Witke 1977: 102).[8]

The success of Jiang Qing's interpretation indicates how the function of the play in China shifted from the early 1920s to the early 1930s. Nora had became a popular heroine in the 1920s because the May Fourth Movement looked to the west for progressive models of emancipation. When she reappeared in left-wing intellectual circles in the 1930s, it was as a symbol of rebellion and revolution. A clear distinction had developed between the reforming agenda of the Guomindang, which sought to reconcile the traditional role of Chinese women within the increasingly modernised society, and the revolutionary agenda of women's emancipation introduced in the communist-held areas. In Shanghai, where the open expression of pro-communist sentiments resulted in imprisonment, it was necessary for artists to work through vehicles that allowed multiple interpretations. Jiang Qing's Nora lived in a conventional European drawing room, but her audience read her rebellion as a symbol of their own revolutionary thinking.

*Plate 3*    Lan Ping (Jiang Qing) as Nora in Zhang Min's 1935 production of *A Doll's House*, Shanghai. Photo reproduced from *The White Boned Demon* with the permission of Ross Terrill.

Once again the text became a displacement for a local political struggle, but this time the model from the west was presented as outmoded, and Jiang Qing claimed that she had gone far 'beyond Ibsen's original conception of the character' (Terrill 1984: 67).[9]

As a symbol of radical thought, Nora retained her popularity until 1949 when the Communist Party gained power. With the introduction of the Marriage Law in 1950, inequalities in the domestic sphere became the subject of legislation and the Party took a direct interest in the emancipation of women in the home. Playwrights were encouraged to write short domestic dramas showing that marriage conflicts could be successfully resolved with the assistance of a third party in order to promote the Party's Marriage Laws. Nora's miracle was transformed into the benevolent intervention of the state in the role of marriage counsellor. *A Doll's House* was still performed in the 1950s, but it had become an example of the pathetically backward nature of relationships between the sexes in the west. To mark the fiftieth anniversary of Ibsen's death, the play was staged in Beijing; the reviewer in the *People's Daily* took the opportunity to celebrate the new position of women in post-revolutionary China:

> In our present time, the life of a couple is built on mutual respect, love, and support. This was the family life that Ibsen longed for. The rights of women are no longer just talk, they are the general standards accepted by our new world.
>
> (Wu 1956)

In post-revolutionary China, then, Nora demonstrated the achievements of the Communist Party and functioned as an exemplar to educate backward elements in the audience. Early productions of the play emulated the west, whereas later productions despised it. In the space of 44 years, Nora transformed from a progressive heroine to a symbol of revolution, to an outmoded relic from an oppressive past, her character functioning as a variable symbol embodying diverse identity spaces.

China is not the only post-revolutionary state to enmesh Nora in an ideological battle with the 'decadent' west. In 1994 she reappeared in a veil, living behind closed doors in a bourgeois suburb of Tehran. If Japan can be characterised as a culture that successfully integrated aspects of European modernity, and China as a culture in which the volatile dynamic between tradition and modernity is still unresolved, then Iran is a country in which the imposition of modernity created a 'double culture'. On the one hand, the upper and emerging middle classes became increasingly westernised; on the other, the majority of the population continued to live by traditional religious practices. The period of imposed modernity in Iran coincided with the Pahlavi dynasty from 1925 to 1979. The second Pahlavi Shah established a royal dictatorship in 1953 with the support of British Intelligence and the CIA, and he maintained his power-base for the next 25 years with the aid of Savak, the political police force.[10] One of the legacies of this period is that feminism is firmly associated in Iran with western imperialism because the legislation improving the status of women was introduced by a regime pandering to foreign interests. Women were given the vote, but for elections that were boycotted for lack of genuine opposition parties. Not surprisingly, the most popular Iranian version of *A Doll's House* does not date from the Pahlavi era; it was released as a film under the title *Sara* in 1994, and explores the position of women within the Islamic Republic.

Dariush Mehrjui, the director and scriptwriter of *Sara*, played a major role in the development of the new Iranian cinema. For 30 years his films have won critical acclaim both within Iran and internationally. Mehrjui's first international success, *The Cow*, convinced the Ayatollah Khomeini that cinema could have a social function (Cheshire 1998: 28). Yet Mehrjui has had films banned by both the Shah's regime and the Islamic Republic. *Sara* is one of four films with strong central female characters made by Mehrjui between 1992 and 1997. In his adaptation of *A Doll's House*, time, place, and culture are all changed, and the artistic medium has moved from theatre to film, but overall the text is extremely faithful to the original, despite some significant deviations. The question we need to ask of this Islamic Nora (renamed Sara, and played by the popular Iranian film actress Niki Karimi) is what identity space does she offer her Iranian audience, and does she hold residual meanings of European emancipatory feminism that transcend the process of adaptation? In order to answer this question, it is necessary to contextualise the film within the ongoing debates about the position of women in post-revolutionary Iran.

Women were involved throughout the coalition – made up of bourgeois, nationalist, and Marxist–Leninist parties as well as religious activists – that caused the overthrow of the Pahlavi dynasty (Shahidian 1997: 8). It took several years for the Islamic Republic

*Plate 4*   Niki Karimi in *Sara*, 1994, directed by Dariush Mehrjui. Photo reproduced with the permission of Dariush Mehrjui and Hashem Seifi.

to silence the secular elements of this coalition. Although there has been a slow resurgence of secular discourse, particularly since Ayatollah Khomeini's death, discussions regarding the position and role of women are still framed through interpretations of the Qur'an and the life of the Prophet. Some commentators argue that the Qur'an provides a strong basis for equality between the sexes, especially with regard to religious duty, and therefore it is not necessary to go outside the traditional belief system to address problems of gender inequality. Moreover, the Prophet's own life indicates Islamic respect for women, because he married a wealthy woman, Khadija, who ran her own business in which he was an employee. Advocates for this approach include Faezeh Hashemi, a popular member of the elected assembly (the Majlis) and daughter of the former President, Akbar Hashemi Rafsanjani. Her father was noted for his views that western-inspired feminism and materialism were responsible for 'severely impairing women's growth and progress' (Organisation for Human Rights and Fundamental Freedoms for Iran 1997). According to Faezeh Hashemi, the real issue is not a bias against women within the Qur'an, but textual interpretations; she argues that men have always been in control of the interpretation of Islamic laws and have 'implemented them due to their own interests' (Organisation for Human Rights and Fundamental Freedoms for Iran 1997).

Regardless of interpretative subtleties, the regulations in the Qur'an concerning marriage, divorce, and child custody are biased towards men. The dower system, or *mahr*, gives women some financial independence (Mir-Hosseini 1993: 60), and as Islamic law regards marriage as a contract, a woman can insert divorce clauses, subject to her husband's approval (Karmi 1996: 75). In contrast, men may marry up to four wives, have numerous mistresses, and can divorce with comparative ease. Child custody rights also favour the father: under Article 1170 a mother is given custody of her daughter until the age of 7, and of her son until the age of 2; if she remarries she loses all rights over her children (Mir-Hosseini 1993: 67). This legal framework provides the background to the narrative shifts that are visible in the Iranian *A Doll's House*.

Nora has become Sara, Mrs Linde is her schoolfriend, Sima, Helmer is transformed into Hessam, and Krogstad reappears as Goshtasb. The forged signatures, blackmail, and revelation letters remain the same, but the threat that Hessam will be implicated in the forgery is magnified. In contrast, the notion that the law is man-made has diminished, and all discussion of sexuality has been removed. The suggestion that Sara might have committed adultery to pay the loan is dismissed as preposterous. There is no hint of Hessam's sexual fantasies, the tarantella is cut, and the Christmas party becomes a promotion party for Hessam where he dances with the men, while the women sit and watch. A close-up of Sara shows her gently swaying to the music as a tear falls from her eye. Sexuality has been displaced on to the sensuality of the food; rejected food congeals on the plates after Hessam has read the blackmail letter.

The film medium gives Mehrjui a locational freedom that allows him to develop the sense of a sex-segregated world. The two spheres are clearly delineated: the home, hidden behind layers of walls, gardens, doors, curtains, and veils, is contrasted with the modern city run by men. Outside the home women are subject to constant surveillance: when Sima and Sara stand together 'immodestly' laughing in the street, a car accelerates towards them, splattering Sima with water from the gutter. The world of work is totally male-dominated, yet Mehrjui's *mise-en-scène* is filled with the products of women's labour. The female body may be totally covered by the *hejab* (the long black veil), but the sensuality of women is present in all their traditional labour: the bazaar is filled with the beauty of the carpet weaving, needlework, and handicrafts; the fruit and vegetables are voluptuous. Sara sleeps in her sewing room surrounded by beads and white satin, though this romantic image is countered by the knowledge that her eyesight is fading. In contrast, there is no beauty in the women's labour at Hessam's bank. At no point in the film is the life of an unmarried, financially independent woman presented as a viable alternative to an unhappy marriage.

Faced with the decision whether or not to leave Hessam, Sara has no hesitation, but she does not follow in Nora's footsteps. She will return to her father's house, but she will not seek employment or education.[11] The most profound difference between Nora and Sara is tied to the fate of their children. Mehrjui cuts all implication from the text that a child can be corrupted by the lack of moral virtue in a parent, and his heroine defies her husband and insists on taking her 3-year-old daughter with her when she leaves her doll's house. This significant shift in the narrative can be interpreted as a challenge to Iranian child custody laws.

To return to the question regarding the identity space offered by Sara to an Iranian audience, we must assess the relative strengths of the religious and secular discourses within the film. An analysis of the adaptations of the narrative would imply that the religious discourse is pre-eminent. It is not the gender division within the Islamic Republic that is problematised, rather it is the specific relationship between Hessam and Sara and their inability to reach equality within their different roles. Two devices frame the film: sickness and sight. Hessam lies in hospital in the prologue, but he is brought back to health through Sara's actions; as the film ends, he is sick once again, but this time he must heal himself. Paralleling Hessam's sickness is Sara's faulty vision: she has partially lost her sight through her secret labours as a seamstress, but her symbolic blindness can only be cured through her realisation of Hessam's true nature. It can be argued that the solution to the problem within their relationship lies in one of the most disputed of the Qur'anic verses, the *gaymuma*, which is interpreted either as giving men authority over women, or the financial responsibility for their well-being (Karmi 1996: 74). This would presuppose an Islamic interpretation of Sara's miracle, in which Hessam accepts that it is his duty to sacrifice himself in order to protect his wife.

Although aspirations for a modernist subjectivity which link women to the workforce, education, and the world outside the home appear to be eradicated from the narrative, a secular discourse is still present within the film through the politics of clothing. The historical link between modernity and clothing codes is particularly strong in Iran. In 1928, the Pahlavi Shah imposed a universal dress code for men that specified western dress and a round peaked cap; in 1935, the *hejab* was banned for women and the male dress code replaced the cap with a brimmed felt hat. Riots broke out in response to these clothing edicts and a number of people were killed in Azerbaijan, where protesters claimed that the brim of the felt hats prevented their foreheads from touching the ground during prayer. Significantly, it was only the obligatory clothing for women, the *hejab*, which was reintroduced by the Ayatollah Khomeini for workers in post-revolutionary government ministries.[12] Women demonstrated in the streets in protest over the imposition of the veil, but they were subjected to stoning and the revolutionary guards were ordered to fire over their heads (Hiro 1985: 132). Mehrjui uses the dress codes within the film to raise questions about power and gender. The *hejab* that Sara wears restricts her physical freedom as she runs through the streets, picks up crates of bottles, cooks, and cleans. In contrast, western clothes denote power. Hessam, at his most successful, wears and receives gifts of western clothing; but when he is sick at the beginning of the film, or stands in the street powerless to stop Sara and his daughter leaving home, he is draped in the long white folds of the bed-sheets. By analysing the dress codes within the film, we can read a subtle questioning of the Islamic premise of equality in difference. By emphasising the physical restrictions placed on women by their traditional clothing, Mehrjui seems to suggest that women will never achieve equality while they are excluded from the secular world of Iranian modernity.[13] If subjective freedom is the essence of modernity, as Habermas suggests (1987: 83), then the character of Sara is as symptomatic of the identity spaces associated with social modernity as the Noras of Japan and China.

In all the productions we have considered, with the exception of the performance in China in 1956, traditional Confucian or Islamic laws dominate the domestic sphere, and these laws are enforced by men who have been catapulted into a modern world. In this context, male identity is dependent on the capacity of women to embody the traditional cultural values that are threatened by social change. As the inevitable contradiction between the domestic and public spheres intensifies, Nora and Sara, and the women they represent, struggle to transcend the yoke of tradition. The paths they take are determined both by social context and the divergent cultural frameworks of their artist/adaptors. Mehrjui's *Sara* appears the furthest removed from Ibsen's play since the plot has been assimilated into an Iranian world and the medium has shifted to film. Yet in another sense, *Sara* is the most faithful of these adaptations and translations because it works as a social-realist text through identification and empathy. In Japan, the Buddhist concept of 'awakening' is predominant, but sexuality and performance are major themes, as indicated by the re-working of the plot in *Feeble Husband* and *Sunrise, Nora in Japan*. All references to performance and sexuality are removed from the Iranian adaptation, which seeks to re-interpret rather than overthrow Islamic law. In China, the text variously becomes, over a period of 44 years, an advocate for westernisation, the embodiment of the communist revolution, and a condemnation of western decadence.

Despite the differences in the translations and interpretations of *A Doll's House*, in each culture the central character functions as an 'interpretive mechanism' (Chun 1996: 69) for the audience to explore the consequences of adopting new identity spaces made available to women through the social changes associated with modernity. It is this acquisition by women of an identity embodying subjective freedom, rather than the adoption of the specifically western form of emancipatory feminism, that appears to traverse geographical boundaries. As the identity space embodied by Nora shifts and adapts to diverse cultural contexts, certain aspects of the character are highlighted and others are marginalised. It is ironic that Nora's decision to leave her children, the most controversial aspect of the late nineteenth-century European productions of Ibsen's play, is treated as a minor rather than a major aspect of the narrative in Chinese and Japanese productions, and it is completely removed from the Iranian version. Hence motherhood is not presented in these adaptations as contradictory to the creation of an identity space embodying subjective freedom; rather it is represented as an adjunct identity that can coexist with new social formations. In order to consider the creation of an identity space within an intercultural text that directly challenges the social order through a re-working and re-defining of mother-hood, we must leave *A Doll's House*, and look instead at a play marked by maternal absence.

## *ANTIGONE* IN THE PLAZA DE MAYO

*Antigone* has become identified in the late twentieth century with one of the most important collective struggles against the violence of the state, a struggle conducted by a group who define themselves first and foremost as mothers. In a paradigmatic version of *Antigone* for the late twentieth century, Griselda Gambaro's *Antígona Furiosa*, mothers and motherhood in Argentina take up a public and even subversive role. It may seem curious that this study of women's intercultural performance returns to *Antigone* as an intercultural site. *Antigone* may also seem removed from *inter*culturalism because ancient Greece is the culture that most Europeans and westerners feel they 'own': it plays a wise ancestor role in the exalted heritage of western culture, when in reality most cultures retain only a distant aesthetic appreciation of Greek theatre.

The narrative of the play pits Antigone against her uncle, Creon, who has contravened spiritual laws by forbidding the burial of Antigone's slain brother, Polynices. Antigone deliberately buries Polynices, and each time an enraged Creon insists that his body be disinterred. Creon's son, Haemon, who is betrothed to Antigone, tries unsuccessfully to convince his father to relent, on the grounds that his decision represents poor leadership. The blind seer, Teiresias, prophesies a bleak future, following Creon's stubborn action (and Antigone's equally stubborn reaction), which prompts a reluctant Creon to relent. He orders the burial of Polynices and pardons Antigone, only to find that he is too late: both Haemon and Antigone have killed themselves out of divergent senses of honour. The tragic day is concluded when Creon's wife commits suicide. The Chorus, composed of elders of the city of Thebes, acts as the bridge between the audience and the actors/action, becoming more powerful as the play proceeds. The role of the Chorus suggests that they hold a possible compromise between the stances adopted by Antigone and Creon, also reminding the audience that the play presents a political dilemma as well as a domestic drama.

The narrative is open to multiple interpretations and recontextualisations, because of its polarising of opinions and its refusal of narrative closure. It demands answers to the following questions: Is Creon to blame for the various deaths? Should Antigone have capitulated? Should Creon have relented on his harsh and strident decree? *Antigone* has thus been taken up for a variety of critical, literary, political, cultural, and even moral purposes. As a means of validating the tenets of the Church of the Latter Day Saints, for example, *Antigone* holds 'a timeless and eternal . . . lesson [that] is grounded in family. Every individual, unless he is truly rootless, experiences in his own context the same conflict that the Theban uncle and his niece undergo' (Waterstradt 1979: 507). From a radically different perspective, Ynestra King has used *Antigone* to justify ecofeminism (King 1990: 107–8). George Steiner chronicles how *Antigone*, rather than *Oedipus Rex*, has intrigued writers and philosophers including Hegel and Kierkegaard (Steiner 1984: 104).[14]

Throughout the twentieth century, the play has been used so often as a vehicle for political resistance that Steiner claimed in 1984 that 'no complete catalogue of the explicit and implicit lives of the Antigone theme, from its mythical, "pre-epic" origins to the present, has been or can be drawn up. The field is too vast' (ibid.: 194). The most famous of the twentieth-century versions of *Antigone* is Jean Anouilh's war-time production, which premiered on 4 February 1944 at the Théâtre de l'Atelier in Paris. In fact, some contemporary productions of the play borrow from Anouilh more than Sophocles. Employed specifically to fight the

Nazi Occupation of France, Anouilh's text was cleverly designed to satisfy both parties: the German officials were pleased with the cultural exhibition and the conclusion which seemed to vindicate their government – because, as Steiner points out, 'Creon *wins*' (ibid.: 193) – while the French audience read it as a warning that Creon's ruthless power would continue if they failed to resist the Occupation.

Since the Second World War, *Antigone* has been read increasingly as an example of a woman defying the patriarchy of the state. The play has been championed for its feminist possibilities, but as we have argued with regard to Nora, the manifestation of this women-centred approach can and does vary depending on the cultural context. Antigone resists political tyranny, but she also represents an individual woman defying patriarchal control and insisting on the validity of her own autonomy. This is particularly true in those adaptations set in repressive states. As Hölderlin reminds us, the attraction to *Antigone* is its marking of 'a moment of "national reversal and revolution"' (ibid.: 81). Among the women writers or directors around the world who have returned to *Antigone* are Ratna Sarumpaet in Indonesia[15] and Somalatha Subasinghe in Sri Lanka.[16] Both their versions highlight state inequity and injustice and investigate how women can help redress state violence. We look specifically at the ways in which Gambaro has adapted *Antigone* to foreground the struggle for women's rights. In contrast to the focus on the resistance of a female protagonist in the private sphere that dominated in the first part of this chapter, we shift here to a focus on the resistance of a female protagonist in the public sphere.

## Griselda Gambaro and the Mothers of the Plaza de Mayo

The most significant adaptation of *Antigone* in recent years is Gambaro's *Antígona Furiosa*.[17] Well known for her novels as well as her plays, Gambaro is unafraid of drawing attention to the violence that has characterised Argentine governments for decades. Her work is closely associated with her country and its complex social politics. Gambaro acknowledges that her culture is quite different from Sophocles' and that she has not studied the extensive intellectual and analytical history of Sophocles' play. Nevertheless, she maintains that *Antigone* is Argentinian:

Antigone belonged to us because we had painfully earned the right to it. Antigone lived and still lives in Argentina, a country which has repeated, in a parallel way impossible to conceal, the old story of unlimited power that takes revenge, kills those whom it considers its enemies and denies them not only a funeral and a tomb, but also the right to be remembered.

In my case, when I had finished telling the story, I could see, not so much of that Antigone who has been present in so many pages, but rather those Antigones who every Thursday, during the most difficult days of military rule, their heads covered with white scarves and carrying photos of their children, walked around the square, shaking with fear.

(Gambaro 1995: 58)

Rather than using Greek theatre to consider rights or wrongs or to explain Argentina, Gambaro deploys *Antigone* interculturally to combine gender with social politics and aesthetics to comment on women's roles in contemporary Argentina. She firmly states her intention to rewrite *Antigone* in 'the voice of a Latin American and Argentinian woman and with the voices of other women who had tried to do in Argentina what Antigone did: disobey omnipotent power and bury their loved ones' (ibid.: 57).

Contemporary Argentinian history is notorious for the highly repressive military juntas that ruled the country between 1976 and 1983. The self-imposed powers of the military government enabled a 'structural transformation of the economy and the extension of an anti-insurgency campaign to all areas of political life. Civil and political rights were denied: the Constitution was suspended, Congress was closed, unions were terrorized, and the judiciary was silenced' (Brysk 1994: 677). The favoured mechanism for ensuring the continuation of power and the quelling of opposition was 'disappearance'.[18] Over 30,000 citizens disappeared, many simply because they were educated. The excuse the Argentinian government gave for this violence was the necessity of preventing further infiltration by supposed Marxist elements. Schirmer explains that

[disappearance] is the perfect crime, as the crime itself is invisible, except to those who are victims or relatives. Both are meant to suffer silently, individually and alone. The victim is denied martyrdom; those left behind are prohibited the final ritual of bereavement. . . . Disappearance then is a form of censorship of memory by the state.

(Schirmer 1989: 5)

Most were young, some were even children, and one-third were women. Most of the victims were savagely and repeatedly tortured before being killed, and only 1,500 people 'returned' from the 342 concentration camps around the country (Taylor 1997: 151). This act of disappearance attempted to reshape the people completely into a more conservative, subservient populace. This culture of silence and blindness, supported by the American government and multinational corporations,[19] was challenged by Las Madres or the Mothers of the Plaza de Mayo.

The Mothers have been an important political and cultural presence since 13 April 1977, when 14 women began their march. The numbers have gradually increased, and the women continue to march every Thursday afternoon at 3.30 pm to remind Argentinians of their recent past and to ensure that history is not repeated. They have always been very visible because of their choice of meeting place: the Plaza de Mayo, well known in Argentina for its patriotic and historical significance, is 'in front of the Casa Rosada, the headquarters of the Argentine government in the center of Buenos Aires' (Femenía 1987: 14). While disappearances no longer occur, the Mothers still march to ensure that their children are remembered, and to demand that the perpetrators of these and other government-sanctioned crimes against humanity be brought to justice.[20]

As they gather into their marching circle, the women don their costume (a white headscarf embroidered with the name of their missing child/children and the date of the disappearance), and they begin to perform the social role of mother. They refuse to accept the state's lies that they were bad mothers, or that their children were deviant, or even that their children never existed (Schirmer 1989: 20). The Mothers deploy the social expectations of mothers looking after – or here looking *for* – their children. In performing motherhood they play, to some degree, with the gender roles available to them as women within the very conservative social order in Argentina, where women's roles are limited to two: madonna-like mother or whore. These women have become activists by default, simply by trying to find out what happened to their children.

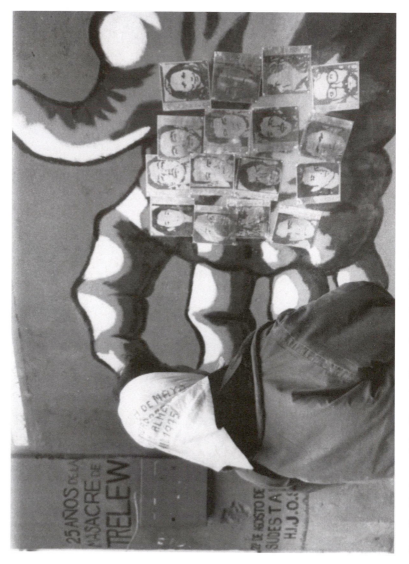

*Plate 5* Mothers of the Plaza de Mayo, Argentina, 1999. Photo credit: Lucila Quieto.

*Plate 6* Mothers of the Plaza de Mayo, Argentina, 1999. Photo credit: Clara Rosson.

The Mothers succeeded both in challenging the codes by which they were represented and in making their children (or at least the memory of their children) symbolically reappear. Success is, however, a relative term here. The Mothers were almost completely unsuccessful in having their children materially or literally restored to them (even in death: their bodies were by and large unrecovered, having been buried in mass, unmarked graves or thrown – alive – from planes into the sea, or chopped into pieces before being burned) but their persistent protest focused international attention on the atrocities of the government.[21]

Not content just to make life-risking statements by turning their own bodies into 'walking billboards' (Taylor 1997: 183), the Mothers have also incorporated their children's 'bodies' into their protest. They pin their children's photos to their clothes, wear photos around their necks, hold small photos and large placards, all bearing the young faces of their disappeared children. Some of the Mothers even say that they feel their children's presence, walking beside them as they march (Agosin 1987: 434–5). The signification of the photos has changed over the years. Most people who witness the Mothers' march comment on the age of the photos: the haircuts, clothes, and styles of, usually, the early 1970s. At first representing both loss and hope, they have come, after the revelation that the children were long since murdered, to represent torture and repression.

This is not, however, the only manner in which the Mothers have deployed 'bodies'. Nora Amalia Femenía lists their tactics:

> they constructed life-sized paper silhouettes, labeling each one with the name of an actual *desaparecido*. These posters appeared on the walls of buildings around Buenos Aires. In another campaign, they circulated paper cutouts shaped like human hands to symbolize the actual hands of their missing loved ones. They released balloons with the names of the disappeared attached to them. Later, they paraded wearing identical masks, to symbolize the common plight of all the victims. . . . [T]he individual nature of their losses was transformed into a collective loss. 'One child, all the children', the Mothers said.
>
> (Femenía 1987: 15)

In the early years, the Mothers carried photos of their own children. Now they take up posters of any of the disappeared, or what they also call their 'living apparitions' (Ortiz 1995: 24).

The effect of this corporeal sleight of hand is to enforce a cultural memory that recalls both the individual bodies and the collectivised body of the disappeared. From these disembodied images comes a material insistence on the danger of forgetting. The Mothers have ensured that traces of bodies and traces of body parts crop up all over the place. People in the centre of the city must continually 'see' the images of the Mothers themselves and their mission. It is against the background of the Mothers in the Plaza and the events they represent that Gambaro's *Antígona Furiosa* was written.

## Antígona Furiosa

Gambaro explains that *Antígona Furiosa* is a

> collage, unified by my own language. . . . [It] does not follow the structure of a classical play, but that of a cantata where it is clear from the beginning what is going to happen. Antígona, who appears strangled at the beginning of the play, revives to tell her story and this initial death somehow renders Creon's actions useless.
>
> (Gambaro 1995: 57)

While Sophocles' play pits the heroine with and against Creon, Gambaro's play figures the relationship in more of a triangle: Antígona (as Gambaro names her), Creon, and the Chorus figures, the porteños (men from Buenos Aires). The porteños, Coryphaeus and Antinous, are party to Creon's violence, but they are also distinct from him. This stripped-down version of the play has only three actors. The roles of Ismene and Haemon are 'played' by Antígona and thus represented through her perspective. Antígona also re-enacts the battle between her brothers. Coryphaeus doubles as Creon, who is represented by a large, hard-framed costume that resembles a protective, armoured shell. In contrast to Creon's stiff, shell-like appearance, Antígona moves with sensuality and fluidity. Teiresias' presence is felt, but he is not represented on the stage. The plague that he prophesies is manifested in slime that falls upon the porteños, and the wings of an enormous bird that represents death to Antígona. When the play begins, Antígona is seen hanging from one of the bars, foreshadowing the end of the play. She then comes to life, but remains locked in a pyramid-shaped cell or cage, with the audience seated around her. Around the cage/cell are several café tables where Coryphaeus and Antinous sit.

*Antígona Furiosa* is based on constructions of power, particularly power divided along gender lines. The most powerful figure is Creon, whose military-style language (and even its rhythm) represents a more authoritarian, fear-based, iron-fisted rule than Sophocles' Creon. When Gambaro's Creon begins to repeat himself maniacally, his power becomes terrifying. He does pardon Antígona, too late of course, but he refuses to bury Polynices, the very thing that she – like the Mothers – demands. Unlike Sophocles' even-handed play, Gambaro's version takes a principled stand with Antígona.

It is in the representation of the two porteños that the nature of absolute power is most apparent. Unlike a Greek Chorus, Coryphaeus and Antinous are differentiated. Coryphaeus has a lugubrious and self-serving sense of humour whereas Antinous is stupid, easily frightened, and confused by both Coryphaeus and Antígona. The porteños are allied to Creon through fear and their common desire to exert power over other human beings. They are complicit in acts of torture with Creon. Their continual mocking of Antígona (as well as Antinous' bumbling confusion) prevents them from acting, like Sophocles' Chorus, as the identificatory bridge to the audience. They believe themselves to be superior to Antígona, because they are male and she is female: they judge her life to be worthless. Neither the porteños nor Creon has the last word in the play because they are complicit in the Argentinian atrocities, and cannot speak dispassionately about human nature (the characteristic choric ending to a Greek play). The inability of the porteños to see the effects of their actions feeds Antígona's fury.

The behaviour of the porteños points to the inhumanity of a corrupt regime where brutal punishment and the complicity of the country's citizens cheapen all lives. Like the symbolic power of the figure of Nora, Antígona represents a subversive collective identity, one figured in Argentina most powerfully by the Mothers of the Plaza de Mayo. This collective identity is designed to force the nation to remember the disappeared in opposition to the very deliberate intention of the disappearances to prevent memory and the marking of either life or death. While Coryphaeus taunts Antígona with comments such as 'Remembering the dead is like grinding water with a mortar and pestle – useless' (Gambaro 1992: 140), she insists on acknowledging the death of her brother. The Mothers' power and right to remember is raised later when

Antinous, in a confused state, asks 'If we know already that she dies, why doesn't she die?' (ibid.: 154). While this acts as a meta-theatrical statement and points to the audience's role in the shaping of future events, Antinous' comments also reveal that the dead do not simply die and go away.


## CONCLUSION

Antígona dares to challenge the patriarchal order and surprises Antinous who maintains that 'Women don't fight against men!' (Gambaro 1992: 145). Both the audiences and the texts we have considered in this chapter prove his statement wrong. The narratives revolve around the fate of two female protagonists who defy male-defined sacred or secular law; the open-ended structures of these texts allow for cultural relocations and multiple rewritings. We have argued that these narratives have an intercultural value to societies gripped by the social upheavals associated with modernity, or the political turmoil triggered by state violence, and that the translations and adaptations we have discussed are motivated by social, more than aesthetic, considerations.

The initial impetus to re-work these narratives is tied to the recognition by artists that women are challenging conventional gender norms within their societies. They also look to other cultures for additional representational vehicles configured as identity spaces to conceptualise these transformations. We do not intend to suggest that these theatrical representations instigate social change, merely that they give symbolic expression to the lived realities of women enacting these changes.

Gambaro re-interprets the actions of the Mothers through the myth of Antigone, a symbolic figure who crosses the important public/private divide, daring to demonstrate publicly, daring to insist that her demands be met. In Argentina, their actions have disengaged motherhood from its association with 'oppression' in a patriarchal culture and re-associated it with political intervention. Gambaro draws on the lived reality of the Mothers to reconfigure the myth of *Antigone* but her adaptation does not function merely as a reflection of the demonstrations at the Plaza de Mayo; the dramatic text engages dialogically with its audience. Towards the end of the play, Creon pardons Antígona and mourns all he has lost, but then Antinous re-defines Creon's actions when he says:

'(theatrical[ly]) Bravo! (CORYPHAEUS *removes the robe, bows*)' (ibid.: 158). In this fascinating play on theatricality, the role of the audience, and the complicity of the witnesses, *Antígona Furiosa* demonstrates that it is, indeed, all an act, an act that can either be played again or adapted, depending on its audience. A dialogic relation linking theatre to political struggle is equally apparent in the relationship between Nora and the writers of *Seito*: they address her literally by name in their critical writings. Censorship makes this process more oblique with regard to *A Doll's House* in Iran, but in China the ongoing dialogic and interactive process between the theatre artists and their audiences is manifested in the changing interpretations of Ibsen's play.

Is it just the narrative and dramaturgical structures of these texts that are crucial to this dialogic process, or is the relationship between the central protagonist and her audience also an essential element in this interaction? Nora and Antigone are constantly re-defined by the lived reality of women engaged in the struggle for social change, but they also offer back to these same women a three-dimensional theatrical embodiment of new identity spaces. 'Bluestockings', 'girl agitators', and 'Mothers' are living images tied to discursive practices; they are also referents for Nora and Antigone. Rosi Braidotti argues that:

> [i]dentity and subjectivity are different and interrelated moments in the process of defining a subject position. This idea of the subject as process means that he/she can no longer be seen to coincide with his/her consciousness but must be thought of as a complex and multiple identity, as the site of the dynamic interaction of desire with the will, of subjectivity with the unconscious.
>
> (Braidotti 1994: 196)

Subjectivity, by this definition, is an amalgam of multiple identities drawn from a culturally specific repertoire. Members of the audience explore these identity spaces as they follow the characters through the dramatic narrative, accepting some elements while rejecting others.

It is our contention that the translation and adaptation of texts across cultures can increase the repertoire of identity spaces available to audiences, and can assist in articulating the shifts in subjectivity triggered by social upheaval. This process is particularly significant when the identity spaces contained within the performed texts are capable of expressing a lived reality that is insufficiently symbolised within the existing frameworks of the host culture. Although the plays explored in this chapter are part of the European canon, we would argue that the intercultural process of translation and adaptation has minimised the cultural imperialist dangers of these texts while maximising their social and political value to women struggling for social change. In consequence, these texts succeed in performing a desirable function for a culturally diverse set of female subjects across both space and time.

In the next chapter, identity spaces and the construction of subjectivity are still central to our critique, but from intercultural texts that aid the construction of female subject positions within modernity, we move to intercultural performances that aim at filling an imaginary lack within this same subjectivity. Our focus shifts from the pursuit of subjective freedom to the perceived lack of spirituality that lies deep within the subjective constructions of modernity, and the concomitant desire expressed by western consumers for products that provide a return to a state of imaginary plenitude. One product that is marketed in post-industrial western cultures as capable of satisfying this need is women's intercultural ritual performance.

# Chapter 2

# Ritual translocations

## Kim Kum hwa
## and Warlpiri women

[A]rtists and Aborigines emerge as the redemptive bearers of the power to heal our spiritual alienation from ourselves which modernity has inflicted. . . . This aestheticising of Aborigines transforms them into the spiritual side of the western self, they become that which the West lacks and must recoup if it is to re-establish wholeness.

(Lattas 1991: 323)

I would not be able to perform any kind of ritual, even in a theatre context, without the gods residing in me. Without the gods that I serve residing in myself, I wouldn't be able to perform on the razor sharp blades. The limited time, the bright light, the audience not being attached to the performance, these things make a difference and can disturb me, but I invite all the gods within myself and that remains the same.

(Kim Kum hwa 1995: 20)

In the previous chapter we argued that the female identity spaces contained in *A Doll's House* and *Antigone* contributed to the successful export of these European narratives to non-western countries. The trading of subjectivities also dominates this chapter, but from western exports we turn to western imports, and particularly to the shifts in subjectivity introduced to audiences through the performance of shamanic and indigenous rituals. Once again we make the distinction between identities linked to the private and public domains. In the realm of the private, we shall consider a performance tour of four Australian cities by the Korean shaman and spiritual leader, Kim Kum hwa; with regard to the public domain, we consider ritual performances in these same four cities by indigenous women from the Central Australian Warlpiri clan. In both these accounts we invite the artists to explain their motivations for performing ritual in an intercultural context, and we explore the meanings derived from their performances by urban Australian audiences. We argue that the Korean performances were consumed as a form of personal spiritual enrichment and the Warlpiri performances were consumed as symbolic gestures in the creation of national identity.

Ritual has long been associated with theatre and, more importantly, with intercultural theatre. Artaud, Grotowski, and Brook incorporated the rituals of other cultures to 'try to shake theater out of the slumber of aestheticism' (Grimes 1982: 539). In addition, ritual has long been an interest for theatre anthropologists who tend to suggest that just by staging rituals, we can 'reacquire' pathways to lost spirituality, albeit in a slightly different, mediated form. There are three major strands in current definitions of ritual. The first and most narrow tends to analyse particular rituals as frozen, unchanging moments associated with non-western cultures that are frequently described by (problematic) words such as 'primitive'. The second situates ritual in the role of the ancient ancestor of contemporary theatre, a location which also makes links between ritual and the primitive very easy, and which implicitly justifies the use of ritual as theatre, regardless of context. The third, more encompassing definition suggests that virtually every activity in which humans regularly engage can be considered a ritual act.[1]

We prefer not to subscribe strictly to any of these three strands. Rather, we see ritual as being an activity performed in a particular location that has been prepared in some way; by an authorised practitioner(s); at a particular time that may not pertain to clock time; for an audience who may or may not share the culture/faith of the practitioner(s); and for the specific benefit of a community. In this context, then, ritual is inflected with religious worship or recognition of religious spirituality: the faith that maintains a culture or a community, whether in worship, re-affirmation, celebration, solidarity, or continuity. 'Ritual action effects social transitions or spiritual transformations; it does not merely mark or accompany them' (MacAloon 1984: 250). Barbara Myerhoff (1984: 155) explains ritual as 'a form by which culture presents itself to itself'. It takes place in a particular timeframe that differs from regular, lived time: '[t]o do their work rituals must disrupt our ordinary sense of time and displace our awareness of events coming into being and disappearing in discrete, precise, discontinuous segments' (ibid.: 173). Just as the time is at odds with conventional, chronological time, so, on occasion, are the participants: many rituals include an audience of ancestors and 'members' of the community who are, as yet, unborn.

Rituals are not impervious to change. As a community inevitably changes, so do its rituals, which, Grimes reminds us, 'have life cycles and life spans' (Grimes 1982: 543). Other socio-political factors (such as the introduction of a colonial presence or a technological shift) can affect the way in which rituals are performed, and, indeed, if they are even performed at all. The major factor affecting the rituals that we are about to consider is the translocation of the ritual site. Removing a ritual from the location in which it evolved, and from the community that gives it purpose, changes not only the form and function of the performance, but also its meaning. When ritual performances are imported into post-industrial western societies, these new meanings are frequently tied to the audiences' perceived lack of spirituality.

Western culture has been haunted by nostalgia for a primordial union, or a return to a state of imaginary plenitude, since reason replaced religion, and the cohesive social body founded on religious observation disappeared from the modern world.

> Since the close of the eighteenth century, the discourse of modernity has had a single theme under ever new titles: the weakening of the forces of social bonding, privatisation, and diremption – in short, the deformations of a one-sidedly rationalised everyday praxis which evoke the need for something equivalent to the unifying power of religion.
>
> (Habermas 1987: 139)

With the Enlightenment, the determining structure of subjectivity became possessive individualism: self-reliance, private conscience, and individual rights to property, person, and body. Deprived of a sense of community, the rational subject of modernity was doomed to search for some panacea to ward off existential isolation and loneliness. The consequences of this shift in subjectivity have been eloquently theorised by Jurgens Habermas: '[s]ome place their hope in the reflective power of reason, or at least in a mythology of reason; others swear by the mythopoetic power of an art that is supposed to form the focal point of a regenerated public life' (Habermas 1987: 139). The nineteenth-century Romantics popularised the view that art was a mechanism for reclaiming social harmony, and they looked to nature as the source of their new-found spirituality. The qualities attributed to the supernatural in traditionally defined religious faith were re-assigned, and an assumption made that in the vastness of nature, it was possible to glimpse the vastness of the soul. In the late twentieth century this conflation of community, nature, and spirituality has found its expression in New Age and neo-pagan movements which almost always have an environmental message, one in which women, and their reproductive capabilities, are central. Carol P. Christ's vision of the world is typical of the relationship between nature, spirituality, and women:

> With many spiritual feminists, ecofeminists, ecologists, anti-nuclear activists, and others, I share the conviction that the crisis that threatens the destruction of the earth is not only social, political, economic, and technological, but is at root spiritual. We have lost the sense that this earth is our true home, and we fail to recognize our profound connection with all beings in the web of life. . . . The preservation of the earth requires a profound shift in consciousness: a recovery of more ancient and traditional views that revere the connection of all beings in the web of life and a rethinking of the relation of humanity and divinity to nature.
>
> (Christ 1989: 314)

It should not surprise us to discover that once a lack has been identified in a western consumer-oriented culture, a product appears in the marketplace that promises to satisfy the need. In the case of a lack that is perceived as spiritual, the postmodern marketplace (with its talent for selling non-western cultures in a borderless global interchange) offers new types of spiritual well-being borrowed from an amorphous mass of different cultures. Spirituality is perceived to be extant in those cultures considered 'other' by the west and variously labelled as primitive and irra-tional. One of the inevitable results of this appropriation of a variety of cultural customs is the collapse of boundaries in the rhetoric of New Age and neo-pagan movements. Indigenous spiritualities become homogenised and then blended with references to nature and environmentalism, all in opposition to mainstream culture.

Leslie Jones concludes that 'the explicit message of the druid-as-shaman' is, then, to 'assume that their spiritual opposition to the worst of culture makes them automatically One With Nature' (Jones 1994: 136).

The packaging of spirituality as a commodity – and particularly the spirituality of an indigenous culture defined by the west as primitive, mythic, and irrational – presents peculiar problems for the marketplace. 'Indigenous wisdom', Piers Vitebsky notes, 'must be packaged into the format of a database: the butterfly must be killed in order to take its rightful place in the glass case' (Vitebsky 1995: 199). The product must be packaged in a form that can be readily consumed, but retain the essence of the raw material of spirituality which may well have been defined as the inalienable connection between a culture and the land. There is an inevitable contradiction implied in the process of translocation of a spiritual essence from an imaginary site of spiritual plenitude to the alienated urban environments of post-industrial capital. Cultural artefacts in the form of live ritual performance have distinct advantages within this packaging process because the spiritual strength of the ritual performers allows them to act metonymically for the land. Ritual can offer a heady mixture of spirituality, nature, and community to the purposive rational subject suffering from existential angst, and the product can be consumed through an intercultural encounter without ever leaving home.

## KOREAN SHAMANISM: KIM KUM HWA

In 1994, Kim Kum hwa performed extracts from a *Kut*, or ritual performance, in four major Australian cities. Evidence suggests that the audience expected an ecstatic experience and personal spiritual enrichment from the performance, but it is not clear whether they were latter-day Romantics, or followers of Nietzsche looking to the realm of aesthetics to undermine the rational and pragmatic basis of all thought and action. Habermas has suggested that Nietzsche opened the door to a postmodern subjectivity by proposing a fragmented subject capable of self-oblivion through an aesthetic encounter with rapture and the unforeseen. He believed that an ecstatic experience could undermine the basis of individualism and open up 'the escape route from modernity' (Habermas 1987: 94).[2] The audiences may have been looking for this 'escape route', but is the modern subject, schooled in self-reliance, scientific rationalism, and personal freedom, capable of breaking down the boundaries of the individual ego to merge into a 'communion' stimulated by ritual performance? In this context, we are using Georges Gurvitch's definition of 'communion' as a state 'when minds open out as widely as possible and the least accessible depths of the "I" are integrated in this fusion (which presupposes states of collective ecstasy)' (cited in Turner 1982: 45).[3]

According to Hahm Pyong-choon, in Korea the 'communion' associated with shamanistic ritual is being eroded by 'modernisation, Westernisation, urbanisation, industrialisation, and the development of science and technology' (Hahm 1988: 95). Shamanistic subjectivity is predicated on a sense of continuity with nature; any boundary created between the individual and the community is feared and abhorred. '[T]he continuum of the human ego is not limited to interpersonal relations and human behaviour: the human ego overlaps with non-human beings as well' (ibid.: 67). But Hahm concludes that this subjectivity has been undermined by the introduction of an industrialised economy. In the light of his comments, it appears impossible for the average purposive-rational subject in post-industrial Australia with no knowledge of Korean culture or language to experience a state of communion in a ritual performed by a charismatic shaman from Seoul. On the other hand, as Hyun Chang, Kim Kum hwa's interpreter during the Australian tour, points out: 'we are culturally conditioned, but spirits are not. If there are spiritual realms which influence our emotions it would not be necessary for the audience to have a good understanding of Korean language or culture' (personal correspondence with authors, 14 May 1999). But the question remains: how was the expectation of this experience manufactured within the Australian audience? To understand this dynamic, we must examine the promotion and marketing of the performance tour, in particular the pre-publicity that appeared in the Australian press, the subsequent reviews of the performance, and the use of Kim Kum hwa's image in a wide variety of publications from daily newspapers to academic journals. In the light of this evidence, we highlight the contradictions that emerged between the press coverage of the tour and Kim Kum hwa's motivations in performing a shamanic ritual for Australian audiences. The gap between the intentions of the ritual performers and the expectations of the audience provides a rich seam of intercultural enquiry. However, before we can examine this gap, we must contextualise Korean shamanism, the infrastructure of Kim Kum hwa's tour, and provide a description of her Australian performance.

There are two distinct forms of shamanism in Korea: the southern part of the peninsula is known for its highly musical form of hereditary shamanism, while the central and northern parts are known for charismatic shamanism and the technique of trance possession by which the pantheon of Korean gods appear.[4] As a folk religion, shamanism holds a place alongside the official belief systems of Buddhism and Confucianism, which were introduced into Korea in elitist and male-dominated forms. After Confucianism was adopted by the Chosun Kingdom in 1392, shamanism became associated with women and the home; today 90 per cent of the charismatic shaman, or *mudang*, are women.[5] The traditional role of the *mudang* is to act as a medium between the worlds of the living and the dead, and to ensure the spiritual well-being of the community. With the growth of the pro-democracy movement in the 1970s, the figure of the shaman became a popular national icon: a representation of the true spirit or culture of Korea. In the political theatre of the 1970s, the shaman figure was ubiquitous.[6] Cultural assertion was a strong element of the pro-democracy movement in South Korea, and the traditional arts of dancing, drumming, and *pansori* (a folk opera form) were learned by many of the student activists. It was with the assistance of the San Maek Theatre Company, which specialises in teaching these skills to students and workers, that Kim Kum hwa was invited to perform in Australia. The Third International Women Playwrights' Conference (3IWPC) had issued the invitation,[7] and the San Maek director, Suh Kwang Seok, convinced Kim Kum hwa that the cultural movement in Korea would benefit from her presence at the Conference.

Kim Kum hwa accepted the invitation on the condition that the Conference organised ritual performances in a number of major cities. These were arranged in partnership with the Perth Arts Trust, the Victorian Arts Centre in Melbourne, and the Museum of Contemporary Art in Sydney. Additional funds were raised from the Australia Korea Foundation, which was actively encouraging cultural exchanges during this period as Korea had become Australia's second largest trading partner. The contractual arrangements were based on Australian entertainment industry standards and were approved by the Media and Entertainment Arts Alliance. In every respect – from the applications for artists' visas, the booking of venues, and payment of performance fees – the Australian tour was designed to conform to entertainment industry standards. At no point was Kim Kum hwa's identity as a spiritual leader considered within these transactions. On a contractual level the performances were treated as secular entertainment; it was only in the subsequent marketing campaigns that they were attributed a spiritual content.

Kim Kum hwa decided to perform a *Taedong Kut*, a ritual celebration for the community, in Australia. According to Suh Kwang Seok, the elements of the performance were derived from the *Ch'olmuri-gut*, or Great Ritual of Good Fortune, which originated in Hwanghae-Do, the province of North Korea where Kim Kum hwa and the older members of her company were born. There are many variations of the great ritual, and its exact form is determined by its function: a community celebration connected to a rural calendar, a birth or death rite for a private family, or a ritual performed by a shaman for initiatory or supplicatory purposes. The basic structure of the great ritual involves a pre-rite of purification, between 12 and 24 discrete episodes, and a post-rite of exorcism through fire. Each of the episodes involves the invocation of a particular deity or set of deities and follows a standard pattern: the deity is invoked, descends, issues warnings regarding the future, and is entertained and dismissed. Specific costumes, props, songs, and dances are associated with each of the deities. Shaman, or *mudang*, become known for their close affinity to particular figures from this pantheon. The great ritual cannot be performed in less than one day (in a rural environment it may take as long as a week) but adaptation is permissible and condensed versions are performed in civic theatres throughout Korea.

In Australia, the performance had to fit into a 75-minute slot and was adapted by Kim Kum hwa to please an audience unfamiliar with Korean language and culture. The performance consisted of extracts from seven episodes, or *kori*, with the emphasis on visual spectacle, music, and comedy.[8] Throughout the performance the musicians accompanied Kim Kum hwa and the junior shaman as they sang, danced, and transformed into the deities. The drums provided the rhythmic structure for the spiralling and jumping movements that preceded these trance states. The company performed three famous spectacles from the repertoire of the charismatic shaman (*mudang*) of North and Central Korea: a male shaman, cross-dressed as a woman, balanced a pig carcass on a trident to symbolise the presence and blessings of the deities; nine yards of white cloth (the road to the other world) was torn apart by the body of a female shaman forcing a pathway through the woven material to demonstrate the interweaving and subsequent separation of the living and dead; and, at the climax of the *Kut*, Kim Kum hwa appeared as the Knife Riding General. The rite she performed is known as the *Chak Doo Ta Ki*, a version of the Warrior Deity episode, which involves dancing on the sharpened blades of ploughshares.[9] This dance is intended to frighten away unwanted spirits attracted to the ritual site by the noise of the *Kut*. A comic interlude followed the *Chak Doo Ta Ki* and provided a transition from the intense concentration of the trance performance to the celebratory conclusion of the *Kut*. A member of the audience was invited on to the stage and, while wine was poured down her throat, Kim Kum hwa impersonated a lecherous farmer with a mock phallus made out of a drumstick. The phallus was thrust at the women drum players and at the laughing members of the audience, until the company, exuding good will, invited the whole audience to join them on the stage. Everyone was dressed in elements of the brightly coloured shaman costumes as they danced to the compulsive rhythms of the drums and cymbals. The stage was packed with exuberant dancers. When the drums stopped, the exhausted audience joined hands with the company and knelt, placing their foreheads on the ground, to receive a communal blessing.

## Marketing the *Kut*

Having described the basic structure of the Australian *Taedong Kut* and the logistical arrangements of the tour, we can now focus on the central aspect of this account of ritual translocation: the construction of audience expectation through the marketing strategies, pre-publicity, and performance reviews. Prior to the commencement of the tour, all the venues were provided with the necessary background material for their marketing and production departments. This included information about the Conference to contextualise the tour, basic factual material about Kim Kum hwa and the importance of shamanism in Korea, the technical specifications for the performance, and a video of a similar performance presented by Kim Kum hwa and her company in a theatre venue in Korea.

Vicki Laurie, a freelance journalist based in Perth, contacted the Conference and requested that an interview be arranged for her with Kim Kum hwa in Seoul. This interview appeared in slightly different forms in *The Bulletin*, *The West Australian*, and *The Advertiser*.[10] In all the versions of her article, the following etymology of the word shaman appeared: 'its origin is obscure, thought to be a native Siberian word for "healer" and probably originating in Sanskrit (from "Srama" religious exercise)' (3IWPC 1994b). Laurie continued, 'perhaps more helpful in grasping the shaman's role are terms like mystic, fortune-teller, and faith-healer'. In fact, the Chinese word for shaman phonetically represents the Sanskrit *sramana*, meaning diligent or laborious, and the Sanskrit root is *sran*, 'to be fatigued' (Turner 1982: 31). *Ch'ach'a ung*, which is Korean for shaman, is also the name of the second King of Silla (Chang 1988: 31), but, in the hands of the Australian media and the venue publicists, the word 'shaman' became increasingly charged with paranormal significance.

Portraits of Madame Kim appeared throughout the Australian media, and an analysis of these images clarifies the role Kim Kum hwa unwittingly began to play in the public imaginary. Not only did her image accompany all the *Taedong Kut* pre-publicity features and interviews, it was also used indiscriminately in conjunction with general articles on the Conference.[11] None of these photographs features any other company member, and only two out of a total of 15 portraits show Kim Kum hwa looking at the camera: both are long shots and the direction of her gaze is unclear. In all the photographs she is dressed in traditional shaman costume, and in ten of the images she is involved in some aspect of ritual performance. She is looking down and her expression is filled with concentration and sometimes verges on pain. In the five photographs that show Kim Kum hwa outside the performance context, two show her dancing and three with her hands together in an image a Christian audience would associate with prayer. In only two photographs is she smiling. The photographs came from a variety of sources: the original press-kit contained photographs from Kim Kum hwa's own collection; four came from the collection taken by Vicki Laurie in Korea; and the remaining ten from photographers working for the media reporting on the Conference. Despite the range of photographers supplying the

*Plate 7*   The Korean shaman, Kim Kum hwa, 1994. Photo credit: Lisa Tomasetti. Reproduced with the permission of Julie Holledge for the Third International Women Playwrights' Conference, Adelaide, 1994.

images, all these photographs have a common fascination with the exotic and spiritual object. The body is always witness to the ritual action: it is always on display for the viewer and, despite the fact that six of the articles that accompany the image are purported to include interviews with Kim Kum hwa, the image distances any notion of direct address from the interviewee. She is a fascinating but strange object, and the introspection and possible pain suggested by her expression signify an inner world which the reader cannot access.

There was a clear bias in the organising and framing of the written material that accompanied these images. The socio-political context of shaman belief and the immediate context of the tour as an adjunct to the Third International Women Playwrights' Conference dropped out of view. The information that appeared in the articles, though loosely based on the material supplied through the Conference publicity unit, included highly selective quotations from various interviews with Madame Kim. It tended to commodify and exoticise the spiritual content of the *Kut*, and offer the experience up to readers as a night of supernatural titillation. Like other reports, *The Bulletin* focused on the 'enigma' of the charismatic shaman; whilst *The Subiaco Post* portrayed the performance as an 'ancient' ritual with the power to 'transport the audience into a world of mysticism and magic'. According to *The Canning/Melville Times*, the shaman was going 'to get rid of evil spirits', and perform 'birth and fertility rites' culminating in 'the skewering of a wild boar and the descent of the god!'

By the time the news of Kim Kum hwa's tour had reached Adelaide, *The Adelaide Ray* was sure that 'the shamans not only become possessed and experience ecstatic trance states themselves but may induce their clients to do the same'. These journalistic excesses reached their height in the article by Nadine Williams in the Adelaide *Advertiser.*

> Kim Kum hwa strongly believes good and evil spirits still exist and her ritual would remove 'bad spirits and spirits with grudges' hampering Adelaide women. . . . A pig carcass may be used to pacify angry gods or dangerous dance on two-edged swords performed to 'threaten' them. The priestess and medicine woman − or shaman − says she also uses divine gods to heal people and forecast the future.

*The Age* in Melbourne was slightly more circumspect:

> When Kim Kum hwa goes on stage, she falls into a deep
> trance. Then she dances on razor-sharp knives, pierces her
> arms, legs, and tongue and balances the carcass of a pig on a
> pitchfork. It sounds like a circus act, perhaps, but she is
> performing rituals that go back thousands of years.

As Kim Kum hwa and her company moved around Australia, a
side-show developed surrounding the carcass of the pig which
was repeatedly described as a sacrifice or sacrificial offering. In the
technical specifications for the show, the venues were asked to
acquire a medium-sized dead pig from a local butcher. In Perth
one of the local radio stations suggested that the pig would be
slaughtered on stage, which resulted in some talk-back radio
outrage. The pig was transformed into a 'wild boar' in Perth by
*The Canning/Melville Times*, and assumed a subject position in *The
West Australian*: '[t]he pig, one suspects, is rather less pleased by it
all.' And by the time it reached Sydney and *The Sydney Morning
Herald*, it had become a little 'white piglet which must have died
of natural causes' and was to be supplied to the company along
with '25 kilos of rice and a bottle of Houghton's White Burgundy'.
    There were two reviews of the *Taedong Kut*: one by Leonard
Radic in *The Age* and the other by Samela Harris in *The Advertiser*.
Both reviewers featured the pig which readers were reassured by
Radic had been 'pre-slaughtered for the occasion', whereas Harris
told readers it had been 'humanely killed' even though it was
'impaled . . . through its neatly gutted belly with a three-pronged
fork'. The visual spectacle of the knife riding sequence was
acknowledged, and particularly the sequence in which Kim 'grace-
fully attacks herself with razor-sharp blades' and 'drew the blades
across her arm, her legs and (for those who could bear to watch)
her tongue'. But the overriding tone of both reviews was mildly
supercilious. The opener of *The Advertiser* piece read: '[h]ow do
you know a person has been to see Kim Kum hwa and company?
Because they're the ones without any evil spirits; spirit nasties have
been driven away.'
    Yet the pieces also revealed a longing or lack for an imaginary
that had not been satisfied. Harris ended her review with the
observation that it 'is more of a visual phenomenon than the soul-
quaking physical and spiritual experience of trance ceremonies

in situ'. Radic mused: 'we were told that in ancient times shamanistic performance went on for three or four days, ending in a celebration, which is probably a euphemism for an orgy.' But the *Taedong Kut* 'lasted a mere hour-and-a-half and there was no orgy or ecstasy – simply a final celebratory dance'; though he admitted that he had been 'curiously invigorated by the experience'.

Given the pre-publicity, then, it was not surprising that the performance was ultimately framed with the expectation that individual audience members would take part in a communal ecstatic experience. The association between ritual performance and sacrificial rites can be traced to the Romantics and their obsession with Dionysus, the Greek god of frenzy, wine, and rapture. Nietzsche inherited the Romantic fascination with Dionysus and tied the god irreversibly to the history of western theatre by linking him with the Greek chorus and the origins of the drama. This connection, coupled with the associations forged by the Romantics between the narrative of the sacrificial Greek god and Christianity, provides a strong framing device for the interpretation of ritual performance in western cultures. This paradigm includes the complete denial of subject-centred reason and the loss of consciousness in some form of madness or frenzy. There is also an unspoken assumption that all such rituals are based on sexual licentiousness, the sacrifice of a human victim, and cannibalism. Viewed through this framing device, the media coverage of Kim Kum hwa's tour assumes a predictable form. The pig, a symbol of a repressed fascination with cannibalism, is transformed into the *white* piglet in such a way that it conjures up images of a human infant. A suggestion is floated that this ancient ritual was connected to sexual orgies, and the possibility raised that audience members might themselves fall into a trance. Finally, the whole performance is undermined by the fatuous statement that Adelaide women have been freed of 'spirit nasties'.

The reviews express a latent desire for a Dionysian ecstatic experience. This aspect of the media coverage, which is symptomatic of more general patterns of ritual consumption, requires further investigation. Popular assertions that ritual performance can stimulate states of communion in purposive-rational subjects rely upon a combination of evolutionary and psychoanalytic theory, which suggests that the evolution of the entire species can be replicated in the development of each individual.[12] This interweaving of evolutionary and psychoanalytic theories makes it possible to argue that a state of communion associated with so-called 'primitive' societies can be retrieved from the dyadic relationship between the mother and child. Even if a mode of subjectivity has been constructed as excessively private or personal, it can be tempered by a retrospective connection to the pre-Oedipal intersubjective relationship. Theoretically, it should be possible for audience members to achieve a state of 'communion' through the memory of this formative experience, whatever the social construction of their subjectivity.[13]

Yet enormous obstacles lie in the way if we are to accept this formulation. The pre-Oedipal has been the source of wide-ranging feminist theory[14] and can function as a conceptual space to theorise an alternative to phallocentric discourse. It is, however, extremely problematic to argue that a parallel exists between the conscious-ness of the child and the lack of ego individuation associated with pre-modern communal societies. Belief in the possibility of the retrieval of early childhood states (and the assumption that these duplicate the psychological states experienced by 'primitive' peoples) is deeply ingrained in the residues of western colonial thinking. But does it offer an acceptable basis for an analysis of audience responses to the translocation of ritual performance?

Although a concoction of evolutionism and psychoanalysis may assert the theoretical possibility of a post-industrial Australian audience experiencing an ecstatic communal state, the reviews of Kim Kum hwa's performance make it abundantly clear that this state was not achieved during the *Taedong Kut*. Moreover, there is no evidence to suggest that the shaman intended to lead her audience to a state of communal ecstasy. But if this was not her aim, what did she wish to communicate to an audience with little or no understanding of the spiritual significance of *Kut*?

## Kim Kum hwa's response

Kim Kum hwa's clearly stated intention was 'to introduce Korean shamanism to Australia'.[15] At no point did she suggest that it was possible to provide a foreign audience, or for that matter a Korean audience, with an ecstatic or deeply spiritual experience in a 75-minute extract from a *Kut*. However, she insisted that her spirits entered her with undiminished strength in Australia and can appear in any place and at any time: 'They come and help us wherever

we are in the universe and live in our bodies and minds just like
Jesus Christ or Buddha.' Even when members of the audience
knew nothing about her belief system, they still benefited from
the blessings of her gods: 'Gods are called different names in
different places. Linguistic difficulties do not have any significance
in the spirit world.' For Kim Kum hwa, the important issue was
whether members of the audience were willing to participate
without cultural prejudice. On her first tour to America, Kim
Kum hwa encountered hostility, particularly from Americans of
Korean descent. She was performing as part of a celebration
of Korean culture in Knoxville. When she began the preparations
for the *Kut*, people started to leave. Her account of this incident
illustrates her response to audience resistance during an intercultural
performance:

> I was not afraid of performing a *Kut* in front of foreigners,
> but of the disappointment in Korea if I failed. . . . I jumped
> up. Instantly I felt a strong spirit coming up from my toes; it
> spread all over my body. Sweat was flowing and I could no
> longer see the audience. My body was as light as a feather. It
> was a rare and wonderful possession by the gods. Without any
> hesitation I climbed up on the ploughshares and danced. When
> the spirit left me I was standing on the blades with my eyes
> closed. The audience seemed too quiet and I felt faint. I
> thought, 'The audience has gone. What can I do? I've done
> my best but it was not enough.' . . . I decided to accept the
> will of my gods and slowly opened my eyes. I could not
> believe it. The audience members, who had been about to
> leave, were all sitting down watching. I could not hear
> anything. Everyone stood up. I saw them putting their hands
> together – they were clapping.
>
> (Kim Kum hwa 1997: 202)[16]

Kim Kum hwa is convinced that the translocation of *Kut* is
possible, but she does not deny that differences exist between
performances in Korea and overseas. In North Korea, where she
began her work as a shaman, she remembers whole villages
laughing, crying, and singing together as a single entity during the
ritual. Everyone knew the rules that governed the performance
and the patterns of the *kori*, or ritual episodes: 'village people are
all shaman.'

In Australia, Kim Kum hwa was impressed by the sincerity of the audiences; she felt they tried to understand the *Kut* without prejudice, but the time constraints and the audience numbers were disappointing. She does not believe that a great deal can be achieved in one visit. A strong pedagogical motivation is clear from her statements, and the decision to perform overseas is driven by the desire to establish shamanism as a formal religion that 'can systematically help poor, hungry, and sick people'. She acknowledges the difficulties of adapting her work for foreign touring, and some Korean theatre critics feel that the spiritual dimension of her work has suffered,[17] but she believes that the spiritual integrity of her performance remains unaffected.

Kim Kum hwa considers that the Australian performances were spiritually efficacious through the blessings of her gods, but she never suggests that the *Kut* could satisfy a spiritual lack associated with modernity within an individual audience member. Hence the contradictions of this intercultural site. Whereas in the previous chapter we suggested that identity spaces could cross cultural borders and influence the constructions of subjectivity by means of an intercultural text, no equivalent process appears to underlie the enactment of the Korean *Kut*. This is not surprising, considering the fact that the audiences' expectations were framed by a classical western view of ritual and were manufactured through the mechanisms of a postmodern marketplace. The audience was encouraged to assume that an intangible spiritual presence would accompany the performance and be registered by individual audience members as some kind of epiphany. Yet as Kim Kum hwa's account of her performance makes clear, her spirits manifest themselves through the body ordeals of the performer. In Australia, where the performance of physical ordeal is associated with circus tricks and side-show magicians, the spiritually inflected identity space offered by the shaman was consumed by her audience primarily as a form of popular spectacle.

## WARLPIRI *YAWULYU*

Our second investigation into intercultural ritual in Australia focuses on the translocation of indigenous women's ritual from the Tanami Desert to the urban periphery of the continent. This account is based on the experiences of Warlpiri women from

Lajamanu and Yuendumu in the Northern Territory who have danced and exhibited art works in the major cities of Australia.[18] They are respected elders within their communities, have considerable ritual responsibility, and represent Warlpiri interests at important land claims. In the wider Australian community they are known as performers and prominent visual artists. Their intercultural performance fills a lack in the national imaginary, rather than in the realm of individual subjectivity.

The research and writing of this account coincided with heated political debates in Australia over Native Title. The High Court of Australia made a historic decision in 1992, regarding Eddie Mabo's case against the State of Queensland, which threw out the premise that Australia was *terra nullius* (a land belonging to no one) at the point of colonisation. It found this claim to be a 'discriminatory denigration of indigenous inhabitants, their social organisation and customs' (*Eddie Mabo v. The State of Queensland* 1992). The Mabo case confirmed that under certain conditions, Aboriginal title and Crown title could co-exist. The High Court decision recognised Native Title, but instead of resolving land rights issues, it opened up a new era of controversy and legislation over Australian land ownership and usage.[19] All interactions between indigenous and non-indigenous Australians in the late 1990s were sensitised by the political debates surrounding this issue. Our research into the translocation of indigenous ritual, the intentions of its performers, the responses of the non-indigenous audiences, and our account of these transactions, were inevitably shaped by these public debates. In an effort to avoid any misrepresentation, we have tried, wherever possible, to quote directly from interviews with the Warlpiri women who are the traditional owners of the rituals that are the subject of this account.[20]

In analysing the reception of these ceremonies, we have had to engage in a level of speculation. The performances are not presented in traditional theatre venues, they are not reviewed, and have no paying audience. None of the conventional indicators of audience response is available to us; there are neither box office figures, nor contrasting reviews from diverse media outlets. The performances are not subject to conventional advertising, they are not commodified in the conventional sense, and they fit neither into the conventional performing arts marketplace, nor into the tourism sector. In fact they fall into a distinct genre of performance that maximises symbolic rather than financial value. This genre we broadly define as 'performance in the service of the state'.

In our analysis we are indebted to Andrew Lattas and his work on the process of 'ventriloquism' (Lattas 1991: 314) through which one culture is forced to speak on behalf of another. Lattas argues that one of the responsibilities of the state is to provide a 'corporate cultural identity for its citizens', and that in Australia, Aboriginal art has been used to symbolise 'primordial truths of origin that have created the fiction of a national identity' (Lattas 1990: 50). Despite the tendency to use Aboriginal art as a national logo, the social and economic realities faced by the indigenous population remain unchanged, and there are still major problems in the areas of health, education, and employment.

The spatial metaphors employed by Lattas are of particular relevance to our analysis. He suggests that the endless angst surrounding the search for an Australian national identity – variously attributed in the popular press to the relative youth of the nation, its diverse population, or its superficial materialism – creates and sustains an imaginary inner void or lack. This void is believed to lie beneath the 'tinsel town' of the urban culture. In contrast, the sparse and empty interior of the continent becomes an imaginary place of spiritual plenitude, the continent's 'red heart'. Thus a fascinating spatial irony is created: the emptiness of *terra nullius* that justified colonial annexation is reconfigured as a spiritual fullness, reaching its greatest intensity in the landscape and peoples of the Central Desert. It is for this reason that we have focused on the ritual performance of Warlpiri women from the Tanami Desert; we argue that urban audiences are encouraged to read the symbolic landscape of spiritual renewal through the Warlpiri performing bodies. It no longer becomes necessary to undertake the journey to the red centre, which in Lattas's terms is the site of the Australian postmodern pilgrimage, because the centre has been translocated to the periphery of the coastal cities. Before we can comment further on this symbolic transaction, we must explore the meanings that the sacred dances hold for the Warlpiri and how they fit within the kinship structure and the system of ritual ownership.

*Yawulyu* are an expression of Warlpiri women's *Jukurrpa* or Dreaming. The term *Jukurrpa* can apply to 'individual ancestral beings, or to any manifestation of their power and nature, i.e. knowledge of their travels and activities, rituals, designs, songs, places, ceremonies' (Laughren *et al.* 1999). The *Jukurrpa* provides the 'Law' for all human and non-human activity and, because it is not fixed in any temporal sense, it is conceived as a continual living presence. In *Yawulyu*, the ancestors from the *Jukurrpa* stories are represented: the ritual performances involve songs composed in couplets, highly codified movements, and the painting of *kuruwarri*, or sacred design, on ceremonial objects, the rock face, or ground, and the upper bodies of the dancers – particularly the breasts and shoulders. A cycle of songs is usually sung by women as they paint the intricate 'designs' on each other's bodies with ochre in preparation for the dancing. The 'designs' are a significant aspect of the story or stories being told.

Performance of *Yawulyu* is strictly controlled through the Warlpiri kinship system, explained here by Jeannie Herbert Nungarrayi:

> The Warlpiri kinship system determines how people – and which particular people – may or may not interact with one another. It determines our obligations to others and our relationships to others. It determines whom we can marry. It also determines what designs we are allowed to paint on our bodies, what stories we can tell, what dances we can do, what songs we are allowed to sing. Problems arise when people attempt to operate outside this system. The kinship system is too complicated to explain in depth like this – it takes Warlpiri people a lifetime to learn – but I'd like to explain a little bit about it.
>
> There are eight skin names in the Warlpiri kinship system:
>
> Nungarrayi/Jungarrayi
> Napaljarri/Japaljarri
>
> Napurrurla/Japurrurla
> Nakamarra/Jakamarra
>
> Nangala/Jangala
> Nampijinpa/Jampijinpa
>
> Napanangka/Japanangka
> Napangardi/Japangardi
>
> . . . I'm a woman of the Nungarrayi skin-group. The skin names starting with 'N' are all female. The names starting

with 'J' are all men. Nungarrayi/Jungarrayi, they're sisters and
brothers; Napaljarri/Japaljarri, they're sisters and brothers;
and so on.
Mothers and daughters are in two groups and they cycle
four times. Starting with Nakamarra, as an example, her daughters are Nungarrayi. Nungarrayi, her daughters are Nampijinpa;
and her daughters are Napanangka; and her daughters are
Nakamarra. And the other group, for instance starting with
Napaljarri, her daughters are Napurrurla; and her daughters are
Napangardi; and her daughters are Nangala. See, it cycles four
times. So, we know who [our] mothers are. On our father's
side, there are four groups that cycle twice. Jungarrayi, his son
is Japaljarri, whose son is Jungarrayi, and so on. It cycles twice.
Japurrurla and Jakamarra. Jangala and Jampijinpa. Japanangka
and Japangardi. Fathers and sons.
                                (Herbert Nungarrayi 1995: 14–15)

The kinship system determines access to ritual knowledge:
it gives each woman in the community the right to perform
particular *Yawulyu*, paint specific designs, and tell selected *Jukurrpa*
stories. There are two forms of ownership or management of ritual:

For each *Yawulyu* re-enactment of a particular *Jukurrpa*, Warlpiri women are either *kirda* or *kurdungurlu*. *Kirda* are owners
or bosses related to a particular tract of country or place and
therefore to a particular dreaming from their father's side.
*Kurdungurlu* are the guardians or stage managers or 'directors'
of the country or dreaming from their mother's side. Both
*kirda* and *kurdungurlu* must be present to properly enact the
*Yawulyu*. The *kurdungurlu* woman paints her *Jukurrpa* designs
onto the body of the woman who is *kirda* for that dreaming,
singing while she paints. Sometimes the women paint all day,
sing all day, for a ceremony. Then, the *kirda* begin to dance.
The *kurdungurlu*, who are guardians of that dreaming, act like
'stage managers' or 'directors'. They are responsible for the
correct enactment of the ceremony and may, at any time, stop
the ceremony or insist it is enacted another way. If the *kurdungurlu* think that the *kirda* are performing any part of the
ceremony incorrectly, they can tell them off, or move them
around, or intervene in the ceremony in any way they wish.
                                (Herbert Nungarrayi 1995: 17)

This doubling of responsibility between the *kirda* and the *kurdungurlu* is of vital importance in any discussion of ritual translocation: it operates as a system of checks and balances ensuring that the ritual retains its essential character. The structural relationship between the *kirda* and the *kurdungurlu* ensures that ritual responsibility is dialogic and is continuously renegotiated as part of the practice of ceremony. It has assisted the Warlpiri in their resistance to the pressures from the dominant commodity culture of Australia to reify ritual inheritance into individual private property.[21]

## Performing for *kardiya*

*Yawulyu* have been performed in city locations in front of *kardiya*, or white Australians, since the mid-1970s. The first invitations came from *kardiya* in Adelaide and were linked to the establishment of the Yuendumu Women's Museum designed, not for the display, but for the preservation of ritual objects. Prior to settlement living, these objects painted with *juju*, the powerful sacred designs, were kept in bough shelters or put up in the trees, but there were no appropriate places to store them in Yuendumu and they were being damaged by the weather. Judy Granites Nampijinpa and Darby Ross Jampijinpa were sent to Adelaide to speak on behalf of the community:

> We asked them to take pity on us because all our sacred objects were in humpies and the water was getting in and damaging them. If they gave us the buildings, we said we would teach white people and try to make them wise by putting [on our designs] and dancing. So the white people, in good faith, promised us, 'We will give you the buildings so you can place your dangerous and sacred things – the important dreamings – inside where they will be protected from the rain.'
>
> We decided to ask the white people to come to the opening of the new buildings and lots of white people came in a big plane. The visitors all put money into the *parraja* and came inside our building to look at the *kuruwarri*, and we began to dance. We were carrying the designs: Nampijinpa and Napanangka carrying our designs, and then Nakamarra and Napurrurla with their designs. The visitors said the dancing was very good. Some time later they rang us up and said,

'Hey, if you get ready we'll give you a grant to come to Adelaide', they paid for the train and we went, men and women, to Adelaide to dance.

(Granites Nampijinpa, interview 1998)

This first performance tour of the Yuendumu Warlpiri to major Australian cities occurred in the early 1970s and was organised through the South Australian Museum. It proved to be the first of many such trips around the country. Through the Women's Museum and, in later years, the Yuendumu Women's Centre and Warlukurlangu Art Gallery, numerous invitations to dance *Yawulyu* have been received from Darwin, Alice Springs, Melbourne, Adelaide, Perth, and Sydney. In Judy Granites Nampijinpa's account of the opening of the Women's Museum, most of the themes that occur in the descriptions of these subsequent tours are present: the *Yawulyu* are performed in the correct sequence by their traditional owners; the performance is intended to educate white Australians and is exchanged for a pre-negotiated fee; the audience is perceived to be appreciative and compliments the dancers on their skills; and details of the itinerary and the mode of transport are important aspects of the narrative.

It is impossible to do justice to the scope and range of the *Yawulyu* performed in urban Australia during the past 25 years. In an attempt to give readers some understanding of this performance tradition, we shall take a detailed look at just one of the *Yawulyu* that has been toured all over the country. Jorna Nelson Napurrurla and her sister, Peggy Poulson Napurrurla, are *kirda* for a *Yawulyu* based on the *Jukurrpa* of the caterpillar, the big yam, and the little yam. Their *Yawulyu* concerns a battle between the little yam (*ngarlajiyi*) people from Wapurtarli and the big yam (*yarla*) people from Yumurrpa, which ends when the leaders of the two armies, realising that further carnage is pointless, agree to a peace. It is this resolution, together with the possibilities of healing that emerge after the battle, that lies at the core of the *Jukurrpa*. The point of reconciliation between the two leaders is told here by Liddy Nelson Nakamarra, who, as a father's sister, shares this dreaming with her classificatory nieces, the Napurrurlas:

Then the two fathers of their people, those two, the two elders sat down to fight each other, the two most important men, Ngardilpi and Wapurtarli, big yam and little yam.

*Plate 8*    Warlpiri women painting up for performance, 1998. Photo reproduced with the permission of Dolly Daniels Nampijinpa. Photo credit:
Kate Ferry.

Threateningly they sat down. Savagely they wounded each
other, savagely they wounded each other.

At the same time many of the others killed each other, many,
many of the other people killed each other in this way, in this
way at that time. Many others continued to defend themselves
by warding off the blows, they warded off the blows.

The two drew close to each other in order to make peace.
They are the two who still stand there, one to the south, one
to the north. They truly still stand there. . . . That is a very
sacred place. In fact, it is a secret place.

(cited in Rockman Napaljarri and Cataldi 1994: 109)

In the account of their performance tour of five major Australian
cities, Jorna Nelson Napurrurla explained that they took with them
'that very big country, that very big dreaming in which they fought
each other', and that they carried the big yam, the little yam, and
the caterpillar 'like relatives'.[22] She emphasised that Napurrurla
and Nakamarra are the only people entitled to carry these
dreamings. In response to questions concerning the performances
she replied that the audiences particularly liked the little yam dance,
and that 'we were very happy and we didn't get nervous. The
white people didn't make us frightened. We danced very strongly,
we kept our kuruwarri designs very strongly . . . and we will go
on dancing like this forever.'

Despite the overriding importance of place in Warlpiri culture,
the Napurrurlas do not perceive it as contradictory to perform
Yawulyu outside their country.[23] They believe that they carry
their Jukurrpa to the urban centres of Australia and that their land
travels metonymically with them. Performing to non-indigenous
Australians is a statement of cultural assertion, not a debasement
or corruption of culture, but the efficacy of the ritual may shift
according to place. When the big yam and little yam is performed
in Warlpiri country, the power of the kuruwarri enters the earth
and makes the plants grow. Peggy Poulson Napurrurla explains:

We sing the song and the designs. . . . It goes in and from
underneath it comes back up. The plant grows, it appears as
the plant, little yam plant with baby leaves, the little yam and
the little green shoots – then the plant and everything grows
up and the same for the big yam. We recognise the whole
thing. We recognise the whole dreaming.

In an urban context, the power of the ritual shifts and is felt within the people. Wendy Nungarrayi, who is *kurdungurlu* for the Napurrurlas, explains: 'as a result of the dreaming, after the dance, as the designs wear off on the body, it is good for people and makes them happy . . . they feel happy.' 'Yes that's right,' echoes Peggy, 'they become happy, the people who belong to the designs and the dreamings become happy.'

The decision to perform the battle of the big yam and little yam is never made by the Napurrurlas in isolation. The choice of *Yawulyu* may be pre-determined by the composition of the touring group, but the precise elements of the performance must be negotiated, as Oldfield Napaljarri explains: 'the *kurdungurlu* tell the *kirda* what they can and can't dance in any given situation.' *Jukurrpa* frame the *Yawulyu*, but the precise dance sequences, songs, and designs are metonymic to the story, and it is possible to select different elements for each performance. This selection process is based on the nature of the event and the composition of the audience: the *Yawulyu* contain many elements that can be viewed by the uninitiated, but the sacred and powerful elements must be removed before the *Yawulyu* can be performed in front of *kardiya*.

A clear instance of this process of selective censorship is evident in the description by Lucy Kennedy Napaljarri, a classificatory mother to the Napurrurlas, of a Sydney performance of a *Yawulyu* based on the Ngarlu *Jukurrpa*. As a major owner of this *Jukurrpa*, Lucy Kennedy Napaljarri describes it as 'a very big story. It's not a lukewarm story this one, it is [a] very important one and belongs to my grandfathers and my father's sisters. My aunties taught me, and we learnt it with our ears in the Warlpiri way.' In the story, a man seduces a woman from the east by singing 'a love song while spinning hair and the hair spins out from the spindle and follows the woman' and draws her back to him. The seduction described in the story involves a liaison between incompatible skin partners and acts as a warning against sexual transgression. The love song, or *yilpinji*, that accompanies the Ngarlu *Yawulyu* is considered extremely powerful, and, while men may watch the dance from a distance, to hear the song would 'make them feel bad in their stomachs'. For this reason the *yilpinji* was not sung at an open-air performance in Sydney.

Despite the exclusion of sacred or powerful elements from the *Yawulyu*, the majority of the women we interviewed were adamant that the performances they give in Australian cities are essentially

the same as those given within a traditional context. According to
Kay Ross Napaljarri, the dancers 'hold' the landscape,

> when they get into the dreaming, and they are singing. The
> actual country may be invisible, but they can still see it. They
> hear it in the ears, in the singing, and in the paint . . . the
> paint takes them towards their country.

On a personal level, the Warlpiri clearly enjoy the experience
of touring and seeing other people's country. Dolly Daniels
Nampijinpa explains: 'I'm a proud woman when I travel. I felt
well in my spirit. It made me happy. I liked seeing different places.'
In Lajamanu, where there is less opportunity to travel, the
prospect of touring is even more welcome: 'We are very keen to
go to places,' explains Liddy Nelson Nakamarra. 'We're very keen
to travel taking the dances. If white people talk to us, and invite
us, we are happy to go.' Maisie Napangardi expresses a strong
desire to see *kardiya* and *yapa* (Warlpiri) working together and
sharing cultures:

> We are very happy to show you everything, and maybe you
> will be happy too, when this happens. We will all be together:
> if we show you these things then we will become one. We
> are quite happy to show our things to Aboriginal and white
> people, we say to people if you want to show us your things
> we will show you ours.

The attitude of Maisie Napangardi is not typical and the women
in Yuendumu are more reserved. They emphasise the importance
of cultural exchange as a means of educating *kardiya* and share
their knowledge in the hope that non-indigenous Australians will
respect and understand their history and become, as Ross Napaljarri
phrased it, 'more pleasant – more friendly'. But do they? It is time
to turn to the other half of the intercultural exchange in the
Australian cities and explore the symbolic meanings attributed to
the Warlpiri performances by non-indigenous audiences.

## Urban symbols

The Warlpiri women are clearly aware of the symbolic value
of their performances and negotiate their fees accordingly. The

contexts within which they perform ensure that the audience is respectful, appreciative, and invests the *Yawulyu* with symbolic significance, even if it is at variance with traditional meanings. Our interest in the symbolic value of the Warlpiri performance is in terms of the overriding contextualisation of these performances as signs that legitimise the state. Warlpiri women are invited to open things. Between them, the women we interviewed in Lajamanu and Yuendumu had performed at the openings of buildings or exhibitions connected with the following state institutions: Araluen Arts Centre and Yirara College in Alice Springs; the Parliament House, Northern Territory University, the Art Gallery, and the New Court House in Darwin; Tandanya Arts Centre and the South Australian Museum in Adelaide; and the Museum of Sydney. The concept of opening an important site is not foreign to the Warlpiri: they describe the process of all ceremonies as the opening of the *Jukurrpa*. The irony is that the Warlpiri, who have never reified their culture by building edifices, provide the ceremonies that legitimise the physical symbols of the culture that has appropriated their land.

The positioning of the *Yawulyu* as rituals to mark moments of civic pride and community celebration places the Warlpiri in the role of celebrants who bless or consecrate symbols of nationhood. They provide these institutions with a sense of history and invest them with legitimacy as the cultural, legal, and political representatives of the people. In a country in which the founding principle of colonisation is still so contested and the process of reconciliation has hardly begun, the inclusion of *Yawulyu* within civic ceremony creates an illusion of social harmony. In addition, it provides a picture of an uninterrupted history, in which the Warlpiri women are cast as representatives of the past while the opening of the civic building indicates progress and the future. Within this narrative, it is possible for the Warlpiri women and the *Yawulyu* to stand for a common ancestral past for the non-indigenous multicultural population. This sense of a historical continuum is only possible in a country in which the popular imaginary contains associative paths, established by psychoanalytic and evolutionary theory, linking the indigenous population with the evolution of the human species (Freud 1938: 15). In his analysis of the most recent manifestations of cultural 'ventriloquism', Lattas suggests that Aboriginal imagery has been used by the state as a symbol of unity to ward off anxieties associated with multiculturalism and its potential for 'ethnic and linguistic divisions created by immigration' (Lattas 1990: 60).

The real contradiction exists not between the performers and the audience, but between the performers and the state. The Warlpiri are trapped within this double bind: in their efforts to educate non-indigenous Australians, they inadvertently legitimise a state that is denying them land rights, and by denying them these rights, it denies them the collective rights to the autonomy of their culture.

*Yawulyu* are not just performed for *kardiya*; they are also performed outside the commodification of the marketplace, through a system of cultural exchange between indigenous clans. The importance of these intercultural sites lies in their contemporary relevance as a living ritual practice by and for women. They maintain a pedagogic function, but hold none of the restrictions or dangers we have identified in the translocations of ritual performances to the urban centres. In this context of ritual exchange, in a sex-segregated environment, elements of the *Yawulyu* that would never be shown in the urban centres become part of the performance. The sharing of sacred and important ritual knowledge among indigenous women is the key function of the meetings. It is for this reason that it is not possible for us to provide readers with any information about the organisation or nature of these events. Certain practices still exist outside the boundaries of the postmodern marketplace. Ritual performances may be threatened with reification through the process of commodification, but the traditions themselves cannot be reduced to museum artefacts: they are dynamic and changing phenomena.

## CONCLUSION

Clear parallels exist in the stated objectives of the ritual performers that we have considered in this chapter. The Warlpiri women and the company of Korean shaman led by Kim Kum hwa share a pedagogic intention with respect to their urban Australian audiences: they perform with the clear purpose of educating audiences to respect and appreciate the richness of their cultures and belief systems. They also perceive their audiences as influential. If Kim Kum hwa is to succeed in raising the status of shamanism as a formal religion in Korea, she needs an international profile; if the Warlpiri are to succeed in their wider political struggle for self-determination, they need the support of non-indigenous Australians. Although the desire to educate is predominant, these performers are aware of the financial value of their rituals and negotiate fees that reflect not only the symbolic but also the spiritual value of the *Kut* and *Yawulyu*. When conflict does occur between the performers and the tour organisers, it is frequently linked to financial disputes. The Warlpiri include in their worst touring experiences confusions over contractual arrangements, and some of the older members of Kim Kum hwa's company complained that their Australian performance fees undervalued the spiritual efficacy of the *Kut*.

There is a clear disjunction between the intentions of the artists and the audience expectations, yet for both parties the actual performance is perceived as satisfactory. It is this contradiction that lies at the heart of this intercultural site. On the one hand, it appears that an intercultural performance can operate at a satisfactory level even when the meanings derived by the one culture have little to do with the meanings invested by the other. On the other hand, it is possible that a subtle shift in these divergent perspectives occurs during the ritual because of the nature of live performance. In a sense, the strategies of the Warlpiri and the Korean shaman are predicated on this assumption: if they familiarise audiences with the realities of their cultural and spiritual practices, they can undermine the more damaging projections that tie them into an imaginary binary relation with Australian urban culture. It is comparatively easy for a void or lack to be filled by an unfamiliar and exotic 'other' – all that is required is a simple act of projection – but familiarity erodes the ability of the exotic 'other' to carry these imaginary constructions. By familiarising audiences with the realities of the *Kut* and *Yawulyu*, it may be possible to increase respect for these cultural practices. But this is a dangerous game: the adaptations necessary to cater for the needs of the urban Australian audience involve the commodification of spiritual practice. If the performance is to be accessible to a general audience with little or no knowledge of the traditional ritual context, it must be edited to emphasise spectacle and must conform to numerous time and venue constraints. These demands threaten to compromise ritual practice, yet the Korean shaman and the Warlpiri women vehemently deny that this has occurred. They consider themselves to be in total control of the adaptation process and place their confidence in their gods or ancestors: as long as they perform with sincerity and maintain their spiritual energy, they believe that the essential core of the ritual remains strong.

We have argued that the *Kut* was marketed to Australian audiences as a postmodern product that could fill an imaginary spiritual lack for the price of a theatre ticket. Framed by this expectation and mode of consumption, it is hardly surprising that the reviews reflected some dissatisfaction with the experience. The spiritual content of the *Kut* was manifest in the physical ordeals enacted by the shaman, but these performance elements were reported as if they were fairground spectacles. On an intersubjective level, the shaman remained an exoticised 'other' engaging in an incomprehensible rite. Individuals within the audience may have increased their understanding of Korean shamanism by witnessing the performance, but their relation to the event remained culturally voyeuristic. The identity space inhabited by the audience was reaffirmed in its difference, rather than altered by this encounter with a translocated ritual.

In contrast, a shift in subjectivity does seem to accompany performances of *Yawulyu*. These indigenous rituals are consumed outside the conventional venues associated with live performance in Australia, and are framed by moments of civic pride. They are re-inscribed by the social context to act as a symbol of national unity. To this extent the *Yawulyu* fit within our genre of 'performances in the service of the state' because the audience identity space shifts to embrace a national imaginary in which the indigenous population function as common ancestors. It is clearly not the intention of the performers that the *Yawulyu* function as a building block for the corporate cultural identity of Australian citizens, but they cannot control this process of ventriloquism that results in their symbolic incorporation.

In our next two chapters, we move away from the larger issues relating to theatre (narrative and ritual) to explore tropes more directly associated with performance: space and bodies. Chapter 3 addresses space in the form of theatre space as well as the more metaphoric and public cultural space. We explore a different register of loss that is frequently ascribed to the postcolonial subject: the loss of space, land, and territory that finds both a literal and symbolic expression in the concept of home. From such constructions of space we begin to draw conclusions regarding the structuring of personal identity spaces.

# Chapter 3

# Layering space

## Staging and remembering 'home'

A culture never repeats itself perfectly away from home.

(Young 1995: 174)

[M]odern drama at first employs, as one of its foundational discourses, a vague, culturally determined symbology of home, replete with all those powerful and empowering associations to space as are organized by the notion of belonging.

(Chaudhuri 1995: xii)

I was homesick with nowhere to go. . . . The place that I missed sometimes seemed like a memory of childhood, though it was not a childish place. It was a place of mutuality, companionship, creativity, sensuousness, easiness in the body, curiosity in what new things might be making in the world, hope from that curiosity, safety, and love.

(Pratt 1984: 24)

In Chapters 1 and 2 we considered the ways in which public and private spaces associated with motherhood and loss provide a useful model for analysing intercultural translations and adaptations of narrative and ritual. This chapter focuses on the specific materiality of space in theatre. Our aim here is to define the public/private dichotomy in terms of real space and imaginary space, especially in the context of 'home' space: both the private home and the more 'public' home of geo-political space to which one feels allied. While the construction of identity spaces has been central to the first two chapters, the exploration in this chapter focuses on a different approach to identity formation, based on several interpretations of 'home'. Charting geo-political and personal home spaces in theatre is the objective of this chapter, rather than providing an economic or feminist subversion of 'home' as a restrictive domain for women. In their explorations of these spaces, the plays that we consider in this chapter provide a journey back to a place that was once 'home' (for both the protagonists and the playwrights), as well as travelling forward to forge a new home that incorporates several intercultural spatial spheres.

'Home' is, of course, an immense category, so we have limited its parameters to postcolonial homecomings in/to Africa. As we illustrate later in this chapter, postcoloniality is one of the most intercultural of sites in social, cultural, and geo-political discourses, even if the substantial power imbalances that colonialism generated cause the intercultural nature of postcoloniality to remain largely unacknowledged. Many of the strategies that former colonies choose to counteract the effects of colonialism include distinctly intercultural techniques, such as the use of cultural hybridities and the rupturing of boundaries (such as those of geography, politics, and identity). Our focus on Africa in this chapter not only helps to restrict our analysis further, but also reinforces the legacy that Africa holds in colonial and intercultural histories. Explorations of 'darkest Africa' – and the continent's subsequent 'settlement' – were ostensible triumphs of European imperialism. Africa remains one of the sites that have been particularly popular among European practitioners seeking intercultural material (whether on the basis of a committed interchange or an appropriative exchange).[1] We look at plays specifically located in Africa in which women return from another continent or from another part of Africa, and in which the space of the maternal body is correlated with theatrical space and with the return home: *The Dilemma of a Ghost* (1965) by Ghanaian writer Ama Ata Aidoo; *You Have Come Back* (1988) by Algerian playwright Fatima Gallaire-Bourega; and *Have You Seen Zandile?* (1986) by the South African artists Gcina Mhlope, Maralin Vanrenen, and Thembi Mtshali. Each play considers some of the difficult historical and current political realities for women in Africa and in the African diaspora.

This chapter works towards an account of the spatialisation of personal/cultural memory in an intercultural context. We investigate three main types of space: location space (or the play's setting), theatre space (architecture and production design), and geo-political space (determined by narrative). As we shall see, however, these spatial dimensions are insufficient for an analysis of intercultural space. As a result, we also consider the place of spaces that have no physical location but nevertheless determine one's surroundings and even one's identity. To that end, we move from real space (geo-political and architectural) to an imaginary spatial construct (triggered by metaphor or metonymy). This chapter is itself a journey through the layers of space articulated by the language and the performance of these plays. We attempt to offer a more deliberate analysis of the ways in which space determines the nature of intercultural encounters and the ways in which space can be manipulated in intercultural performance. First, we must address the composition of space itself.

## CONSTRUCTIONS OF SPACE

The construction of space in culture (and theatre) helps to determine social systems of meaning and representation. In one of the most basic and insightful arguments about spatiality, Michel de Certeau asserts that '[s]patial practices in fact secretly structure the determining conditions of social life' (de Certeau 1984: 96).[2] One need only consider the effect of various architectural designs – including the architecture of theatre buildings – to understand how the organisation of space governs social existence. To demonstrate the particularities and types of space, Edward Soja breaks down spatiality into a tripartite interrelationship which provides a formula for understanding the components of space: social, physical, and mental (Soja 1989: 120). These components helpfully delineate the more specific uses of theatrical space wherein theatre as social space encompasses both the physicality of the theatre building and the mental spaces by which the audience structures meaning. Such mental spaces are constructed by means of metonymic associations primarily from the language of the text and, secondarily, from associations generated by the performance text.

Space is frequently considered to be elusive and even empty, making it extremely difficult to define with any finality. We can, however, consider how space structures social reality and meaning, particularly where the meanings that it constructs reflect a dominant ideology. It is more difficult to perceive how alternative or marginal ideological formations are excluded through spatial determinants. Developing this perceptual sense is part of the project of contemporary feminist and postcolonial theories – to name just two – which highlight the socially constructed ways in which space restricts women and/or colonised subjects.

Ironically, while space may be structured in such a way as to exclude women, it has also come to be associated *with* women. Space's definitional association with women has resulted partly from the general hegemonic perception that space is passive and less dynamic than the ostensibly masculine action *in* or *on* space, and partly from the creative maternal potential of the womb, as a reproductive space within women's bodies.[3] Sue Best explains the recurring metaphor thus:

> The female body delivers a conception of bounded mappable space, space which can still be understood as a totality even if it is internally fractured or carved up. Recourse to the female body in this example seems to deliver and secure the idea of space as still a bounded entity, still a sort of container.
>
> (Best 1995: 184)

The enclosed maternal body thus overlaps with the enclosed material theatre space which is also frequently depicted as a container. Our analysis combines these two notions of enclosure: spaces identified with women merge with theatrical space (the space that is generated by the imagination of the playwright, the concepts of the designers and directors, and the spatial associations of the audience) and with theatre space (the theatre building and its location in a social context).

While they share a common cultural delimitation of space, at the very point of sharing a representation of enclosure, maternal space and theatrical space also raise questions about the dominant symbols associated with the maternal body as enclosing. In the maternal body, such boundaries are problematic in a different way. Best points to the dilemma in using a metaphorised female body to signify space.

> [F]eminizing space seems to suggest, on the one hand, the production of a safe, familiar, clearly defined entity, which, because it is female, should be appropriately docile or able to be dominated. But, on the other hand, this very same production also underscores an anxiety about this 'entity' and the precariousness of its boundedness.
>
> (ibid.: 183)

The 'precariousness of its boundedness' does not diminish its metaphoric value: rather, the anxiety associated with its use can serve to destabilise the docility apparently attached to the image of women.

This imbrication of the space of the body with the space of the theatre offers a potential intercultural meeting point for women from different cultures who come together in a theatre building. This is not to say that the space of the maternal body (or how that space is represented) will mean the same thing to all women, regardless of their cultural backgrounds. Certainly definitions of theatre space – and the accounting for time and space within that building – also vary widely from culture to culture. Rather, it is to say that at an intercultural meeting point, women from two different cultures at least are likely to have an understanding of how the maternal space intersects with the theatrical space in their own cultures. From this point of encounter, each culture can begin to understand how the other culture structures personal and public space: this is a first step towards working within the spatial dynamic of another's culture.[4]

The next four sections discuss the intersecting real, imaginative, symbolic, and 'theatre' approaches to space, using *You Have Come Back*, *The Dilemma of a Ghost*, and *Have You Seen Zandile?* as illustrations. In focusing on these specific spaces, this analysis attempts to offer a phenomenological understanding of space in intercultural performance in order to reinforce how spatial dynamics can structure the intercultural encounter.

## Real space: colonial displacements and postcolonial homecomings

Real space in the theatre, the space commonly associated with a performance's setting, its socio-political context, and its author's/company's context, is the principal way in which audiences understand performance in the context of the outside world.

### Geo-political space and its 'imaginary' effects

One of the most important real spaces underlying the plays considered here is the complex socio-political 'real space' of decolonisation. The postcolonial contestation of territorialisation is itself an intersecting and overlaying spatial concept, as Robert

Young has described (Young 1995: 173–4).[5] Colonialism has always been about intercultural exchange, although the imposition of colonial rule over a population hardly creates the basis for an equitable exchange. Colonialism's cross-cultural encounter frequently resulted in a cultural double-cross, with the colonised culture duped or forced into relinquishing to the colonisers their cultural autonomy and political self-determination. Postcolonialism, defined as any type of resistance to colonialism that colonised peoples have mounted, is circumscribed by a specific contest for literal and metaphoric space. Postcolonialism's direct strategy of redressing colonial spatial organisation – the 'discovery', mapping, bordering, and carving-up of the world from about the fifteenth to the early twentieth centuries – provides an alternative to marked, bounded, defined colonial space. This site of intercultural tension is central in the ongoing negotiation between an invading culture and a pre-existing culture.[6]

The postcolonial context we are concerned with here is the return to Africa popularised by the 'roots' metaphor (primarily associated with the African-American diaspora), in which descendants of African slaves return to Africa to search for their ancestral roots. There have been numerous 'back to Africa' movements in the US, the Caribbean, and elsewhere, which have variously promulgated the importance of returning to Africa permanently as a means of correcting the disruption and destruction caused by the colonial spatial and political enterprise. Frequently, such movements disintegrate when they mount literal returns to Africa only to find that the continent (whether as a whole or a more specific location within Africa) proves not to be the (impossible) idyllic homeland.

Intercultural plays that generate an encounter between an African country and another location invariably confront the all-pervasive western cultural imaginary that figures 'Africa' as the 'dark continent', the repository of the primitive and the dangerous, and/or the originary space from which *homo sapiens* as a species is thought to have emerged. The Orientalist imaginary of Africa provided – as any cultural imaginary does – all the possible signifiers for European deployment or consumption, regardless of their stereotypic qualities or even their veracity. For example, early twentieth-century theatre artists 'translated' the popularity of 'primitive' African art and images into an originary moment for contemporary intercultural theatre. The African continent is, of course, composed of numerous discrete countries, cultures, and languages, rendering a reading of a unified 'Africa' virtually impossible.[7] Afro-American or Afro-Caribbean movements to reclaim the idea and imaginative space of 'Africa' must also acknowledge the effects of such mythification of the continent.

One of the enduring legacies of Africa's function as an imaginary space from which westerners mine symbolic signifiers is the figure of Mother Africa, encapsulating an idealised version of women as culturally regenerative but passive. The plays that we assess here retain a sense of the rich images of the matrilineal tradition, but they contest the validity of 'Mother Africa', the overarching category that attempts to define women according to a static and idealistic model.[8] The artists we examine here attempt to re-work creative space through a female line. This is, however, quite a different activity from creating often limited and stereotyped symbols of a nation or assuming that women act as agents of the land or as mother earth figures. While *The Dilemma of a Ghost* addresses the 'Mother Africa' image most overtly, *Have You Seen Zandile?* also focuses on mother figures – including the struggle between competing mothers. *You Have Come Back* takes place in Algeria, where, not surprisingly, the role of mothers in the strict Islamic world of this play differs from their representations in the other two plays. In all the plays, women endeavour to re-assess motherhood and national space in female-centred contexts. One of the effects of this re-assessment is that they also raise questions about the ways in which restricted space is regulated.

## The plays

We briefly outline the plays' narratives and the political contexts of their home spaces here.

Aidoo's *The Dilemma of a Ghost* concerns the return of American descendants of slaves to Africa. Eulalie Rush marries Ato Yawson, a Ghanaian student studying in New York, and returns with him to Ghana when they graduate. Her naïve expectations of Africa are not met, and the expectations that Ato's family has of both young people are also unfulfilled. The play takes place over the course of about a year at the family's rural clan house which the couple visits for festivals and holidays from their apartment in Accra. After a year passes and no children are produced, the family decides to perform a ceremony on Eulalie's stomach to ensure fertility, ignorant of the fact that the couple has been practising birth control. Ato finally reveals this news to his stunned family, who (bearing in mind that the play is set in the 1960s) cannot believe that a couple could possibly control fertility, let alone wish to. Both the family and Eulalie are shocked by the inadequacy of Ato's explanations and his lack of concern. The play concludes with the possibility of a reconciliation between Eulalie and her mother-in-law, once they both realise that they must work around, not through, Ato. As the title suggests, the play is in the mode of a Ghanaian 'dilemma play' which offers several different perspectives on a particular issue, leaving it up to the audience to 'solve' the dilemma for themselves.

Gallaire-Bourega's *You Have Come Back* addresses the legacy of religious and sexist bigotry that has followed Algeria's 1962 independence from France. As a country on the northern edge of Africa, Algeria has been more heavily influenced by other cultures and religions than central and southern African nations. Independent Algeria has been dogged by conflict between secular and Islamic forces,[9] and Gallaire-Bourega's play is firmly positioned within a secular discourse. The play uses this political backdrop to highlight the disjunction between birth and adopted cultures. It begins as another text working in the standard 'return-home' genre: having moved from the periphery to the imperial centre, the postcolonial artist visits home for the first time in years. Lella returns from France to visit her country of birth shortly after her father's death. Bearing heavy suitcases and wearing western dress, Lella has long since left Algeria, making a happy life in France with her non-Islamic, French husband. Lella and the younger women who welcome her recall old times when they were children. Then the elder women enter the courtyard and pronounce a harsh judgement on Lella for abandoning her religion. Lella does not heed the warnings that a number of sympathetic people try to give her; as a consequence, she and these few supporters are brutally beaten to death by the community's female elders. Acting on behalf of the men in the community, the female elders carry out these murders to honour her father's last wish for her death because of her apparent betrayal of her religion. Lella's father's wish is sweetened by his will, which stipulates that his fortune will be left to the community once this dying wish is realised. The play concludes with order apparently restored as the muezzin's call to prayer is heard: the home culture rejects the attempted intercultural encounter.

*Have You Seen Zandile?* is a play for two actors which considers the spatial manifestations of a variety of social divisions within the cultures that formed apartheid South Africa. The play describes a conflict between several South African women about who will care for a young girl, Zandile. The rift occurs when they disagree about where and by whom Zandile ought to be raised: her mother in rural Transkei or her beloved grandmother near the distant coastal city of Durban. Each 'mother' feels that she has the rightful claim to the girl. The play begins with Zandile living happily with her grandmother, Gogo. She is abducted at age 8 by her mother, whom she hardly knows, and is forced to move to the Transkei where she is prevented from contacting her grandmother who has no idea where she is. In the Transkei, where she has to learn farming techniques to till the poor soil that her mother tends, her future lies in her mother's hands, and her mother is preparing to marry her to a traditional, local boy who will demand Zandile's subservience. Years later, the adult Zandile manages to return to Durban only to find that her grandmother, Gogo, has died. Gogo has kept for Zandile all the gifts that she would have given her, including a collection of dresses in increasingly large sizes. The play closes with Zandile weeping over the gifts. We consider this play intercultural because the two 'cultures' in which Zandile lives are vastly different. Apartheid only recognised culture in terms of colour: white, coloured, and black. Like colonialism before it, apartheid made a crude division which ignored the complexity of the cultural diversity within South Africa and this complexity is exemplified by the two divergent cultural location spaces and their differing habitus in which Zandile resides. Interestingly, the play also stages a reversal of the conventional play structure wherein the older generation upholds traditions and the younger generation embraces modernity: here, Zandile's grandmother lives in the city, while her mother farms in a 'traditional' mode.

For an analysis of the spatial dynamics in these plays, these plot outlines are, as such, insufficient. An account of the plays' locations space(s) is necessary to demonstrate how – initially – intercultural space is constructed in the plays.

## Location space

Each play foregrounds the staging of an interculturated journey to a memory space. We set out a brief description of the location space in each text before demonstrating how these worlds intersect with one another and with the operations of the theatrical building. In each case, location space constructs a sense of physical restriction and confinement that intersects with the space of imaginary plenitude and the socio-political context of the plays' narratives.

In Aidoo's *The Dilemma of a Ghost,* the location space of the play is the courtyard of the new wing in the large clan home. This courtyard is a communal family space but Eulalie can only occupy the space when she is alone. She seems unable to access the communality of the space which, to her, is as imprisoning as her misguided impressions of Africa and her already fragile marriage to Ato. The courtyard location reinforces the historical confusions that Eulalie represents to her in-laws. While Eulalie finds it impossible to be in the courtyard with the family because she doesn't understand their language or their ways, they too find it difficult to interact spatially with her: Eulalie's African-American heritage represents to them the return of the repressed in relation to the slave trade of previous centuries.

The location space of Gallaire-Bourega's *You Have Come Back* is also created via a courtyard, a deceptively simple space: the play takes place entirely in the courtyard of Lella's family home, but this courtyard operates differently from the courtyard in *The Dilemma of a Ghost.* This walled, interior space is the traditional sphere of women. The courtyard's female space is ultimately controlled by misogynistic men, but Lella remembers this space as a safe retreat exclusively for the use of women. The courtyard is a highly social, female space, but, with its high walls, it also acts as an imprisoning space: when she returns to the world within the courtyard, Lella is metaphorically imprisoned by the religious culture of Algeria.

Other types of prisons appear to operate in *Have You Seen Zandile?* The play sets up audience expectations that the circumstances of apartheid will pit white against black, but both the worlds of this play are 'black worlds'. Such investigations of African customs and values are rare in apartheid South African theatre, which characteristically constructed apartheid as the main (and sometimes the only) antagonist. Apartheid is responsible for Zandile's situation because of the travel restrictions and the living/working arrangements that it erected in order to control blacks by controlling their movements. The play does not, however, operate only in terms of apartheid. The actual location space counterpoints two places: the more urban Durban and rural Transkei, both of which are depicted with only the barest of props comprised of suitcases and boxes. When Zandile is taken by her mother, the place where her grandmother remains is transformed into a memory space in Zandile's mind, and the two characters try to reconnect almost telepathically.

The location spaces contextualise the action, establishing a basis for the 'real space' worlds essential to the plays' narratives. *You Have Come Back* and *The Dilemma of a Ghost* stipulate a closed social space by means of a fixed location. The courtyard for both plays denotes an enclosed area, but one that can be 'realised' theatrically in a variety of ways that are open either to extreme naturalism or a more abstract conceptualisation. *Have You Seen Zandile?* differs from this model. The minimal props and the direct address to the audience provide a very limited spatial illusion and allow the presence of the theatre building to be always readily apparent. The play relies on the ability of the audience to create spatial locations metonymically through the two actors' bodies; this points to the importance of 'non-real spaces' layering with 'real spaces'. In addition to 'real spaces', the audience creates what we call memory spaces by generating images from the language of the text. We turn next to a more detailed analysis of such memory spaces so that we can situate an account of the plays' uses of imaginary spaces.

## Memory space

Since, as de Certeau maintains, humans tend to think in spatial terms, the imaginative facility for spatial generation is activated within the theatre experience by numerous associative mechanisms. Imaginary spaces are created in the minds of the audience through associations of language (including the body language of the actor), sound, and music. This reliance on real space and an imaginary spatial dimension is clearer in an account of postcolonial homecomings and displacements.

As Una Chaudhuri (1995) outlines in her study of space in contemporary American and British theatre, a preoccupation with home and homelessness is a part of the late twentieth-century condition. The definition of home and the consequences of homelessness in postcolonial contexts are, however, often substantially exacerbated. Despite their attempts to recover a pre-contact space, many postcolonial writers are prevented from living in the spaces in which they or their ancestors were born. If they are able to return to their ancestral homeland, they are generally faced with a conflict between at least two competing identity spaces: the ancestral culture and the contemporary culture in which they now reside. This conflict can play itself out within the realm of personal subjectivity. The restricted access to the space of 'home' can also have repercussions for the creative process: in the attempt to write a space for oneself, postcolonial writers – like those we consider here – frequently turn to an imaginary space between 'home' and homelessness. This imaginary space has the potential to be significantly empowering in stage practice when such artists make spaces – or create new spatial dynamics – from the intercultural amalgamations of postcolonial space. This intruding, multi-layered space often takes the shape of memory space.

For an even more particular analysis of memory spaces in the context of 'home', we draw on Gaston Bachelard's *The Poetics of Space* (1964). Bachelard explores the place to which we all desire to return, the space that contains memories of home. His theory of home, 'topoanalysis', explains that most people's lives are spent, at one level, attempting to recover the shape, smell, or feel of rooms that they first knew as a child, or even the comfort of the womb.[10] This attempt to recapture the essence of childhood space is both physical and psychological: one may not find a house or space that actually does resemble the space of home, but one may eventually be able to re-create that safe, protected, secret shell for oneself. Memory space, or space that sparks memories of the past, is 'space that has been seized upon by the imagination [and which] cannot remain indifferent space subject to the measures and estimates of the surveyor' (Bachelard 1964: xxxvi). This combination of fixed space and memory space creates what Bachelard calls 'the dramatic tension between the aerial and the terrestrial' (ibid.: 22). Home and space, then, are physical locations as well as psychological dimensions. Home space is able to be represented physically, even if the space being remembered is not itself real but rather generated by a feeling or sensation. It is literal in that it is tied to the literal spaces of those locations we have known and lived in. Bachelard's space is also crowded: it is complicated by other spaces (even other memory spaces), many of which impact upon home space. Such a memory of home inevitably becomes romanticised and can never be reproduced exactly as it was, which is precisely Bachelard's point. This failure to reproduce completely memory space does not stop memory space operating as a crucial perspective from which we view our worlds.

How does this occur in the theatre? In the plays that we have chosen, each playwright uses this search for a memory space as a crucial part of the narrative: the longing for a lost 'home', in the sense of a physical dwelling, a national or cultural site, and a psychic location of safety and comfort. One of the most important and recurrent personal and social spaces is the re-emergence of an imaginary perception of 'home', a place that may be accessible only by means of memory. It is sometimes such imaginary spaces which provide the sharpest redefinition of personal and social space. The playwrights explore the spatial contexts of two cultures, usually attempting to find a space from which to mount a reconciliation – of sorts – of times, spaces, cultures, and/or homes. Memory space in each of the plays is figured slightly differently. At times it exists literally in the location space(s) of the plays, while at other times (e.g. in *You Have Come Back*) it is more metaphorically rendered.

Lella's early childhood memories of home, of life in the court-yard, and of her long dead mother are happy ones in *You Have Come Back*. The recent death of her father makes a return to this world possible because Lella could not return while he was alive. Lella recalls her memory space easily, once she returns to the court-yard of her childhood, which her mind fills with sweet smells and with laughter. For Lella's memory spaces, the walls of the courtyard present no encumbrance: everything she needs is within these walls. She wants a life that continues to hold laughter, but one of the elders is anxious to destroy this space by proclaiming, 'Love? Joy? What do these have to do with life? Life is misfortune and oppression, constraint, servility, and despair. . . . We do not speak the same language. You have abandoned our tongue and adopted the foreigners' (Gallaire-Bourega 1988: 204). Lella's pleasure at returning to the memory space of her home blinds her to the dangers that the courtyard now holds.

Like Lella, Eulalie has expectations of a pleasant memory space which is substantially compromised. In *The Dilemma of a Ghost*, Eulalie's memory space of her own childhood is presented as a place where she felt that she belonged. This space is dominated by memories of her dead mother who supported her intellectual endeavours. It is staged spatially by means of the courtyard in the new wing of the clan house where ceremonies are held and where Eulalie spends most of her time. She does not, however, join the family for ceremonies in the courtyard: whenever they are present, she is conspicuously absent. Her presence in the courtyard is primarily connected to the sense of belonging she experienced with her own mother and that she expects to feel in her idealised view of 'Africa'. Eulalie believes that she can recover this nurturing memory space in the physical location of Africa, the place she believes to be her primordial home and the place to which she has a historical connection through her slave ancestors. Since her own mother is dead, she asks her husband if his mother can 'be sort of my Ma too?' (Aidoo 1965: 3). She assumes that the memory space occupied by her dead mother can be augmented by a new, living relationship with Ato's mother, but the two women speak different languages and seem unable to interact on any level. She is, of course, disappointed with the reality of 'Africa'. As the play proceeds, she fills out her courtyard with more and more cigarette smoke, Coca-Cola, and whiskey – all frowned upon by Ato's family – in a desperate attempt to transform the space into her memory space. By the end of the play, Esi Kom sees that she must create a maternal space for her daughter-in-law that can incorporate Eulalie's memory space of her dead mother as well as offer her a way of living in the present. Esi Kom deploys a symbolic space to ameliorate Eulalie's adjustment problems, as we describe later in the chapter.

Memory space is frequently connected to a dead or distant loved one. The memory space that Zandile desires is associated with Gogo in *Have You Seen Zandile?* She is unable to return literally to her grandmother, but she is able to retain some of the characteristics and abilities that they share, specifically Gogo's storytelling ability, a skill that is passed on to her granddaughter. Zandile's failure to be reunited with her grandmother must be seen in light of her success at retaining a memory of her grandmother and a way of deploying her grandmother's knowledge and talents in a new way. The transformational nature of this memory and of the denial of access suggests ways of working around prohibitions to find a means of self-expression. By learning the techniques of praise songs, Zandile also learns to conjure the image of Gogo, as contained within the stage directions: '*on the other side the spot light shines on Gogo, who comes in with some presents for Zandile, wrapped in colourful paper and she thoughtfully packs them in a suitcase'* (Mhlope *et al.* 1988: 64). When Zandile belatedly finds where Gogo had been living prior to her death, she is given Gogo's suitcase which becomes the tangible representation of memory space that is central to Zandile's life. She attempts to re-capture home via letters and stories but it is not until she holds her grandmother's suitcase that she can firmly lay claim to the memory space by means of this tangible and symbolic object.

The narrative of these plays is substantially affected by the ways in which the memory space manifests itself physically and symbolically. The memory space that is at the core of each of these plays is more than merely a location of childhood remembrance. The women in these plays are attempting to return to that which they have lost. The central characters seem determined to merge – however roughly or inconclusively – the two cultures and 'homes' into a single, containable space. The playwrights are also engaged in a project of reclamation as they consciously try to generate the recombinative space of a hybrid, intercultural community. The playwrights fill this breach by drawing on the possibility of creating a *chora*.

## Chora

We are using Elizabeth Grosz's rendering of *chora* which recovers one form of positive, recombinative spatial location for women (Grosz 1995).[11] While men also construct memory spaces, *chora* in Grosz's assessment is specific to women. It also questions male definitions of space and femininity. Grosz isolates *chora* as an opportunity to

> return women to those places from which they have been dis- or re-placed or expelled, to occupy those positions – especially those which are not acknowledged as positions – partly in order to show men's invasion and occupancy of the whole of space, of space as their own and thus the constriction of spaces available to women, and partly in order to be able to experiment with and produce the possibility of occupying, dwelling or living in new spaces, which in their turn help *generate new perspectives, new bodies, new ways of inhabiting.*
>
> (ibid.: 124, our emphasis)

Spatiality is at its core. *Chora* is creative, regenerative space, but not necessarily the reproductive space of the womb. It is 'the space in which place is made possible, the chasm for the passage of spaceless Forms [*sic*] into a spatialized reality, a dimensionless tunnel opening itself to spatialization, obliterating itself to make others possible and actual' (ibid.: 116). *Chora* is an imaginary construction and is within the symbolic realm that is accessed by writers in their creation of imaginary worlds.

While Grosz does not refer to theatre, her characterisation of *chora* offers a provocative opportunity for recognising the ways in which space can be staged: the discovery and staging of a productive space that helps define identities between and across cultures. Conceptually, *chora* can act as the synthesis of the theatrical, memory, and locational spaces within these plays, even as it is sought outside the body, but in association with maternal space.[12] The combinative potential in *chora* thus renders it an ideal tool for establishing contact in the intercultural encounter.

There are a number of ways in which this *chora* can be achieved. The courtyard of Lella's memory provides a *chora* that is ultimately thwarted in *You Have Come Back*, because it is violated by outside forces. Now that her father can no longer invade the women's space in the courtyard, Lella returns, expecting to find in her courtyard a space where she can safely interact with women. The influence of her father has, however, extended far beyond the grave as the courtyard transforms to become an imprisoning space. Any creativity and happiness that could possibly emerge from this space is curtailed by the elders' determination to control women at every point. Lella repeatedly attempts to explain that there is life outside the confines of this metaphoric house and its restrictive religion, but the courtyard of her desire is in a different place than the courtyard she currently inhabits in Algeria, where the women's lives and bodies are completely circumscribed by the men. The play is dominated by women, initially suggesting a matriarchal structure, but Lella's dead father and the male elder who appears briefly at the end of the play firmly control the social context and frame the narrative. Any sense of *chora* that Lella feels she might be able to generate is refused by the sexual and cultural repression and by the brutal murders that conclude the play. The two cultural spaces in this play cannot mix, despite Lella's best intentions. Even dialogue between the two cultures is impossible: Lella's attempt to re-work creative space through a female location results in her death. The remaining women also have no possibility of a metaphoric creative space, only a purely literal reproductive function. The restrictions of the community extend to a form of communal control of women's bodies: most of the young women with whom Lella exchanges memories are mothers, but those women who have been unable to bear children have been divorced and/or rejected. Gallaire-Bourega implies that any alternative is refused by the Islamic patriarchy, whilst deviations from the restrictive norm are monitored by the female elders of the community. The area once designated as a women's area is now circumscribed by men.

Zandile's attempts to create a *chora* are also thwarted. She has little chance of transforming the signifier of her memory space – Gogo's suitcase – into a *chora*. The suitcase is also a metaphor for the womb, particularly because it represents the traits (as well as the clothes and gifts) that Gogo tries to pass on to Zandile. As in *The Dilemma of a Ghost*, the clash between women is essentially over reproduction and who ought to raise the child. Lulama, Zandile's mother, had an unplanned pregnancy by a secret lover. Married to someone else, Lulama could not take her child home. Zandile's paternal grandmother, Gogo, was left to raise the child. Lulama's only choice is to take Zandile by force, after her husband leaves her. The older women in the play cannot even lay claim to the space of their wombs, which are controlled by their husbands; much as the land and the rights to travel are controlled by the apartheid government. By examining the nature of the lives of several women in the context of apartheid, *Have You Seen Zandile?* demonstrates concretely the problems that arise when women are forced to act as agents of the land or as 'mother earth' figures. The suitcase stands as a variable symbol that encompasses the magnitude of apartheid by simultaneously referring to the displaced person, restrictions on travel, and the control of reproduction through the womb. This state control means that the space of the suitcase and the space of the womb can never be a *chora*: both spaces are too circumscribed by prohibitions to be a liberated space under apartheid. Zandile's spatial world is reduced to the suitcase.[13] Zandile's access to the past through storytelling may prove useful, but any sense of *chora* eludes her at the end of the play.

Like Lella in *You Have Come Back*, Eulalie confuses her memory space with a *chora* in *The Dilemma of a Ghost*. She assumes that she

will be able to make a new home in Africa that will contain her
memory space and offer her a place where she can belong. She
fails to recognise that Ato's family has expectations and precon-
ceived ideas of her as well. Keen to preserve their traditions as
they choose to remember them, they are not willing to embrace
Eulalie who represents a history they would like to forget: Ato's
grandmother, Nana, calls slavery the 'Unmentionable' (Aidoo 1965:
14), and Eulalie's slave ancestors seem to be a liability to the family
and its reputation. Yet for Eulalie, this slave-history connection to
'Africa' is what ought to make it understandable to her.

Eulalie's confusion between memory space and *chora* is brought
to a head over reproduction. This women-centred community
that she initially idealises creates a variety of problems for her when
the family's sphere of influence focuses on the space of Eulalie's
body: since she has not conceived a child after a year, the extended
family feels that it is up to them to assist her by applying a
herbal remedy to her stomach. Eulalie considers her body and her
fertility to be her own business. For the community-oriented
clan, however, Eulalie's apparent infertility is their business too.
The contest over space extends well beyond the courtyard to the
comparable enclosed space of Eulalie's womb.

Both Eulalie and her mother-in-law, Esi Kom, come to realise
that whatever else divides them, the major barrier between them
is Ato. When they remove this obstacle, the play suggests that they
will be able to learn to occupy the same space at the
same time. This reconciliation will inevitably be fraught, but Esi
Kom decides that she must begin it and that it is necessary to
incorporate Eulalie's mother in this reconciliation as well. She
explains to her son:

> And we must be careful with your wife
> You tell us her mother is dead.
> If she had any tenderness,
> Her ghost must be keeping watch over
> All which happen to her.
>
> (Aidoo 1965: 50)

Aidoo resists the temptation to provide a space of reconciliation
where all the women are united, in favour of individuated characters whose personal and social space has the *potential* to intersect
usefully; in doing so she offers a possible solution in the link

between the two women from divergent cultures who can cohabit the same space. Esi Kom and Eulalie thus aspire to a *chora* at the play's conclusion. Their readiness to bridge the divide that separates them spatially and culturally suggests a more productive future.

All three plays use a genre in their dramaturgy that involves a variety of individuated women, many of whom attempt to control their own lives in a manner that is counter to the traditions of one of the two cultures to which they have a claim. Each play attempts to recover (or adapt or even generate) a creative space and, in doing so, formulates a stage space that is heavily layered with multiple physical and psychic levels. The elusiveness of *chora*, the ultimate memory space, does not diminish the effort to reconcile divergent spaces in *Have You Seen Zandile?* and *You Have Come Back*. More importantly, the plays do achieve a type of *chora* for the playwrights who find in writing and producing theatre their elusive creative space. Each play constructs a memory space based on the playwrights' own lives: through these plays, *chora* becomes not just a physical location but also an equally tangible creativity manifest in the play itself. On one level, this helps mitigate the tragedy of *You Have Come Back*: Lella is unable to change her circumstances, but Gallaire-Bourega has expressed her dissent from the tenets of Algerian politics.

It is possible to see *chora* as a common, basic spatial experience through which women from a variety of cultures can meet. The imaginary, creative space is linked to sexuality, but not just to reproduction. In many parts of Africa, the maternal body frequently symbolises fertility, community, and an idealised female figure.[14] Yet as these plays illustrate, the construction of the maternal body in plays by women disrupts the idealism of this role: they refuse to situate motherhood and fertility as *chora* itself. While the representation of sex and the sexual(ised) body is not the same in every culture, the plays we have discussed here deploy enclosed spaces associated with the female body to stage a search for a further possible way to spatialise the intercultural interactions between women.

Even more significantly, the search for a *chora* in these plays offers a way of combining space and female bodies in a manner that does not replicate the outdated and patriarchal view of women as passive vessels of space in opposition to men who act in/on space. In an attempt to redefine women's relationship to space, Sue Best argues that the combination of women and space evolves

new and multiple meanings for each, rather than limiting either
to predetermined, contained representations.[15] Because *chora* is
spatial but not restricted to the womb, it offers manifold ways of
spatialising women and women's desires.

## Theatre space

So far in this chapter, we have been considering theatrical space,
as opposed to theatre space, because theatrical space acts metonymically for other, extra-theatrical spatial arrangements. However,
we must also take into account the literal rendering of space in
theatre and how the memory or symbolic spaces operate on the
real stage. Developing de Certeau's concept that space determines
the structures of social life, Michel Foucault explains that space
actually controls us. His famous examples of state-controlled sites
of containment underscore space's surveillance function (prisons,
sanatoria, or similar sites). While attendance at a theatre production
generally involves an audience watching actors, both performers
and audience are controlled by spatial sites of power which operate
differently, depending on the type of theatre, its conventions,
the performers, and the play.[16] The location of the audience (geographical, as well as distance from stage, or interactive possibilities
with the actors and the stage) can affect the audience's subject
positioning. Theatre space, like any space, exists in a particular
physical and metaphysical place within the social sphere.

    This is perhaps easiest to see in the context of South African
theatre space during apartheid. The stage where *Have You Seen
Zandile?* first played helps complicate the ostensibly simple apartheid
world in a way that mirrors the narrative. The play was first
performed in 1986 at the Market Theatre in Johannesburg, which
then operated without any form of government support and often
presented plays that were critical of apartheid. More importantly,
the Market Theatre provided an opportunity for blacks and whites
to sit in the same theatre, an inter-mixing of races specifically
prohibited by apartheid. As a result, the Market had the potential
to generate a very special sense of unity in the audience: sitting
in the theatre could itself be a political statement. That *Have You
Seen Zandile?* also expresses a rural–urban binary rather than 'just'
a black–white dichotomy compounds its political significance. The
main space holds about 450 people in raked, bench seating around
almost three sides of an unembellished thrust stage (Fuchs 1990:

44).[17] The original production of *Have You Seen Zandile?* has also played at the Edinburgh Festival, London, and Switzerland while an American production was mounted in Chicago. When the play is performed in these different countries, it does not necessarily retain the social and spatial meaning that the Market Theatre provided in the first production: it accrues new spatial references associated with the new locations to add to the constructions of meanings through space. The performance of Mhlope's play outside South Africa may communicate some political and social opposition to apartheid or to social conditions in South Africa in the 1970s and 1980s, but its social effect is bound to be educative rather than specifically resistant.

For *You Have Come Back*, theatre space communicates on a slightly broader level. The implications of a performance's geographical location can be enormous, as Fatima Gallaire-Bourega's *You Have Come Back* demonstrates. Given the persecution that many Algerian writers and artists experience, this play cannot actually be performed in Algeria. Its performance in other parts of the world serves to inform audiences about current events in Algeria. *You Have Come Back* has been staged in New York (as part of a women's theatre season in 1988), in Australia (by students in Adelaide in 1994), in Uzbekistan (organised by the Alliance Française in 1992), and it has been broadcast on radio in Paris. The play's history is in alternative theatres which place the audience in opposition to censorship. The audience's response is already conditioned by the knowledge that this is a banned play that cannot be shown in certain (political) spaces.

*The Dilemma of a Ghost* is designed to speak specifically – but not exclusively – to Ghanaians, and its theatre space context reinforces this point. First performed in Legon, Ghana, in the Open-Air Theatre at the University of Ghana in 1964, *The Dilemma of a Ghost* was written to raise awareness in Africa about the African diaspora. Ironically, the architectural style of its first performance location conflicts with its message. The theatre (on the university campus that is itself designed to imitate Oxbridge quadrangle architecture) recalls 'a Greek amphitheatre at the top of Legon Hill [which] offers, unfortunately, no more than a weak imitation of the real thing. Acoustics are not adequately considered and the sightlines are poor' (Rubin 1997: 144). The play works to bridge the Ghanaian culture with the diasporic American culture in a venue that aspires ineffectually to classical European grandeur.

The location of performances of this play, particularly the structuring of space, helps determine which of its dilemmas are foregrounded. When it is performed in the city, Ato's dilemma is no doubt centralised. This play continues to be a popular teaching text in schools across western Africa to educate Ghanaians strategically about their own history and the roles that their ancestors played in the slave trade (Wilentz 1992: 45). When the play travels to rural schools, it actually returns to the point of origin of its narrative setting: rural Ghana. In this context of rural performance, the figures of Ato and Eulalie become as foreign to the audience as they are to Ato's family. Here the audience's subject position shifts with regard to the actual location of the play in the real time of the performance. In this situation, the audience is likely to share the same confusion over the behaviour of Ato and Eulalie that Ato's mother experiences. When this play is performed in the US or other countries with large diasporic communities, it takes on a third dilemma function: beyond that of simply identifying with Eulalie, this third dilemma creates an opportunity for the audience to recognise the similarities and the significant intercultural differences between diasporic subjects and the subjects who remained in Africa.

The narratives of these plays work differently depending on the real-time performance, the plays' location in specific theatres or specific cultural/political contexts, and the subject positions that such performances predetermine. We have not discussed the particular design implications of the plays or their productions: rather, we have raised some of the intersecting spatial questions that must be considered in intercultural theatre productions. Chaudhuri's perception of the polytopian nature of space (Chaudhuri 1995: 138) is especially noteworthy here, given the numerous spatial dimensions that interact with one another in each play. We have seen how the real space of the narrative interacts with memory space, which can produce the space of a *chora*. This is not to say that all intercultural plays prefigure home, memory spaces, and *chora*: rather, we offer in these plays a point of agreement and intersection amid the challenges of staging intercultural theatre. Such complex layers of space represent only one of the puzzles for intercultural performance.

We now move to an account of bodies in space, and particularly to the ways in which bodies become 'layered' within the multiple dimensions of space to signal intercultural difference. We outline three specific types of intercultural bodies which, like the layers of space, help provide points of intersection across cultures for intercultural performers at the same time as expanding possible subjective identity spaces.

# Chapter 4

# Intercultural bodies
## Meetings in the flesh

[N]omadic consciousness consists in not taking any kind of identity as permanent. The nomad is only passing through; s/he makes those necessarily situated connections that can help her/him survive, but s/he never takes on fully the limits of one national, fixed identity. The nomad has no passport – or has too many of them.

(Braidotti 1994: 33)

This chapter is concerned with meetings in the flesh: bodies as sites of the intercultural encounter. We begin our investigations with cultural taxonomies, move into hybrid worlds, and finally trace the pathways of nomads. There are three bodies that weave through this text – the subjective body of the performer, the artificial performing body, and the body of the audience. We do not intend to re-visit the plethora of recent writings on the body, but the basic premise underlying our approach falls within Rosi Braidotti's definition of the new form of 'corporeal materialism':

the body is seen as the inter-face, a threshold, a field of intersection of material and symbolic forces; it is a surface where multiple codes of power and knowledge are inscribed; it is a construction that transforms and capitalises on energies of a heterogeneous and discontinuous nature. The body is not an essence and therefore not an anatomical destiny: it is one's primary location in the world, one's primary situation in reality.

(Braidotti 1991: 219)

The body of the performer and the performing body interrelate to present a surface where 'multiple codes' are inscribed. This doubling is perceived as a binary like those of sex and gender, and race and culture: the body of the performer is the natural element while the performing body is the artificial or imposed term. But where does the performing body begin and the body of the performer end? How clearly does the audience's body read this doubling in the foreign body? Can an actor acquire multiple performing bodies that represent different cultures? In an effort to untangle these questions before re-entangling them in a variety of women's intercultural performances, we begin with our definitions of the three bodies under scrutiny.

The *body of the performer* is the subjective body of corporeal materialism located in a specific historical time and geographical space, embodying the ethics and beliefs of a particular place. It has been subjected to social coercion, legal inscriptions, sexual and economic exchange, and carries its past in its habits, gestures, and demeanour. More importantly for our purposes, this body is sexually differentiated. We are not arguing that the body of the female performer holds some essence of universal womanhood, but we are asserting that every society organises differences between the sexes into structures of signification. These structures may order perception in culturally specific and power-impregnated ways, hence the corporeal reality of the sexed body is always present. Each of the female bodies in this chapter is differentiated by its particular ethos: its unique political, social, and cultural placing (Diprose 1994). Yet in one respect all these bodies are the same: they have all been positioned as other to privileged male identities within their societies. All too frequently the bodies of female performers serve the needs of these privileged male identities. In this chapter we explore the work of artists who defy the rigid boundaries that mark their particular cultural configuration as Woman. They use their performing bodies to explore what is excluded, the elements that cannot fit within these rigid boundaries. They traverse culturally defined gender structures and work interculturally.

It is a truism to say that *the performing body* is a body of artifice. Every genre or tradition of performance involves the codification of body language and vocalisation, and these codes coalesce into performance conventions. These conventions extend from the familiar iconic representations that dominate naturalistic genres to the obscure abstractions of highly symbolic theatrical forms. Performance genres are frequently classified through physical and vocal codes, but they cannot be reduced to these indices because every act of performance also requires that the performer heighten or alter her state of consciousness. These inner states are acquired through the study and practice of techniques designed to shape and concentrate thought processes, emotion, and energies. The construction of an artificial performing body can involve immense rigour and discipline, but it can never escape the corporeal reality of the body of the performer. Consequently, the distinction between these two bodies is always blurred, and the precise nature of the double act is never clear even when the body is wrapped in the powerful signifiers of costume, make-up, or mask. In intercultural performance these doublings find new expressions.

By convention *the body of the audience* is generally referred to in the singular, although it is made up of separate individuals. To shape their performances, actors use the feelings, sounds, and sensations that emanate from the collective body of the audience. This is not to imply that all the members of an audience have an identical response, but that time and place tie a live audience together, so its members will always share some responses based on their common ethos. Probable readings unite the majority of the spectators and form the basis of the relationship between the audience and the performer. Audience members watching an intercultural production tend to share an awareness of the unfamiliar: strange gestural and emotional expressions, alien performance energies, vocalisations, decorative codes, spatial relationships, or the slowing or speeding of perceptual time. When confronted with a foreign body, they are likely to indulge their scopophilic drives, but they will draw on more complex mechanisms to decode this body if the narrative or emotional trajectory of the performance demands an empathetic relationship.

As these brief definitions imply, every performance involves a complex interrelational dynamic between bodies. To avoid being overwhelmed by possibilities, we shall confine our discussions to three genres of women's performance. The first genre we refer to as *taxonomic*, because it seeks clearly to demarcate the boundaries between cultures; the second as *hybrid*, because two cultures in some way merge together; and the third as *nomadic*, because boundaries of identity are transgressed. We consider the bodily assumptions that mark each of these genres. The body of the performer and the performing body merge in the taxonomic genre to create a reified cultural essence that can be identified and categorised by the audience. The hybrid genre is a mass of contradictions in both production and reception: artificial performing bodies from diverse backgrounds are juxtaposed, and qualities of two or more cultures mix and merge as cultural signifiers jump from one body to another. Finally, amongst the nomads, we encounter an intercultural site that capitalises on the physical communication between the audience and performer to challenge radically the boundaries of identity. Our investigations draw on production histories, rehearsal processes, performance analyses, training systems, and the subjective experiences of intercultural artists.


## TAXONOMIES

Our analysis of taxonomic theatre begins with Robert Young's assertion that it is impossible for a western audience to 'read' the 'raced' body, without using the classification system that is deeply imbedded in western discourse (Young 1995). 'Race' was synonymous with lineage until the eighteenth century, when it assumed its current meaning as a system of natural categorisation. This semantic shift reflected the desire of European imperialists to categorise the 'other' in such a way as to justify colonial rule. The 'other' became the negative image of the colonising self and fuelled the obsessive cataloguing and classifying of supposed difference between races that accompanied colonial expansion.[1] In the nineteenth century, gender became a key term within this system of racial differentiation: a masculinist Aryan race with a conquering intellect was contrasted with a wide variety of feminised brown and yellow races that were intuitive and passive. Young argues that classificatory tables of racial difference reveal a deep anxiety that the impregnation of the feminised 'others' would result in the degeneration of the 'white race'. He demonstrates that these fears of miscegenation resulted in the obsessive naming of racial groups, and cites as an example the 1873 table of 'Peruvian Mongrelity' which included the following categories: mulatto, mestiza, chino, cuarteron, creole, chino-blanco, quintero, zambo, quintera, and chino-cola (Young 1995: 176).

A similar obsession with the classification of performing (as opposed to racial) bodies characterises the theatrical taxonomic 'masterpieces'[2] of the late twentieth century. The intensification of the global arts markets and the proliferation of international festivals produced a vogue for extravaganzas with multicultural casts. These intercultural productions resembled theatrical versions of the 1851 Great Exhibition at Crystal Palace, a modern day Expo, or a Coca-Cola advertisement in which the richness and diversity of humanity is displayed in a panoply of coloured bodies and national costumes. In the theatrical expression of this global diversity, the performance technologies of the world were placed side by side: the Indian Kathakali dancer with the New York method actor, the Tokyo Kabuki onnagata with the Ghanaian court dancer. Rigid boundaries isolated the different performing bodies and framed them as supposedly pure and authentic cultural essences. Like safe sex, this safe theatre refused to let fluids and flesh touch. It was as if the anxieties generated by globalism were the repressed underlying this work. On the one hand the fear of conflict was ameliorated by a utopian vision of global collaboration and harmony, and on the other, economic injustices and inequalities were justified by a re-affirmation of the innate and essential differences between races and cultures.[3]

Inevitably this taxonomic genre spread to women's intercultural performance. In Australia a number of productions were created for the national touring circuit. One of the most successful works, *Salt Fire Water*, was produced by the Top End Girls in Darwin, and first performed at the Space Theatre in Adelaide on 7 July 1994, in conjunction with the Third International Women Playwrights' Conference. This production had a strong connection with an earlier work, *Akwanso Flies South*, which toured Australia in 1988–9. Venetia Gillot, the assistant director on *Akwanso*, was a key figure in the creation of the Top End Girls; Robyn Archer, the director of *Akwanso*, booked *Salt Fire Water* for her 1995 Canberra Festival.

A number of common factors link these two works, not least of which was the desire to build enduring bonds between women of different races and cultures. This utopian vision was enhanced by the pre-publicity, particularly of *Salt Fire Water*, which emphasised the cultural diversity of the cast. The culturally marked bodies of the performers were used to attract an audience, instead of the more conventional marketing ploy of publicising the unique performing skills of the company. It could be argued that this emphasis on the bodies of the performers and their corporeal realities was justified by the content of the productions. *Salt Fire Water* and *Akwanso Flies South* were both created through improvisation: the performance texts were shaped out of the cast members' experiences as indigenous or immigrant Australians. The *Akwanso Flies South* cast of four black women included an indigenous Australian, a Ghanaian, a Jamaican, and a North American.[4] The pre-publicity for *Salt Fire Water* listed the cast as follows: two indigenous Australians, one white Australian of Irish extraction, one Papua New Guinean, a Filippina, an East Timorese, and a Mauritian (via South Africa). The project originally included a Maori woman whose family moved in the process of the project's development and an Indonesian dancer who left the company for political reasons three days before the first performance.[5]

The women found sharing their life histories, in the creative development stages of both projects, enjoyable and re-affirming. It was the second stage that proved more difficult, when the women had to decide on the performance techniques they would use to represent their personal histories to an audience. There had been an assumption in both projects that diversity, or cultural identity, would be the overriding factor in the creation and delineation of the performing bodies. In the early stages of *Salt Fire Water* the women shared cultural knowledge through dances, storytelling, and traditional performance. Implied in this approach was the presumption that cultural identity could be meaningfully condensed into a series of physical gestures, dance steps, sound patterns, and costuming decisions. In *Salt Fire Water* the performers constructed costumes based on three elements: the wrapping of cloth around the body in the form of a sarong, skirt, or *malong*; colour-coding according to symbolic associations – green for Irish, red for Aboriginal, etc; and additional jewellery, scarves, and body paint with traditional or contemporary cultural significance, including shell and seed necklaces, beadwork belts, earrings, and bangles.

The dramatic structure of both works further highlighted the cultural differences of the performing bodies. In *Salt Fire Water* the linking metaphor was the arrival of the seven women in Australia, their meetings with the indigenous people, symbolic greetings, and exchanging of gifts that denoted their cultural origin. *Akwanso Flies South* began with the Aboriginal performer Rhoda Roberts alone on the stage, performing an emu dance. The three remaining cast members were introduced to the audience in quick succession and their signatures were defined by paradigmatic dance steps

*Plate 9*    Top End Girls, Adelaide, 1994. Photo reproduced with the permission of Venetia Gillot.

and percussion, instantly recognisable to the audience as from 'the Caribbean', 'Africa', or 'New York'. During the performance, these signatures were highlighted, combined, and structured into a choreographic whole. Life stories and cultural histories were told through dance, song, and direct address: they ranged from the history of slavery to an ironic look at a return to Mother Africa; and from the stolen generation of Australian Aboriginal children to the experience of black nurses in England.

Venetia Gillot maintained in an interview in 1997 that all the women in *Salt Fire Water* were 'in control of how they were represented' but this did not prevent them from feeling over-whelmed by the difficulties of rendering their subjective experience and cultural background into performance. All the participants had a strong sense of personal and political identity but were lost when it came to shaping this identity into a performing body. Their inexperience as performers and the lack of funded rehearsal time encouraged them to resort to cliché, even when the project was designed to prevent this from happening. While none of the women claimed 'just' one cultural affiliation, most of the women attempted to represent an impossible, 'authentic' version of one facet of their cultural identities. Gillot explained in the 1997 interview that Alison Mills felt that she had to represent an 'Archetypal Aborigine on stage. . . . Aly fell into the trap of deliv-ering [to the audience] exactly what they wanted. She sat there in full traditional paint when she's an urban woman.' Mills sub-stituted the complexity of her lived reality with a simplistic and predictable role intended for others: ultimately she was forced into the condition Jean-Paul Sartre defined as 'bad faith'. To contex-tualise her decision, it is useful to listen to her sister, June Mills, discussing the predicament of many urban indigenous Australians:

> We are the walking wounded, and each time you fail to recog-nise us and accept us as Aboriginal, no matter how white we are, no matter how blonde-haired, blue-eyed we are, no matter how we dress, no matter where we live, you are deepening the wound, and you are assisting in our eradication.
>
> (Mills 1994)

Gillot would have liked to have seen the work develop to the point where one woman would tell her story using the perfor-mance techniques of another's culture. As it was, they melded stories but not performance traditions. Gillot concluded that *Salt Fire Water* was a multicultural as opposed to an inter- or intra-cultural work, to use the distinctions outlined by Patrice Pavis (1996b). She explained that it was multicultural because the performers 'still remain[ed] enclosed within our own culture and our own performance piece[s]. . . . We just sat our work side by side' (interview 1997). The cast of *Salt Fire Water* had hoped to stage a clash of cultures, and the mermaid dance of the Balinese dancer, Desak Putu Warti, was deliberately rehearsed to 'clash' with Alison Mills's representation of Aboriginality, but Warti was forced to withdraw from the project. The background to her decision to leave the production provides fascinating insights into the doubling of the body of the performer and the performing body, and raises major questions about probable readings in taxonomic theatre.

Three days before the first performance of *Salt Fire Water*, Warti was contacted informally by a staff member of the Indonesian Consulate and, Gillot reports, told that to appear on the stage with the East Timorese actor – Maria Alice Casimiro – would place her in a position of 'high risk' (interview 1997). Despite the fact that the production was being rehearsed and performed in Australia, Warti felt she had no choice but to leave the company. The attitude of the Consulate reflected the embarrassment of the Jakarta Government over the growing international condemnation of the (then) Indonesian military occupation of East Timor.[6] It was not the performing bodies or the representation of culture in *Salt Fire Water* that the Consulate wished to influence, but the freedom of association of the bodies of the performers. The (then) Suharto Government considered even the placement of an Indonesian on stage next to an East Timorese to be an act of political subversion. The implication was that the audience would read the contiguity of these 'real' bodies as an open challenge to the Jakarta administration and as an incitement to protest. If Warti had ignored the informal warning and insisted on performing with Casimiro, would the audience have responded in this way?

To answer this hypothetical question, we must return to Young's assertion that it is impossible for a western audience to 'read' the 'raced' body, without using the classification system that is deeply imbedded in western discourse. While racial classifications remain a mechanism for justifying global power relations, any taxonomic theatre designed for western audiences is in danger of triggering a neo-imperialist gaze. This gaze encourages the audience to indulge in the cataloguing and categorising of the other in order to re-affirm the superiority and centrality of the self. However hard performers try to escape this gaze, any decision to assign fixed cultural essences to their performing bodies will make evasion difficult. Once this gaze has been triggered within an audience, the body of the performer and the performing body can collapse into a single entity, which is read for cultural and racial generalisations.

In naturalistic theatre the doubling of the body of the performer and the performing body blurs the actor/character divide but still produces the illusion of a unique individual; in taxonomic theatre this doubling reduces the body of the performer and the performing body to a single cultural paradigm. The skills of the performers, their command of aesthetic conventions, and their physical idiolects all merge and are read as symptomatic of a generalised racial or cultural category. As Peter Brook has observed, 'Why should an actor have to come on stage as a symbol of his people? Once he does so, there's no chance of his being perceived as an individual' (cited in D. Williams 1996: 73). By means of this process of recognition and labelling, the audience engages in the policing and patrolling of the boundaries that separate the self and its other, an activity that characterises all dominant groups. If this is an accurate description of the probable audience response to taxonomic theatre, it is unlikely that sufficient empathy can be generated in the body of the audience to reach the level of subversive protest that the Indonesian Consulate imagined possible with *Salt Fire Water*.

A subversive potential does lie dormant within women's taxonomic theatre, but it was not the one envisaged by the Indonesian Consulate. Rather it exists in the aporia of the taxonomic genre: miscegenation. Whilst classificatory tables of racial difference seek to impose order and fixed boundaries, the reproductive power of the female body can undermine these structures by producing children who do not fit the classificatory tables. This might imply that a taxonomic theatre could subvert the neo-imperialist gaze by introducing an unruly maternal body with the potential for anarchic reproduction. This subversive figure remained an unrealised possibility in *Salt Fire Water*, except in a parodic form during the South African laundry sequence, when a group of workers confront the impossible task of sorting the whites from the coloureds. In a literal sense, the unruly maternal body disrupts taxonomic systems by its potential to produce hybrid offspring; in a theatrical sense this same disruption can occur in symbolic worlds through the creation of hybrid performing bodies. Once the rigid cultural delineation that characterises the taxonomic genre begins to break down, new possibilities of intercultural performance are unleashed. Hybridity has long been associated with the operations of cultural or racial exchange[7] and it is to hybridity, our second intercultural body site, that we now turn.

## HYBRIDITIES

In response to his own question – 'What is hybridisation?' – Mikhail Bakhtin answered:

> It is a mixture of two social languages within the limits of a single utterance, an encounter, within the arena of an utterance, between two different linguistic consciousnesses, separated from one another by an epoch, of social differentiation, or by some other factor.
>
> (cited in Young 1995: 20)

In our investigation, social languages become performing bodies, their encounters occur within theatrical utterances, and the factors that separate them are sexually and racially determined. When re-applied to performance, the concept of hybridity does, however, have substantial risks. Popularised in the last part of the twentieth century as a way of positively re-reading the miscegenation and cultural intermingling resulting from postcolonial and diasporic encounters, it is frequently criticised for its idealising, or essentialising, or even assimilating tendencies.[8] Yet, as Helen Gilbert and Jacqueline Lo explain, hybridity is about more than merely identifying two separate cultures in one entity. For hybridity to remain a productive form, the two parts must generate an energy that is almost chemical in its recombinative effects:

> [T]he concept of hybridity stresses the productive nature of cultural integration as positive contamination. . . . [I]t is not a simple fusion of differences but rather a volatile interaction characterised by conflict between and within the constitutive cultures of a colonised society.
>
> (Gilbert and Lo 1997: 7)

In search of these volatile interactions as they occur within the body, our focus shifts from intercultural performances within Australia to the intercultural relationship between Australia and Japan, thus linking a national identity of multiculturalism to a national identity of mono-culturalism. Yet, despite the projected image of Japan as a homogenous society, its contemporary culture is the product of a highly conscious form of hybridity incorporating elements from Europe, America, and Asia. It is not surprising, therefore, that our discussion is largely focused on Japan. We shall begin with the rehearsals for *Masterkey*, an Australian/Japanese production, adapted and directed by the visual artist, Mary Moore, from the thriller *Oi Naru Genei* by Masako Togawa.[9] Following this investigation into the production process of an intercultural work, we will look at sexual and racial cross-dressing in the famous Takarazuka Revue. Our discussions will lean heavily on visual considerations, particularly costume codes, in the creation and reading of hybrid performing bodies.

## *Masterkey*

*Masterkey* falls within the category of experimental intercultural women's performance created for international performing arts festivals: it was commissioned through the 1998 Adelaide and Perth Festivals, and additional investment was provided by the Australia Council, the Sydney Cultural Olympics, and the Sydney Myer Foundation. The mixed-media production used video, object animation, soundscape, and a dramatic text to enact a conventional thriller narrative. In the prologue a man and woman are seen burying a child in the basement bathhouse of the apartment block; simultaneously, a news report is heard about the kidnapping of a child. The mother's search for her lost child brings her to the apartment block occupied by single women working in central Tokyo. She has learned that her son's schoolteacher, a resident in the complex, may have a connection with the kidnappers. The mother enlists the help of a friend and together they trace the mystery of the missing child only to discover that the body in the bathhouse is the schoolteacher's own deformed child. In the final images of the piece it becomes evident that the mother is a present-day Madame Butterfly. Her husband, a major in the US military, left her soon after the disappearance of her son; it is clear that he now lives in America and that the child is with him.

The artistic intention of this production was to create a hybrid performance world, in which a range of culturally determined performing bodies could collaborate to tell a story using a variety of different gestural and expressive performance techniques. Our analysis of this production is located within the pre-production period and the rehearsal room, and therefore does not involve the body of an audience. Instead, it is concerned with the problems of cultural interaction that Homi Bhabha suggests emerge 'at the significant boundaries of cultures, where meanings and values are (mis)read or signs are misappropriated. Culture only emerges as a problem, or a problematic, at the point at which there is a loss of meaning in the contestation and articulation of everyday life' (Bhabha 1994b: 34). The 'loss of meanings' that emerged during the rehearsal period, and the subsequent negotiations to resolve potential conflicts, are the focus of this discussion.

The female performing bodies that entered the 'everyday life' of the *Masterkey* rehearsal room were expert in a variety of performance technologies involving different approaches to interiority and exteriority, emotion, vocalisation, and gesture. The oldest of the Japanese performers, Tomiko Takai, was a *butoh* dancer who had danced with Tatsumi Hijikata; the youngest had been a member of the contemporary *butoh* company Dairakudakan. The remaining two Japanese performers were *shingeki* actors in their sixties who practised a variant of the Stanislavski system. The Australian actors similarly spanned three generations: the oldest were trained in an English-based Stanislavski tradition, the middle generation were influenced by Brechtian alternative performance modes developed in Australia in the 1970s, and the youngest were experienced in the physical theatre of the 1990s.

The pre-production period focused on the creation of a performance space that would allow these diverse performing bodies to interact, while not denying them their different modes of expression. *Masterkey* was set in the early 1950s in a western-style apartment block for single women, based on the Otsuka Women's Apartments in Tokyo.[10] A key design factor was the similarity in the accommodation provided for Japanese and western women entering the industrialised workforce in the first half of the twentieth century. It was this spatial link that provided the performing bodies with a common physical starting point in the rehearsals. As director, Moore wanted to provide each actor with a private space, part Japanese and part western, which could be wrapped around her like the exoskeleton of a crustacean. Her design solution was the wardrobe, an item of furniture which Gaston Bachelard connects with the intimacy of the poetic imagination:

> Wardrobes with their shelves, desks with their drawers and chests with their false bottoms are veritable organs of secret psychological life. Indeed, without these 'objects' and a few others in equally high favour, our intimate life would lack

a model of intimacy. They are hybrid objects, subject objects. Like us, through us, and for us, they have a quality of intimacy.
(Bachelard 1964: 23)

The Foucauldian strategy of concentrating on the body/space created for this new class of professional women had considerable success. The aesthetic hybridity of the interiors was accepted by both the Japanese and Australian actors. In the first rehearsals, the actors explored physical patterns of work and rest within the restrictions and isolation of their rooms/wardrobes, and embodied the characters through this creation of physical habitus. This containment was expressed in all the diverse performance codes of the performing bodies, but these differences were read as signifiers of individual character, rather than culturally designated performance styles. The wardrobes acted as a unifying extension of the performing body, the personalised interiors reflected the lives of the characters; in a sense they acted as prosthetics connected to the performing body, animating and defining its parameters. Framed by this spatial conceit, the performing bodies were provided with an exterior uniformity that could embrace extreme differences of physical expression within the spatial interiors.

In contrast, there was another element of the visual hybridity that was to prove more controversial. The conflict evolved around the costumes, emerging several months before rehearsal began, and was still unresolved in the final discussions after the Adelaide season had finished. During the pre-production period, the *shingeki* actors were particularly keen to see the costume drawings, given that their work practice included active participation in the definition of their physical image. The costume drawings were sent to Japan and the following questions were received by return post: How much adaptation of Japanese clothing was intended? How important was the historical period? How wealthy should the characters appear to be? Michiko Aoki, one of the cast who was also acting as the Japanese producer, offered to provide more costume research material and added: 'We have seen many productions with exotic costumes by foreigners claiming that they know Japan. We all wish that this does not happen in our project' (personal correspondence to M. Moore, 15 December 1997).

In response, Moore explained her costume designs were not intended to reproduce a naturalistic or realistic world; instead they were meant to reflect the intercultural nature of the production.

*Plate 10* Costume designs from *Masterkey*, Adelaide, 1998. Photo reproduced with the permission of Mary Moore.

All the main characters were dressed in a hybrid version of western/Japanese costume, which drew on the clothing of post-war Tokyo, without attempting to be an accurate historical reproduction. The silhouettes were intended to integrate the wrapped form of the kimono and the western tailored jacket and pencil skirt. The colour scheme was tied to the wooden wardrobes, which were the physical extensions of the characters.

In the second response from Tokyo, significant boundaries emerged. Aoki wrote:

> Fifty years ago, during 1945 to 1955, Tomiko was 14–25 years old and I was 12–22 years old. It is already history to the younger generation, but for us it was an unforgettable experience and we still remember it as yesterday. After the Second World War, for 10 years or more, we had many difficulties: shortage of food, house, clothes, and the Americans brought great changes to many Japanese customs.
> (personal correspondence to M. Moore, 17 December 1997)

While stressing that the production was non-naturalistic, Moore (together with the members of the Australian team who were involved in the pre-production period) acknowledged in reply that they lacked a full understanding of the post-war period in Japan. They reiterated that the adaptation had followed the *huis clos* nature of the thriller, which contained little reference to the wider social context. At this point it became clear that everyone was swimming in a sea of lost meanings, trying to understand the problematic relationship between embodiment and identity. The language of theatre was proving inadequate; it was clearly understood by all parties that they were not involved in a realistic or naturalistic production and that the costumes did not need to be authentic replicas of 1950s Tokyo clothing. Although the problem had surfaced as a concern about the embodiment of character through costume, the real issues concerned the bodies of the performers and their corporeal realities solidified through memory.

The youngest members of the *Masterkey* team shared generational time and some geographical space: Yumi Umiumare and Verity Rice spoke each other's languages and lived and worked in each other's countries. The hybridity expressed in the production fitted their corporeal realities, but the oldest members of the company – Miriel Lenore, Audine Leith, Tomiko Takai, and Michiko Aoki – had been alive during the war, and the socio-historical contexts and symbolic structures that had forged their identities were totally different. Underlying the discussions about the costumes was a much deeper ambiguity about the imposed cultural hybridity of the Japanese post-war era. Since the Meiji Restoration, Japan had assimilated many aspects of European culture, but the post-war period saw the uncontrolled imposition of western culture through the American occupation. Ironically, funding for the *Masterkey* project had come from the Hybrid Committee of the Australia Council.[11]

The discussions over the costumes and the resistance to an imposed hybridity brought to the surface the deep ambivalence to hybridisation that was lurking in the original text. The initial transgression that drives Togawa's thriller is miscegenation. Thus the text can be interpreted as placing a taboo on miscegenation through the narrative doubling of the hybrid child and the deformed child, which creates an associative path linking the mixed marriage with the birth deformities of the post-Hiroshima/Nagasaki era. The older Japanese actors in *Masterkey* were in a double bind: their performing bodies had consciously embraced the intercultural nature of the production, but the debate over costumes revealed their ambivalent feelings about imposed hybrid identities. Eventually the conflict over the costumes was resolved by giving the Japanese performers total control over their body image, though in reality they made only minor changes to the original designs. In retrospect, the artists working on the project concluded that the pre-production work on *Masterkey* had focused too exclusively on the performing body and the embodiment of performance technologies. Efforts had been made to find parallels in the Stanislavskian techniques used by the older actors and to trace the links between *butoh* and European expressionist dance. Too little time had been spent addressing the performers' personal and ethical relationship to historical time and geographical space. Of course it was silently acknowledged that the participants over 60 years old had lived through the Second World War, but this shared history was barely discussed. Whenever this subject emerged, whether in discussion about particular textual meanings or the relative positioning of women in the two cultures, the company drifted towards those significant boundaries where, to paraphrase Bhabha, meaning is lost (1994b: 34). Hybrid performing bodies triggered past memories in *Masterkey*, but the personal histories of the bodies of the performers were repressed to facilitate the successful creation of an intercultural work. For the younger generation of artists living and working outside of their birth cultures, the aesthetic hybridity of the production reflected their corporeal realities, but for the older generation, it silenced memory and experience.

## Takarazuka Revue

Following this theme of repression, we move outside the rehearsal room to examine the hybrid performing bodies of the Takarazuka Revue and their ability to release repression, not only in the bodies of the performers, but in the body of the audience. The Revue is arguably the largest and most popular women's performance company in the world. Kobayashi Ichizo – railway magnate, entrepreneur, and cabinet minister – established the company in 1913. The management and the artistic control of the company have always been in the hands of men; but the performers, with the exception of a brief period in the late 1930s, have always been women. There are a number of histories of the Takarazuka Revue, the most illuminating of which, by Jennifer Robertson, situates the company within an analysis of Japanese popular culture (Robertson 1998). We do not intend to re-visit these histories; our interest lies in the particular form of the racially and sexually hybrid performing bodies that mark the company's present-day success.

Cross-gendering and 'cross-ethnicking', to use Robertson's term, have been the trademark of the Takarazuka since its inception. In the 1920s and 1930s, when the Revue attracted mixed male and female audiences, this 'cross-ethnicking' fed imperialist fantasies of the Great East Asia Co-Prosperity Sphere.[12] Since the 1960s, the majority of the 'cross-ethnic' roles have occurred in western or 'red-haired plays' in which the male impersonators, or *otokoyaku*, play occidental men. Assumptions about western masculinity, rather than Japanese masculinity, inform these performances; they are based not on the observation of European or American men, but on physical and emotional gestures codified by western film stars. Although the Takarazuka male impersonators are trained within a Stanislavskian acting system which stresses the use of observation and verisimilitude, their major referents are the performing bodies of James Dean, Jack Nicholson, Clark Gable, Elvis Presley, Marlon Brando, Maurice Chevalier, and Alain Delon. In the creation of their occidental male characters, they merge racial and sexual stereotypes into complex codes of costuming, physical gestures, and vocal qualities. Over many years, these codes have been fixed by the Takarazuka actors into a series of *kata* or steps, a term used throughout the performing arts in Japan to indicate a physical repertoire out of which individual performances can be constructed.

The standard elements of the *kata* for the occidental *otokoyaku* are an open body with a wide stance, square shoulders, with the chin held slightly down. Strong hand gestures are used with fists or open palm and extended thumb stretched away from the fingers. The walk has a long stride and at moments of extreme emotional tension, the body literally falls into a run. The vocal delivery relies on an artificially lowered larynx, slight huskiness, and maximum chest reverberation. The standard costuming, which is based on the three-piece suit, frockcoat, or tailcoat, is beautifully cut to create the illusion of wide (as opposed to padded) shoulders, a waistcoat which disguises and flattens the chest, and high-waisted trousers and heeled boots to increase the leg length. Romantic characters effect a pose with hand on hip, elbow wide, holding back the jacket, thus exaggerating the narrow hip, and wide shoulder silhouette. The standard haircut involves a front quiff to add height with the remaining hair slicked back to the nape of the neck; younger characters may have auburn or blonde hair, whilst older characters tend to have dark hair with grey highlights; and hats are used even if they obscure part of the face. Facial hair is used occasionally, but make-up is used to apply moustaches, sideburns, heavy eyebrows, a hard hairline delineating the temples, as well as a pronounced bone line to emphasise the nose.

In addition to these costuming and physical codes, there are a number of elements that confuse the cross-gender and cross-race illusion. The most interesting is that the front fly or zip line in the cut of the trouser is omitted; with the marking of both the breasts and the genitals removed from the clothing, the performing body becomes pre-pubescent or anatomically sexless. On the other hand, the most interesting additions to the *otokoyaku* are the false eyelashes, use of heavy red lipstick, and visible high heels which, if read through Hollywood iconography, signify *female* desire. The double readings generated by these anomalies may account for responses which characterise the *otokoyaku* as either totally sexless, or *chusei*, the third gender idealised for its beauty.

The *kata* and costuming we have described create the illusion of the aestheticised hybrid body, and all the members of the Takarazuka Revue who specialise in occidental male roles use these signifiers. But if we are to separate out the stars from the chorus players, we must consider two further performance qualities employed by the *otokoyaku*: charisma and *iroke*, erotic appeal. In other words, we must consider how the *otokoyaku* practise the art of seduction. According to Baudrillard, seduction relies not on nature but artifice; it thrives on illusions, disguises, and masks:

> Is it to seduce, or to be seduced that is seductive? But to be seduced is the best way to seduce. It is an endless refrain. There is no active or passive mode in seduction, no subject or object, no interior or exterior; seduction plays on both sides, and there is no frontier separating them.
>
> (Baudrillard 1990: 81)

The *otokoyaku* must seduce the audience and be the object of its desire, while at the same time embodying an active desiring subjectivity on the stage. Just as the *kata* for the occidental *otokoyaku* is drawn from the performing bodies of Hollywood stars, so is an art of seduction which relies heavily on narcissistic desire, following the Freudian principle that self-love attracts the love of others.

Narcissism for the performer involves the active display of the performing body, which invites scopophilia and the ability to take conscious pleasure in exhibitionism. This body is available to the gaze; it holds this gaze and indulges it at moments of heightened dramatic tension, but at the same time it remains active and dynamic as it shares emotions and intimacies with the audience. In the Takarazuka Revue, this narcissistic desiring performing body, masked in the *kata* and costume of the *otokoyaku*, interacts with the audience: visually in the display of its physical features, literally in direct address, and empathetically through emotional states. If the trick of passive display and dramatic action is to work, a plot line providing strong goals, obstacles, and traumatic events must be provided.

To find suitable vehicles for the occidental *otokoyaku*, the Takarazuka writers have mined the western canon for romantic tragedies: their repertoire includes adaptations of *Antony and*

*Cleopatra, Hamlet, La Traviata, Romeo and Juliet, Carmen, Manon Lescaut, Turandot, Tristan and Isolde, The Great Gatsby, Wuthering Heights, Gone with the Wind*, and *East of Eden*. These stories provide *otokoyaku* with characters who yearn for impossible loves, are forced outside the social order, express violent sadistic feelings only to be tortured by remorse, and grieve over the dead bodies of lovers and friends. In addition they give the performer an opportunity to improvise on the standard *kata* and incorporate more idiosyncratic elements from the gestural repertoire of the western film stars associated with the roles. In the Takarazuka version of *East of Eden*, the *otokoyaku* plays James Dean, not Steinbeck's character; when the Revue presents *Gone with the Wind*, Rhett Butler disappears within the impersonation of Clark Gable.

Successful Takarazuka productions play to over one million people. The most popular productions in the repertoire are the romantic narratives and the musical revues; the average audience member may have seen as many as 20 previous shows. It is beyond dispute that the major attractions of the Revue are the company's male impersonators. To understand the lure of the *otokoyaku*, we must take a closer look at the body of the Takarazuka audience. Data collected in 1987 by Zeke Berlin suggest that 90 per cent of the audience are women under 30, four-fifths of whom are unmarried; these findings are contested by Robertson who places the average age at over 30 and the majority as married (Berlin 1988; Robertson 1998). For western critics of the Takarazuka Revue the first and overriding impression of the company is the uniqueness of its audience. It is difficult to sit in a 3,000-seat theatre packed with women watching the Takarazuka performers and not find the atmosphere electric. Robertson describes the 'mostly female audience whose intense absorption . . . made the auditorium sizzle with eroticized energy' (Robertson 1998: 3). Lorie Brau (1990: 90) describes an 'adoring' audience with their 'beloved' stars and observes that 'female homoeroticism may be the essence of some spectators' pleasure in the theatre'. She details the flirtatiousness of the *otokoyaku* and their practice, during the performance, of winking at particularly devoted fans. Berlin (1988: x) refers to 'the fervour of the audience's reaction': he is interested in the response of the young women in the first five rows of the auditorium who 'exhibit an intensity of involvement and fervency that is extraordinary' (ibid.: 150). In the late 1970s, he reports, they would 'wriggle in their seats', 'appear to swoon', and scream when the

*Plate 11   Gone with the Wind*, Takarazuka Revue, Kobe, 1988. Photo reproduced with the permission of Takarazuka Revue.

*otokoyaku* appeared on the 'silver bridge' or *ginkyou*, the walkway that crosses through the stalls of the auditorium (ibid.: 165).

There is little doubt that the Takarazuka Revue operates as a theatre of desire, but there is a great deal of argument about the nature of this desire. In the officially sanctioned accounts provided by the Company, the infatuation or adoration of the fans is depicted as an adolescent phenomenon, like an attack of the measles. Older women in the audience, it is asserted, introduce their daughters to this harmless and innocent entertainment to provide them with a safe vehicle for erotic feelings. In contrast, Robertson argues that the eroticism is not restricted to adolescent girls or unmarried women and fits within a more general pattern of desire for the androgynous body that appears in various guises in popular Japanese culture. Our own observations would support this assertion, because the body of the audience as a whole contributes to the charged atmosphere of the performance. The catalyst for this pleasurable release of energy is the *otokoyaku*. But how does this catalyst work? The combination of seduction, narrative, *kata*, and costume are the tools of the *otokoyaku*, but why is all this artifice necessary to release the erotic energy of the audience? To answer this final question, we must turn away from the body of the audience and the performing body and look at the off-stage corporeal reality of the body of the performer, particularly the way this body is represented by the Takarazuka publicity machine and Revue's critics.

It would be hard to imagine a profile of a performer more at odds with the image of the *otokoyaku*. The company emphasises that these young women are virginal and unmarried, they come from wealthy families, and undergo a two-year training that has more in common with a military academy than a fame school. It is frequently asserted that the *otokoyaku*, by increasing their understanding of men, are training to be good wives and mothers. The performers do not choose whether they will play men or women in the Revue; instead they are assigned their on-stage gender by the company management in the second year of their studies. Even when the *otokoyaku* become leading performers, they have little or no voice in the artistic running of the company. In every way these young women who express an active desire on stage are depicted off-stage as passive, dependent, and the embodiment of the Takarazuka motto: Be Pure, Be Right, Be Beautiful. If this image of passive femininity is in any way symptomatic of traditional gender divisions in Japan, it can be inferred that in the past, the expression of active desiring positions by the female body has been subjected to repression. If this is the case, then the female body of the performer must undergo a complex layering of disguise or masking before it can overcome social taboos. As the taboos lift, so the layers can be removed.

The cross-gender mask allows the performer to inhabit an active male desire, but it is the cross-racial mask that allows her access to the sexual excess that is so frequently invested in the racial 'other'. The eroticisation of the racial 'other' is a familiar trope within western forms of representation and, as we have argued, is tied in western discourse to the genealogy of racial classification. Hence it should come as no surprise to find that an equivalent process exists in Japan for the displacing of sexual pleasure on to the occidental 'other'. Popular Japanese culture abounds with eroticised images of occidental men and women in cartoons, pornography, and advertising: ample proof of the eroticisation of the western body can be found in the advertisements on any Tokyo subway. The Hollywood male stars that provide the raw material for the *otokoyaku* are invested with an eroticism usually reserved in Anglo-Saxon cultures for the 'Latin lover'. There is no doubt that the cross-dressing of the *otokoyaku* is in itself erotic, but we would argue that the additional element of the cross-racial disguise adds a sexuality expelled from the culture and displaced on to the imaginary of a romantic foreigner.[13]

Critiques of the Takarazuka Revue contain endless discussions about whether the audience perceives the star *otokoyaku* as a lesbian, an androgen, or a heterosexual woman transgressing gender boundaries, but it is never suggested that members of the audience believe themselves to be watching an occidental man. The presence of the female body of the performer beneath these gender and racial masks is never denied. The performer and the audience gain their pleasure from the undeniable fact that it is a sexually differentiated female body that is actively engaged in the expression of desire. Ultimately the hybrid performing body of the *otokoyaku* is merely an intercultural fabrication which functions as a conduit; it brings together the female body of the performer and the female body of the audience to join in the illicit pleasure of occupying countless variations of desiring subjectivities.

The *otokoyaku* gives pleasure by the release of repression, but the rigid sex and race binaries that underlie her/his construction are never shaken. In order to find a performing body that can challenge these binaries, we must investigate registers of performance that go beyond the purely visual, and focus on a group of artists whose performing bodies embrace a cultural nomadism.

## THE NOMADS

Conventional notions of spectatorship have dominated our thinking within this chapter. All of our examples of taxonomic or hybrid theatre have assumed that the audience is seeing rather than feeling the presence of the performer's body. In the final section of this chapter we move away from this exclusively visual reading of the performing body to explore interculturalism as it exists within the corporeal presence of the solo artists. The solo performers Yoko Ashikawa, Tomiko Takai, and Pol Pelletier transgress corporeal boundaries in their fluid movements between cultural and gender paradigms.

To escape the tyranny of the visual, we must assert the possibility that the female performing body can exceed its metaphoric function within the phallic economy. This function is graphically described by Braidotti (1991: 157): 'Woman is other – excluded, alienated, denied, a blank screen onto which man projects his anguish terror of death, his contempt for, and fear of, all that is pre-rational and corporeal.' Useful though such an understanding of the symbolic representation of the female body has been to feminist performance theorists – particularly with regard to its function as a fetish to ward off castration anxiety – it is ultimately self-defeating for the feminist practitioner. Subjected to the visual tyranny of the psychoanalytic model, the only strategy of resistance for the female performing body has been to look back, to address the audience directly. Rebecca Schneider has taken this version of the 'laughing Medusa', the explicit sighted female body, to its logical conclusion by claiming the power of double sight for the female performer:

> If one could see while being at the same time positioned as seen, there would be no fear of being blinded when seen, no fear of losing authority in locating oneself. If the feminine could wield prerogatives of vision there would be no threat in feminization. Put another way, there would be no reason

to fear 'castration'. If women can see as well as be seen, then castration anxiety – fear of loss of the prerogatives of vision as linked to *gender-marked* prerogatives – becomes patently absurd.

(Schneider 1997: 83)

Important though this strategy of defiance is, it still exists within a visual economy of representation derived from film theory, and therefore lacks an extensive investigation of the differences that exist between spectators' perceptions of projected images and audiences' perceptions of living performing bodies. Audience members not only see, but *sense* and *feel* the presence of the body. Describing a satisfying theatrical experience they will say that they were 'touched', 'moved', or even 'electrified' by the performer. There is a kinaesthetic dimension to live performance that integrates body-to-body awareness.

In searching for a model to explain this kinaesthetic relationship, we are drawn to the writings of Deleuze and Guattari and their concept of desiring machines. Whereas Freud tied desire to a phallic, and therefore visual, economy through the story of Oedipus, Deleuze and Guattari free desire from this familial plot and allow it to traverse all forms of production. In their model, desire is no longer internal to the subject, nor is it directed exclusively to an object. Desiring–production occurs as part of all social activity, when any part of the body connects with any other part, inside or outside, and it can be measured by a flow, whether it is of matter, or information. The parts of two separate bodies are as connected as two parts of the same body; a body is no longer hermetically sealed within its largest organ, the skin. The fixed boundaries of corporeal presence are undermined. Words flow from the mouth to the ear, milk flows from the breast to the mouth; both of these movements from one body to another constitute a desiring machine. When this model is applied to the theatre, flows become sensations, as well as words and information. Of course, there is an inscribed surface of the body that is read visually, but in addition there are sounds, affects, and the invisible, but palpable, energies and intensities. Tomiko Takai, one of our three nomad performers, describes the relationship between the audience and the performer as a 'united space' in which 'one breathes out, and the other breathes in' (interview 1998).

By configuring theatre as a desiring machine, which links audience body parts to parts of the doubled performer/performing body, we can examine the composition of the flow that moves between them. If this flow is organised through lines of rigid stratification, the meaning that is created is homogeneous and will coalesce into fixed identities for all the body parts that make up the machine. But Deleuze suggests that by avoiding this ordered stratification, the flow can move along escape lines or lines of transgression and can open up multiple and heterogeneous meanings and identifications. Within this concept of escape lines to the multiple lies the possibility of envisaging a theatre desiring machine that can fragment and blur sex and race boundaries of fixed corporeality and open up a multiplicity of positions. But before we can adopt this model, we need to heed a warning from Rosi Braidotti:

> Can there be a 'multiple sexuality' without sexual difference? What is the point of multiplicity if women are absorbed into a new neutral model that grants them no specificity? The fundamental issue in women's demand for sexual difference is the need for everyone, woman or man, to express a non-phallocratic sexuality. . . . [W]omen have a profoundly different relation to their bodies than do men: a bio-cultural difference, or a socio-symbolic one, which has yet to be assessed positively.
>
> (Braidotti 1991: 123)

In positing the possibility of a theatrical desiring machine that can create 'escape lines' to traverse fixed gender or cultural boundaries, we do not intend to suggest that there is a universal body on the stage or in the auditorium. Like Braidotti, we are aware of the dangers of creating idealistic and utopian models that deny the specificity of corporeal reality. In theorising the body as a site of intercultural performance, even at the point where the boundaries of fixed identity are at their most permeable, we must never lose sight of the sexually differentiated and culturally specific nature of the bodies in question. To do so would result in the theorising of a universal performing body, and a universal audience body, cut loose from the materiality of the flesh.

To pursue the possibility of escape lines while heeding this warning, we stay in Japan, but move away from the character-based dramas that have dominated this chapter to look at a form of pure physical expression, Ankoku Butoh.[14]

## The female *butoh* body

At first glance it may appear bizarre to include the female *butoh* body in an account of interculturalism, particularly as this dance form is usually defined as uniquely Japanese. Yet the genealogy and practice of *butoh* is profoundly intercultural. *Butoh* was born out of a post-war resistance to the enforced 'Americanisation' of Japan which affected every aspect of the culture: industry and technology, popular culture, the political system, even traditional art forms. Kazuo Ohno and Tatsumi Hijikata, the *butoh* founders, were inspired by western avant-garde artists who were hostile to bourgeois morality and industrial modernity.[15] Moreover, in Japan, the success of *butoh* has been tied to the globalisation of the performing arts markets.[16] To date there are companies, run by Japanese and non-Japanese *butoh* dancers, in countries as diverse as Argentina, Australia, Canada, England, France, Germany, Holland, New Zealand, Switzerland, and the United States.[17]

The most intriguing intercultural aspect of Ankoku Butoh is its practice of metamorphosis, a technique that can be described as the engine of this performance 'desiring machine'. Hijikata, who invented this technique, directed and choreographed the early works of Yoko Ashikawa and Tomiko Takai. Before we can consider the solo performances of these two women, we need to ask why the performing body that Hijikata created, and in particular the female performing body, was perceived by critics as 'beyond cultural fixations and social meanings' (Ko Murobushi cited in Kuniyoshi 1997). And if this body did transcend cultural fixations, what can it tell us about the possible shape of an intercultural body and its reception by an audience? To answer these questions, we must retrace the steps that led Hijikata from the art of metamorphosis, to the feminine inside his own body, and finally, to the body of the female performer.

Hijikata believed that the performing body was capable of transforming itself into any organic or non-organic matter because 'there is a small universe in the body' (cited in Takai, interview 1998). This did not mean that the dancer only observed, imitated, or mimed animate or inanimate objects; rather the dancer imagined the specific nature of matter – its inner essence – and allowed this to permeate the performing body.[18] It can be argued that this transformation technique is predicated on a phenomenological account of reality. Certainly Hijikata believed that 'if we, humans, learn to see things from the perspective of an animal, an insect, or even an inanimate object, the road trodden everyday is alive [so] . . . we should value everything' (Viala and Masson-Sekine 1988: 60). The *butoh* dancer thinks, feels, and moves her way into the creation of a performing body that encapsulates the essence of the observed object. Yet it is not the moment at which the transformation is completed that was of importance to Hijikata, but the indeterminacy of the performing body as it flowed between the embodiment of two distinct states. His stated aim was the fragmentation of time and being, and he achieved this by presenting his audience with a series of physical transformations without causal connections or a linear narrative.

Through the process of metamorphosis, Hijikata sought to undermine the basis of individualism and the rational subjectivity he associated with western philosophy and imposed modernity. He attempted to eradicate a fixed and unified subject position by constantly transforming his performing body. To some extent his theories paralleled those of the European avant-garde: like the German expressionists, he was drawn to the ecstatic, dreams, and the surreal in his attack on rational subjectivity. In the early choreography for his own and other male bodies, the dance is violent and homoerotic; the sado-masochism attempts to break the mould of the male body. In these performances Hijikata punished his own flesh in an attempt to obliterate its existence; to eradicate the unified male subject, the body itself had to be destroyed. In relation to this work, Takai reports Hijikata as saying that Christ, with his suffering and humiliation, was his 'greatest rival' (interview 1998).

In flight from the discredited construction of masculinity that typified the war years, and the imposition of western individualism that characterised the Occupation, Hijikata turned first to a pre-modern construction of masculinity encapsulated in the writings of Yukio Mishima. From this homoerotic world of poet warriors, Hijikata turned increasingly to the marginalised figures of Japanese history: the criminals, the diseased and deformed, the *burakumin* underclass responsible for every abject task, the blind shaman musicians, the geishas, and the actors known as *kawara mono* or riverside beggars. This search for the body of an 'other' which could express his aesthetic ultimately led Hijikata to the female body and to the feminine within himself. He believed men were 'prisoners of the logical world' whereas women were 'born with the ability to experience the illogical part of reality and are consequently capable of incarnating the illogical side of dance' (cited in Viala and Masson-Sekine 1988: 84). From the mid-1960s, Hijikata began to grow his hair, in memory of his eldest sister who had been sold into prostitution when he was still a child. He wrote:

> I keep one of my sisters alive in my body when I am absorbed in creating a *butoh* piece, [and] she tears off the darkness of my body and eats more than is necessary of it – when she stands up in my body, I sit down impulsively.
>
> (ibid.: 73)

This strong female identification is repeated in Ohno's work:

> When you are in your mother's womb, your mother is moulding and shaping your feelings. When you are born, you become an individual with an independent existence. When she dies, you are again subject to her sub-conscious influences.
>
> (cited in Philp 1986: 63)

In their collaborations Hijikata encouraged Ohno to assume a female performing body: he directed *Admiring La Argentina*, Ohno's most famous solo work inspired by memories of the Spanish flamenco dancer, Antonia Merce; and after reading Genet's novel, *Notre Dame des Fleurs*, he told Ohno 'you will be Divine, you will be a transvestite' (cited in Viala and Masson-Sekine 1988: 34). From this initial fascination with the feminine inside his own body, and the creation of female performing bodies to clothe the male dancer, Hijikata became convinced that it was the female body of the performer that could best express his art of metamorphosis.

In the mid-1960s Hijikata began exploring the choreographic limits of flexibility in the female body with a small group of dancers including Yoko Ashikawa and Tomiko Takai. Together they developed a series of *kata*, many of which are still present in Takai's choreography: *warau hana*, the smiling flower; *kanzashi o sasu*, placing an ornament in the hair; *senkoh no kemuri*, the wafting smoke of incense; *han-nya*, the demon mask; and *hangan bishoh*, the female demon's smile. The *kata* gave *butoh* form, but were never allowed to become fixed or repetitive. Takai remembers Hijikata telling the dancers:

> Forms exist so that we can forget them. . . . We should shed our skins like snakes, to emerge from what we have learned. Everything should become our own creation, not just a repetition of what we have been taught.
>
> (interview 1998)

A number of extraordinary female performers emerged from Hijikata's studio in the late 1960s and early 1970s. *Emotion and Metaphysics*, or *Keijijyogaku*, presented by Takai in 1967, was one of the first works by a female *butoh* dancer directed by Hijikata. This title, chosen by Hijikata, was used by Takai for eight of the solo works she choreographed in the next 30 years. Takai wrote:

> My search in dance is to catch that momentary vacuum in the body after the wind passes through it. I select a season, and take the clouds, the rain, and the snow into my body. The smile of an old woman, who has erased passion, becomes a stone or dew. . . . I want to float like the seed of a dandelion. How do I dance? I cannot choose 'how' anymore. The choice never comes. All that is visible in the light I have left are the worn-out soles of my feet.
>
> (personal correspondence to the authors, 25 September 1998)

A year after the performance of *Keijijyogaku* in 1967, Hijikata directed Ashikawa in *Cat – a dance to pinch a fish, a dance to eat rice from a cauldron*. In Ashikawa's performing body, Hijikata found the perfect vehicle for his art of metamorphosis. The critical literature on *butoh* suggests that their collaboration reached its peak in Ashikawa's solo work performed as part of the 'Ma–Space/Time' exhibition at the Autumn Festival in Paris in 1977. The critical response was overwhelming and it appears that the impact of the performance was profoundly visceral:

> Alone on stage, accompanied by silence or the music of a koto, she changes substance – now flower, now stone, now water – endlessly creating a multiple and polymorphic body

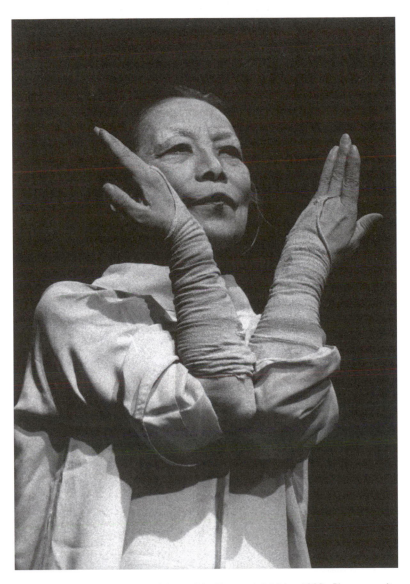

*Plate 12* Tomiko Takai in *Nobana No Tsuyu*, Adelaide, 1999. Photo credit: David Wilson.

in a mysterious ceremony never to be forgotten by the few
spectators fortunate enough to have witnessed it.

(Viala and Masson-Sekine 1988: 88)

The French critic Alain Jouffroy wrote of the same performance:

Ashikawa's powers of communication are so intense that spectators felt their bodies tremble, and tears flowed unsummoned.
Everything explodes at once. The ruling character of the exhibition – discipline, brevity, and mild reserve – flees in the face
of explosion, shudders of fear, the blinking of eyes suddenly
exposed to burning sunlight, the palpitations of the heart in
the grip of an oppressive emptiness. Everyone present experiences the real feeling of aloneness, and isolation such as they
have never felt before.

(Jouffroy in Kuniyoshi 1997)

Ashikawa asks her audience to enter a flow in which her performing body defies signifying boundaries. She is not demonstrating
that these bodily boundaries are constructed by assuming a number
of fixed identities during the course of an evening; instead her
body is in a state of constant flux. Her body moves seamlessly
through categories that are usually presented as fixed and stable.
Inscription traverses the body's surface, while the energies and
intensities of the performing body give it a depth of field. If the
audience registers the body's journey through time and space and
these constantly changing states, it is as if the body is moving in and
out of focus. In the most extreme version of this shape-changing
art, Ashikawa provokes just enough associative connections to
risk the audience locating her in a fixed identity, before her body
blurs and sets off on a different path. She says of her dance:

Butoh is not something you can do casually. The body must
be in a constant state of change. I want the body to be reduced
to a single core of spirit, to disappear, to be beautiful even in
contortion. I believe you must be very harsh, very disciplined
in finding the body's ideal expression.

(cited in Butoh 1993)

Butoh is credited with giving back 'nomadic happiness to the
body' (Murobushi cited in Kuniyoshi 1997), and Hijikata believed

that his dance could break up the principle of individuation. In order to achieve shifting perspectives, it is conceivable that the *butoh* performer uses the perceptual system that has been theorised by the phenomenologist Maurice Merleau-Ponty as the postural schema. Merleau-Ponty (1968) argued that we have an internalised sense of bodily alignment to our environment that orients us to surrounding material objects. This postural schema is a perceptual rather than a visual image that we hold of our physical reality: it is built up through our awareness of our own muscularity, motor capacities, and energies, and it draws on our sensory responses to stimuli and our physical understanding of emotional states. We interpret the actions and intentions of other bodies through our knowledge of our own corporeal reality. In other words, we read the intensities, intentions, energies, and traces on the other body by replaying them imaginatively within our own, and through this imagined physical mimesis we interpret the other's actions. The *butoh* dancer uses an equivalent system to engage in the art of metamorphosis; the body of the performer reflects, observes, almost meditates on the animate or inanimate objects that are, quite literally, the subject-matter of her representation. The body of the performer must imagine her way into the representation, and then use her performing body to sense the pathway that will allow her to transform into the next embodied state.

To follow this metamorphosis from one form of matter to another, the audience cannot rely on a narrative or an iconic system of representation. If members of the audience wish to engage kinaesthetically with the performance, they have no choice but to employ *their* postural schema to interpret the body on the stage. By observing the energies, traces, emotions, and physical contortions on the performing body, and replaying them imaginatively through their own postural schema, members of the audience can experience the dancer's journey from state to state along the pathways of indeterminacy. The intense physiological reaction to Ashikawa's work would indicate that at a visceral level, audience members disturb their *own* corporeal boundaries by physically reading her performing body. In Ashikawa's performances, conventional visual spectatorship breaks down as the performing body begins to create 'escape lines' or 'lines of transgression' through the process of metamorphosis. The body of the audience, or rather the bodies that make up the audience, read the performance through the energies and physical states that they sense emanating from the performing body. Through this physical mimesis, the bodies in the audience and the doubled performer/ performing bodies on the stage become multiple parts in a Deleuzian desiring machine.

However, the danger in advocating a visceral reading that spans cultural difference is that the spectre of the amorphous universal body appears. To rescue us from this possibility, we shall return to the corporeal reality of the body of the performer. Hijikata and Ashikawa created an art of metamorphosis, but they never denied the specificity of the body of the performer. The *kata* developed in Hijikata's studio were based precisely on the anatomical specificity of the female body; these movements were grounded in the muscle and bone structure. The reality of the body of the performer is always present within a specific cultural habitus, even though the performing body is in a state of constant flux. Hijikata sought to release in his dance the deep consciousness of the body that can only come from a corporeal reality tied to both time and place. The bodies that fascinated him belonged to the rural poor of Akita, a northern province on the island of Honshu, where he had spent his childhood. The most obvious characteristics of this body were the *ganimata* or bow-legged walk, and the *namba* movement, apparently symptomatic of rice-planting cultures, in which the arm and leg of the same side of the body move together. This was the raw material or culturally specific flesh that Hijikata was moulding, but the forms he gave it were inspired by diverse sources. These were the images that became the raw materials for the choreographic patterns. In Hijikata's studio, they created a dance form based on the specificity of the Japanese female body out of artistic influences that were thoroughly intercultural. Takai still possesses some of the scrapbooks that Hijikata assembled when he was working on the *kata* for the female performing body: they are filled with reproductions of paintings of bodies, animals, and landscapes by an extraordinary range of artists including Bacon, Picasso, Turner, Brueghel, Klimt, de Kooning, and Goya. The objective may have been to undermine the rigid boundaries that delineated identity in both the audience and the performer, but neither Hijikata nor his dancers ever denied the materiality of female Japanese bodies or their cultural habitus (Takai, interview 1998).

For readers who are dubious about any female performing body constructed or inspired by male artists, it must be said that Hijikata was not a feminist: in fact Frida Kahlo is the only female western artist who appears in his scrapbooks. Hijikata's revolt against modernity acknowledged the sexually differentiated body, but his approach was deeply impregnated by the contradictions surrounding gender identity in post-war Japan. He rejected the constructions of masculinity associated with the defeat of militarism and the Occupation, but his working relationships with Ashikawa and Takai were still patriarchal. Takai describes with some humour life at Hijikata's studio, where she and Ashikawa were expected not only to dance but also to cook and clean. In order to find a resolutely feminist performing body, which employs an intercultural process to create a theatrical desiring machine, we must leave post-war Japan and find a performing body forged out of the second wave of the women's movement in the west.

## Pol Pelletier

Pol Pelletier is a French-Canadian solo performer and playwright; she was a co-founder of the Théâtre Expérimental des Femmes in Montréal, and worked as the director of the company from 1979 to 1985. In many ways her work echoes the *butoh* experience: she has created a theatre desiring machine which binds the performing body to the body of the audience through a 'carnal, psycho-physical link'.[19] Her work is predicated on the notion of the transformation of the performing body, but she employs an intercultural body practice which never denies the corporeal reality of her French-Canadian identity. Like Hijikata, Pelletier believes that the body holds a deep consciousness of its genetic past: 'You cannot leave your culture. Your culture is how you move. You carry your ancestors with you.' Transformation into the performing body involves the abandonment of the everyday body. However, in this altered state 'you have access to your own culture, and to your own culture's collective unconscious'. In defining her cultural habitus, Pelletier includes her identity as a feminist and as a theatre practitioner. *Joie*, one of her major solo works,

> [tells] the story, in the feminine voice, of 10 years in the life of a woman of the theatre. . . . The theatrical dream which I lived throughout the 1970s was characterised by the following elements: faith in a better world, a fierce desire to change life and people.
>
> (Pelletier cited in 3IWPC 1994a: 41)

At the Third International Women Playwrights' Conference, Pelletier's presentation included a demonstration of her transformation into the 'performing body': the body she believes is necessary for 'seducing, fascinating, and truly connecting with other human beings'. She explained that she reaches this altered state through an intercultural body practice that combines techniques from Bali, China, India, Indonesia, Japan, North America, and Taiwan. Her work has been significantly influenced by Eugenio Barba's anthropological observations regarding the physical dynamics of performance. Her performing body has a flexible and sensitive spine, achieves a state of excitement or danger through a lack of equilibrium or psychic imbalance, is always pulled by two or more opposing forces, and expends high levels of energy. She practises a form of Indian meditation to silence the 'chattering in her head' and to discipline her mind to exist in the actual moment of performance. Pelletier formalised these physical and psychological dynamics of performance into a training system, and established a 'Dojo pour acteurs' in Montréal. In choosing this title for her training school, she acknowledged the Japanese influences in her work and asserted the need for an actor training programme that was as physically and mentally rigorous as the Dojo for Zen meditation and martial arts. Her objective is to assist actors to achieve a physical transformation into a hyper-conscious state: 'I tell actors – if people do not fall in love with you, you're not doing your job right.'

Although Pelletier has never studied *butoh*, one of the key examples she uses when describing the state of hyper-consciousness in the performing body is Kazuo Ohno:

> I don't think anyone who sees Kazuo Ohno has a doubt about the existence of the soul or the link to the cosmos. This man is 94 and he plays a woman – he is a woman. You sit there and cry watching him. It's not necessarily sad . . . he plays a little girl, he's running, with his wrinkled knees, he plays a baby . . . the absolute essence of being a baby or child. . . . It's a total connection to the roots of life.

Pelletier admires Ohno because of the link or tie he creates with his audience. If there is one element that she strives for in all her solo work, it is the creation of a tangible connection between her performing body and the body of the audience: 'I'm talking, there's

*Plate 13*  Pol Pelletier in *Joie*, Montréal, Canada, 1993. Photo credit: Fabienne Sallin.

an audience, I'm literally going out there, I'm literally, literally touching them.' She describes her theatrical desiring machine as a 'pure energetic thing' that connects each member of the audience and causes them to 'vibrate in unison'. She visualises threads coming out of her body, she can feel these threads connecting back to her, and she 'can see the energy': 'This is not cerebral stuff but a joined physical and psychic energy.' Pelletier never implies that there is a universal body of the audience. She has toured Australia, Europe, and South America, and finds the physical dynamics of audiences, and theatre venues, culturally specific. In Paris, she performed to an initially unresponsive audience of 300 people and used so much energy to reach the audience that she claims she cracked the cement wall at the back of the theatre:

> I'm a very strong person, but I've never done that. The energy, the whole theatre was full of it, and after an hour on stage, a wall crumbled. Only then did they start communicating with me. And I thought, come on! . . . The next day, it was exactly the same, it was like lifting a car.

Just as Pelletier recognises the cultural specificity of her audiences, she never disguises her French-Canadian corporeal reality. Her interculturalism is invisible to the naked eye. It exists, not in the layering of cultural signifiers on the performing body, but in performance methods drawn from non-western training systems that she uses to focus her physical energy and propel her performing body into heightened states. This technique of visceral communication creates a desiring machine through which the energy dynamic of the performance can be experienced by the audience in the form of bodily sensation.

Our investigations into the solo work of Pelletier, Takai, and Ashikawa have taken us a long way from the global arts markets, where intercultural performing bodies are recognised either as personifying authentic cultural essences in taxonomic systems, or as visible hybrids created out of the layering and combining of disparate cultural signs and symbols. We have argued that in taxonomic theatres the body of the performer and the performing body are merged, and that the process of recognition and identification of cultural difference encourages the body of the audience to solidify the boundaries that delineate self from other. Rigid boundaries of cultural difference begin to break down in the productions we have identified as aesthetic hybrids, but in unpredictable ways. Theatre artists from all cultures find enlarging their repertoire of theatrical signification stimulating and many indulge in the pleasures of intercultural bricolage. It is impossible to summarise all the probable audience readings of aesthetic hybridities, but some general points are worth making. The processes of identification and recognition that mark taxonomic theatre are still at work in the hybrid genre, yet combinations of disparate elements within the single performing body can challenge notions of cultural authenticity. A further distinction can be made between the readings of organic hybridity that reflect the corporeal realities of the bodies of many bicultural performers and the artificial hybrid performing bodies created by monocultural artists. The former will probably be read as a postcolonial or a migrant arts practice, the latter as fantasy creations constructed from non-contiguous semiological material. These fantasy beings can serve many functions. In the Takarazuka Revue, for example, the *otokoyaku* is designed to stimulate an erotic response in the body of the audience, but her ability to create new desiring subject positions is predicated upon the sex and race binaries specific to her cultural habitus.

Finally, in moving beyond hybridities, we have suggested that the performing body can still be described as an intercultural site even when it lacks visible traces of an intercultural performance practice. Nomad performing bodies unsettle the fixed boundaries of their audience through techniques of transformation and metamorphosis. In a Deleuzian sense, they establish desiring machines that connect the doubled performer/performing body to the body of the audience. In describing their desiring machines, our nomad performers speak of a single organism breathing, of touching and being touched by the body of the audience, of connecting threads that link at psychic and physical levels. The construction of these machines has been intercultural, and the machines have drawn on performance and arts practices from across the world. They share a common objective to undermine the rigid boundaries that define the body of the audience, and to open up a kinaesthetic relationship that can challenge fixed corporeal boundaries. Yet at no point do these nomadic bodies deny their own corporeal materialism either in terms of their sexually differentiated bodies or their personal ethos. Through their exploration of diverse body states, they offer the body of the audience access to multiple identities and a fascinating journey through a labyrinth of indeterminacy. By suggesting that an intercultural performing body can be defined through kinaesthetic as opposed to visual or linguistic communication, we hope to open up new theoretical avenues for the body as a site for intercultural women's performance.

# Chapter 5

# Intercultural markets

## The female body and censorship

The hallmark of commoditization is exchange. But exchange opens the way to trafficking, and trafficking in human attributes carries with it a special opprobrium.

(Kopytoff 1986: 85)

The world exhibitions glorify the exchange value of commodities. They create a framework in which commodities' intrinsic value is eclipsed. They open up a phantasmagoria that people enter to be amused. The entertainment industry facilitates this by elevating people to the level of commodities. They submit to being manipulated while enjoying their alienation from themselves and others.

(Benjamin 1978: 152)

The boundaries and issues of interculturalism and multiculturalism can only be considered today within the context of the specific geopolitics of the cultures involved. A multicultural festival may be considered 'successful' in Los Angeles because of the particular cultural and political environment of that region. A cultural festival in Sharjah [United Arab Emirates] will not be accorded the same 'freedom'. This is a sobering reality for the third-world theatre scholar and practitioner.

(George 1994: 148)

Although most assessments of theatre are preoccupied with aesthetics and, increasingly, the political implications of aesthetic choices, we have found it necessary to broaden our perspective from the creation of performance to its distribution in a global context. The distribution of theatre is subject to the economic rules that apply to any commodity, particularly the laws of international economic exchange in a globalised world. While many critics do recognise that the available resources to produce new theatre determine the type and scale of theatre produced, and many performers involved in the making of theatre necessarily heed the dual roles of production and distribution, few extend that economic argument to its social relations. The practicalities of packaging and marketing theatre can profoundly alter the potentially delicate collaborative work accomplished in the rehearsal room. This chapter focuses on interculturalism's markets and the difficulties a number of women performers have faced in their attempts to engage with those markets, which have traditionally been controlled by men. Inevitably, then, a question of agency arises when women performers sell their art. The question becomes particularly urgent when the explicit female body – or the body that consciously and conspicuously displays itself in performance as female – enters the market. The explicit body in performance disrupts accepted behaviour models for women, both on and off the stage.

We are using Rebecca Schneider's concept of the explicit body, a body which 'in representation is foremost a site of social markings, physical parts, and gestural signatures of gender, race, class, age, sexuality – all of which bear ghosts of historical meaning, markings delineating social hierarchies of privilege and disprivilege' (Schneider 1997: 2). Schneider reads in explicit body performance 'an effort to make apparent the link between ways of seeing the body and ways of structuring desire according to the logic of commodity capitalism' (ibid.: 5). She 'look[s] at the ways in which perspectival vision and commodity fetishism are played back across *the body as stage*' (ibid.: 6–7). We might ask why the explicit female body is a site of social anxiety when, as Lynda Nead argues, '[t]he framed image of the female [nude] body . . . is an icon of western culture' (Nead 1992: 1). The very fact that this image is 'framed' as an icon of High Art codes the nude as a means of maintaining patriarchal authority over women. Yet Nead explains that there is a potential danger associated with the female nude:

> The female nude marks both the internal limit of art and the external limit of obscenity. . . . It is the internal structural link that holds art and obscenity and an entire system of meaning together. And whilst the female nude can behave well, it involves a risk and threatens to destabilize the very foundations of our sense of order.
>
> (ibid.: 25)

The explicit performing body recognises this structural link, and its performance actively attempts to destabilise a sense of order that denies a complex and empowering subjectivity for women. The regulations associated with High Art do, however, continue to intervene in the presentation of explicit body performance, particularly in the international marketplace.

We are especially interested in the contradiction between women with control over their performances and women without such control. In our consideration of the large international arts market that engages in the trade of women's performing bodies well beyond arts festivals, we draw some parallels between women who use explicit body practices in their artwork and women who are instructed to use explicit body practices in their performance. The difference is determined by who conceives and controls the performance and its cultural context.

International performance tends to be marked by two opposing poles which are two key distribution networks used by performing artists globally: 'high culture' (best known in terms of international arts festivals comprising events like chamber music, classical ballet, theatre produced by national companies, and many examples of contemporary art) and an entertainment 'underworld' at the opposite end of the spectrum (the domain of dancers, strippers, nightclub performers, and, at the extreme, trafficked women whose entry to the world of performance is by means of illegally procured dancers' visas). The entertainment underworld can be seen to work in much the same way as the trade in high art, as we demonstrate later in this chapter in the discussion of trafficked performers.

Our main interest is in international arts festivals, which can mark the epitome of women's intercultural performance, and, more practically, provide access to funding for expensive performance genres which involve collaboration by artists from different countries. Intercultural theatre is a lucrative drawcard for international arts festivals, particularly when one of the intercultural partners can claim an 'exotic' background. But before we consider how such a market works, we must clarify the three different cultural contexts in which these festivals – and the performances within them – are situated. Each is inflected with specific gender attitudes which determine the representational freedom of women performers. The simplest is the cultural milieu or social sphere in which a festival is located. This includes the (often large) proportion of a festival city's population that may not participate directly in the festival but can affect and be affected by the workings of the festival. The second is the particular dominant cultural heritage of the country holding the festival. This cultural context tends to be defined by national borders and/or ethnic categories. As an entity, it tends to be celebrated at festivals. The distinction we are making between the first and second contexts is between a general social order on the one hand and a specific ethnic/racial identification on the other. While the population in both locations may overlap substantially, the operations of each of these two contexts (especially in relation to the third context) can be quite divergent. The third context is 'high culture' or art forms perceived to be artistically superior to more populist genres like cinema or stand-up comedy or performances at fringe festivals. Each of these cultural contexts can be termed 'culture', and each plays a significant role in the social and aesthetic framing of arts festivals. We refer to the first as cultural milieu, the second as culture, and the third as Culture.

The intersection of these three cultural contexts is not always straightforward, and a performance's interplay within these contexts can result in aesthetic and/or legal difficulties for artists, artistic directors, and audiences. Interventionary censorship and/or regulation can also be the result, raising questions concerning levels of control that women have over their performing bodies, how they use them in representation, how these representations are sold, and the varying forms of censorship they encounter. An ill-defined panoply of regulations and representational dilemmas shapes the artistic product distributed in the entertainment market. The regulations, which tend to stipulate what can and cannot be performed, are not necessarily transparent. This lack of transparency disguises possible differences in the agency allowed to the male and female body. The regulations can be set by the laws of the country in which the art is performed, or by what appear to be nebulous social rules of taste and decency.

Following a discussion of the operation of arts festivals generally, we argue that festivals' socio-political setting continues to have a significant impact on the framing, marketing, and distribution of the female performing body in the international arts market. The first two examples are the arrest of actors from the Ilotopie group and Annie Sprinkle's constant flirtation with censorship. We develop this argument further through a discussion of the opposite end of the performing spectrum, trafficked performers who work in the underworld of international performance and whose artists' visas keep them just within the bounds of national and international law. Finally, we consider the intersection of all three cultural contexts in the marketing of an image of the Virgin Mary to advertise the 1998 Adelaide Festival.

## ARTS FESTIVALS: CELEBRATING OR REDISTRIBUTING CULTURE?

Social structures like the museum and the exhibition have been extensively studied by historians and cultural analysts, but the comparable structure of the arts festival remains largely outside theoretical attention. We cannot offer an economic analysis of arts festivals in this chapter, but we can provide a sense of their regulatory and representational significance for intercultural performance. Arts festivals, which combine local and international performances to excite and entertain a given audience, have the ability to compress time and geography, leaving patrons to take advantage of as many performances as ticket-prices (often high), time, and endurance allow. The public relations machines surrounding arts festivals promise entertainment, excitement, and evenings that audiences will not forget. Contemporary arts festivals bring performances from a variety of countries to one place, introducing audiences to different cultural artefacts, while artists from a range of cultures meet and may be involved in productions with each other. Usually, at least one large mainstage performance in any given arts festival will produce the relatively standard intercultural format of actors from different cultures performing together.

The origin of festivals lies with commerce, in the centuries-old tradition of touring theatrical productions. Most European theatre traditions began with travelling troupes, but from the eighteenth century onwards, touring developed a political dimension and operated as an extension of colonisation: the centre toured to the colonies, replicating the metropolis touring to the provinces, and, in the process, articulated the colonial power's theatrical and behavioural standards. In today's labour-intensive theatre industry, where the time and effort exerted in the creation of work must be recouped by maximising audiences, artists move to the peripheries in search of new audiences once they have exhausted the audience base at their centre, rather like their antecedents. The costs of production can be amortised through syndicating the artistic product over two or three festivals. The publicity and marketing machines connected to these events attract far wider coverage than a one-off marketing campaign can ever achieve.

The best-known festivals include Edinburgh and Avignon, both of which began shortly after the Second World War with a view to uniting European countries post-war. Edinburgh in particular was chosen because its civic buildings were not bombed during the war. Avignon's location outside Paris also reinforces a non-metropolitan ethos. Edinburgh attracts audiences of 300,000, while Avignon maintains a smaller profile with audiences of over 100,000. Arts festivals of all types proliferate around the world these days, but some of the key festivals include Adelaide (100,000), Hong Kong (100,000), Singapore (70,000), and Tokyo (90,000), each varying in numbers of productions and lengths of runs. Most festivals are funded by a combination of government subsidy, corporate sponsorship, and ticket sales, the proportions differing from country to country.

Governments recognise that festivals bring to their cities/states/countries artists and tourists who will spend money not just on theatre tickets but also on accommodation, restaurants, associated exhibitions and tourist venues, souvenir shopping, and, in all likelihood, follow-on tourism. Festivals have the potential to generate considerable revenue for local economies and, as a result, the often large public subsidy makes good political sense. The continued success of a country's or region's tourism industry can depend heavily on such festivals, and the effects of these economic considerations are often apparent in festivals' merchandising and promoting of associated events. Performance groups who tour overseas to arts festivals are also frequently invested with promotional duties: they often wear the ambassadorial and tourism mantles of their home countries. Other important factors that differ from country to country include the breakdown between government funding for festivals and funding for other arts ventures (and the competition between these varied groups), and the elaborate funding formulae that may determine which productions tour from city to city within a country, and which productions tour overseas. Most festivals rely heavily on government subsidy because box-office returns alone cannot support the cost of production and distribution.

Corporate sponsorship is also essential to festivals, and sponsors vie to display their logos in association with prestigious productions. Even the names of many festivals recognise major corporate sponsors, such as The Telstra Adelaide Festival and The Standard Bank National Arts Festival in Grahamstown, South Africa.[1] While few people would admit that such sponsorship affects the artistic choices in any festival, these economic considerations determine how much money is available in the first place, and, therefore, the scale of the productions which will be booked, for how long, and from how far away. The larger arts festivals tend to be competitive marketing and re-distribution enterprises. The variety of regulations that governments and corporate sponsorship in effect place on festivals (whether acknowledged or not) influences the definitions of 'culture' that festivals promulgate.

Arts festivals are often assumed to be celebrations of culture (and Culture). Festivals isolate, frame, translate, and market culture as exoticised difference by producing, re-distributing, and selling performance. Ivan Karp (1991a: 283) maintains that festivals contest the 'ownership of culture and how it is defined'. The 'living' quality to art in festivals – in which performances are composed of live actors, unlike cinema or painting, for instance – contributes to the myth that performers embody culture.

On the stage, culture as difference quickly becomes a commodity that operates slightly differently from the tourist souvenir, or any tangible consumer item. A culturally identified commodity product in performance sometimes comes to be recognised as a metonym for a culture. While a representation can 'stand for' that which it denotes in a metaphoric fashion, it can also 'stand in for', or occlude, that which it might otherwise denote, metonymically. For example, *wayang kulit* outside Bali comes to mean 'Balinese performance' to the virtual exclusion of any other type of performance. Kathakali dance, one of numerous Indian dance techniques and one specifically associated with a particular region in India, frequently comes to represent 'Indian' dance or performance to non-Indians. In both instances, the cultural 'essence' of the other tends to be extracted for western consumption. This 'check–mark' approach to cultures on stage recalls the taxonomic performing body that we described in the previous chapter. In the context of the international festival, such a taxonomic exercise often obscures any awareness of cultural specificity or identity politics. This inevitable commodification process reduces culture to an ever-shrinking signified that begins to resemble a sound-bite. Once such a sound-bite becomes circulated widely enough, it takes on the role of 'culture' in a variation on Baudrillard's (1988: 166) simulacrum. If it becomes unalterably associated with a culture, to the exclusion of other markers of the culture, its commodification is complete until the process begins again, shifting and again shrinking the 'meaning' of a culture to a new marketable entity that possesses novelty value.

There is a factor of recognition associated with these 'exotic' signs: once recognised, they are 'understood', but they are thereby emptied of any signification as difference. While the signs that mark a culture in a form of 'international sign language' are useful to a degree, they become meaningless very quickly.[2] There is no room for the negotiation of identity politics in this cultural sign language, even though all the performers inevitably occupy multiple subject positions. Arts festivals tend to tour productions around the world to maximise investment and amortise risk, resulting in audiences being fed a relatively common diet of theatre that appears to have a global seal of approval. Festivals' manipulation of art and culture culminates, for Adorno, in the generation of a cultural shell. Festivals, he argues,

> are all embraced and controlled by a single comprehensive organization. . . . Administrative reason which takes control of them and rationalizes them banishes festivity from them. This results in an intensification into the grotesque which cannot escape the notice of the more sensitive nerves present at these so-called cultural offerings – even at those of the avant-garde. In an effort to preserve a feeling of contrast to contemporary streamlining, culture is still permitted to drive about in a type of gypsy wagon; the gypsy wagons, however, roll about secretly in a monstrous hall, a fact which they do not themselves notice.
> (Adorno 1991: 102)

While Adorno's depiction of festivals is very bleak, artists are generally obliged to continue to perform in them for economic reasons: the labour-intensive nature of live performance makes mass markets, touring, and subsidy necessary to survival. Festivals continue to thrive, if at the expense of local art that is not (yet) part of an international touring circuit. Most arts festivals set out to present intercultural performance as a showcase of how cultures might intersect and interact, but the underlying financially driven structure of any festival and the resulting commodification of its art forms generally compromise the best intentions to promote interculturalism.

The performances in the international markets that we describe in the following sections demonstrate a clash between at least two of the cultural contexts on the one hand, and explicit body performance on the other. Our efforts to determine the nature of these clashes assist us in delineating the parameters of arts festivals and international performance, and particularly how they affect the production, marketing, and distribution of women's intercultural performance. The analysis that follows begins with the problems of distributing and framing explicit female body performance in the international market, which is necessarily intercultural. We continue to add different specific cultural contexts and performative sites that embody the argument that women performing in the international market are constantly at risk of sanction.

## FRAMING PERFORMANCE IN AN INTERNATIONAL MARKET

### Ilotopie and Annie Sprinkle

Both performances outlined in this section conflicted with the cultural milieu of the festivals in which they performed, challenging cultural assumptions about the female body. Furthermore, both involved women artists choosing to employ explicit body practices. Ilotopie, a French company composed of five men and one woman, was not prepared for their reception in Adelaide. The troupe brought their street theatre performance, *Les Gens de Couleurs* [*Coloured People*], to the Adelaide Festival in 1992, following a successful season at the Perth Festival several weeks earlier. Their eye-catching work frequently uses brightly coloured body paint or foam, drawing attention to the performing body. For this performance, the actors, who had performed around the world, were completely covered in very thick, brightly coloured body paint and wore only G-strings. In their performance, they walked through various public areas in central Adelaide, enacting a sedate, silent piece for approximately 90 minutes in which they left human 'traces' such as handprints and footprints to foster reconsiderations of humanity and peace after the performance was completed.

At their first performance in the Adelaide city centre, the female artist, Myriam Prijent, was arrested for 'behaving in an offensive manner in public' (*The Advertiser* 1992a: 1) because she was bare-breasted. One of the men in the company, Raymond Blard, was also arrested for hindering police, resisting arrest, and damaging police clothing; the latter charge arose from the transfer of some of Blard's body paint to police uniforms in the process of his arrest. Blard was arrested because of his alleged actions, while Prijent was arrested solely for the display of her body. The police, who asserted that unnamed members of the public had complained about the troupe, disregarded the fully clothed stage manager equipped with a walkie-talkie who tried unsuccessfully to intervene in the arrests. Communication between the festival and the police was thus made virtually impossible. As to prior warning, Rob Brookman, the artistic director of the Festival in 1992, exclaimed following the arrests that he did not feel such a warning was necessary, because 'I did not, in my wildest imaginings, think this [the arrests] could happen' (ibid.). Members of the company had only encountered difficulty with the law once before, at a performance in Canada, where they were arrested on charges of indecent behaviour and found not guilty. In Adelaide, the charges were dropped the following day. Concerns regarding whether other performances at the Festival might also be censored were raised by Festival guest performers.

The law regarding the prohibition of bare breasts in Adelaide is only selectively enforced. It is imperative in Aboriginal women's performances and ceremonies that the women expose their ochre-painted breasts, which are arguably less concealed by paint than were Prijent's breasts. Aboriginal women are not arrested, nor are they required to be more fully dressed when they perform in Adelaide (which is a common enough occurrence). The law for Aboriginal women who are performing seems to apply differently to non-Aboriginal women performing bare-breasted: the white western woman who tries to take to the public, global arena in such a way is censored for being obscene. The intercultural dilemma is that the display of Aboriginal women's breasts in public is seen to be acceptable, whereas Prijent's exposed body is offensive, when both are circumscribed by the boundaries of performance.

The location of the performance is the crux of this example: the clash is between the cultural milieu (the Adelaide city centre) and Cultural space (a theatre or enclosed performance location that charged an admission fee) over the representation of Prijent's explicit body. If Prijent had been performing in a space labelled 'Cultural', the police would probably not have arrested her because her performance involved a relatively passive display of her body that could be reinscribed in Culture as maintaining a conventional social (patriarchal) order. Her performance outside the frame of a theatre was more likely to be read as disruptive to the social order. Had she appeared in other cultural milieu spaces but not been performing, the response would likely also have differed. If she had been sunbathing on an Adelaide beach, she probably would also have avoided police intervention because the codes that threaten a patriarchal social order that are associated with explicit body practice do not necessarily apply to a performer when she is not performing the explicit body. That Aboriginal women performers (and nursing mothers for that matter) generally don't attract the attention of the police suggests that they signify a different, non-threatening relation to public space, Culture, and performance. Ilotopie's performative breaching of the boundaries of Cultural space was construed as breaching legal boundaries as well, specifically with regard to the display of the female body.

Annie Sprinkle's performances are more explicit than Ilotopie's, and Sprinkle recognises that she must take very careful precautions to ensure that her work is not censored, even if it is performed in a theatre. Known around the world for her forthright demonstrations of sexual pleasure, Sprinkle has toured *Post Porn Modernism* at international arts festivals for close to ten years, including Adelaide in 1996. The performance is probably best known for the scene entitled 'Public Cervix Announcement' in which Sprinkle inserts a speculum in her vagina on stage in front of the audience and invites audience members to come to the edge of the stage to see her cervix, with the aid of flashlights provided by attendants. The final scene is also notorious: Sprinkle simulates an orgasm on stage in what she calls a moment of collective ritual cleansing during which the audience 'joins in' by shaking paper-cup rattles. Schneider explains that Sprinkle's ritual masturbation is 'designed to transcend "sex-negativity" and offer a healing, spiritual union through mutual "sex-positivity" – a mutuality achieved, ironically, in a display of auto-eroticism' (Schneider 1997: 58).

Sprinkle maintains that her work is intended to educate audience members about sexuality by being very frank about her own body, her experiences as a prostitute, and the pleasure humans can derive from their own bodies. For Schneider, the nexus between art and pornography is the most important aspect of Sprinkle's performance:

> It is the politicized *link* she is making explicit between sexuality, vulnerability, and power that is 'hardly able to be seen' – out of the bounds of vision for a society habituated to maintaining 'perspective' by maintaining distinctions between sexuality and politics, nature and culture, or porn and art.
>
> (ibid.: 77)

Sprinkle's work is no doubt controversial in its public exposure of the interiority of the female body and in its self-conscious collision between pornography, the apparent taboos concerning the prostitute as feminist artist, and 'art' itself. In doing so, Sprinkle takes the clash over space further. She performs in a theatre, yet she exposes the interior and exterior of her body in a way that confronts conventional notions of performance spectacle. In Sprinkle's case, the naming of her performance as 'art' (in the context of High Art or Culture) challenges the norms of female representation.

Sprinkle recognises that her performances can cause offence and, in order to circumvent any accusations of censorship and any accidental affront to members of the cultural milieu, she issues substantial explanatory notes to the presenters in the technical specifications about her work well in advance so that she is not misrepresented and that no audience members are unpleasantly surprised. In order to avoid censorship and minimise the disruption to her touring programme, she issues detailed instructions to each venue about exactly what is entailed in her performances, and exactly which responsibilities promoters and producers must accept for the performances to be executed. Her publicists discuss it carefully with the presenters at every location. She makes it clear that her shows are not intended to titillate: people who are expecting to be sexually aroused will be disappointed. She also advises that very conservative people ought not to attend the performance to avoid any offence they may take (Scobie, interview 1998). The whole production is highly managed well before

Sprinkle arrives in town. This management of Sprinkle's work – and specifically the representation and display of her body – shifts the marketing of the performance from 'mere' entertainment for redistribution to a tightly controlled object divorced even from Sprinkle's own highly exposed body. The management surrounding the performance of *Post Porn Modernism* subordinates the performative and/or artistic dimensions to her work.

The notoriety associated with Sprinkle's performances also attracts more attention than the performances themselves. There is the opportunity for local conservative elements to attempt to prevent the presentation of Sprinkle's work, which is frequently dismissed in outrage – generally by members of the public who have responded to media provocations about the more controversial aspects of her work. Likewise, the media are implicated in misrepresenting Sprinkle and inciting disapproval everywhere she plays, regardless of how clear her technical specifications are.

There is always the possibility that Sprinkle relishes this notoriety, in the context of all publicity being good publicity. However, both Sprinkle and Ilotopie illustrate that attempts by women to control their representations in performance are subject to authorities outside the sphere of their artistry. These women are free to perform in so far as arts festivals require a product, but they are not entirely free to work as they wish, because their work defies normative values in the conventional display of the female body.

Not all women performers are able to control the representation and nature of the display in which they engage, even to this extent. Our next section moves from the highly visible arts market to the black market in order to address a group of performers whose work is rarely discussed in the context of art, and is almost completely hidden from international attention.

## Trafficked women

Ilotopie and Sprinkle are examples of the power of the cultural milieu to intervene in the construction of the high Culture that arts festivals tend to signify when the explicit female body is perceived to be inappropriately placed. The next example reverses the situation: female dancers who are trafficked around the world on dancers' visas enact a display that is perceived to be appropriately placed, out of general view in 'red light' districts and for sale to 'consenting adults'. The performers manage to avoid the very censorship that entraps other performers in the intercultural arts world because they are thought to be in their appropriate cultural milieu. Their display abides by the rules governing the cultural milieu, including the reinforcement of established power relations between the sexes, particularly when the employer controls the performer's every action, even to the point of owning her body. The mechanisms of the international performance market provide the channels for Culture to collude with the cultural milieu to contain the representational frame of these women and their bodies. We do not intend to trivialise the plight of these performers (who are almost always tricked into prostitution under the guise of being recruited as folk-dancers); rather, we intend to provoke discussions about the regulatory parameters for women performing in intercultural markets, and the commodification of both cultures and humans.

The trafficked women[3] are trapped in (usually) western countries by multiple (false) identities, poverty, legal loopholes, and uninterested media. They are generally overlooked by social and legal agencies because technically they comply with the legalities outlined for touring international performing artists.[4] To the extent that it is used by women artists, the global arts market could be described as the legitimate wing of a widespread international trade in women that can be more lucrative than trafficking in arms or drugs, and considerably less risky for the traffickers (Skrobanek, cited in Circle against Sex Trafficking 1997: 3).

If Wagner's Brünnhilde or Shakespeare's Portia are at the top of a western artistic hierarchy, the dancer recruited through the black market with a dancer's performance visa holds a position (often unwillingly) at the opposing end of the market. While the intercultural international trade continues to buy and sell intercultural products in a global marketplace, there is a growing business involving the international movement of many more performers than are currently involved in the major arts festivals. The international market in trafficking in women deploys the same language and channels as the international arts markets dealing in 'legitimate' intercultural performance since the trafficked women are hired as dancers and travel around the world on performers' visas.

The typical trafficked woman is poor. She is invariably told that she is being employed to perform either folk-dance or ballet. The audition frequently consists of no more than an inspection of her naked body. Characteristically, the young artist travels on a fake passport under a new 'stage name' (arranged to facilitate the preparation of fake travel papers). Once she arrives at her destination, her passport is confiscated, she is told that the type of dance now required is striptease, that prostitution is also essential, and that her first three months' salary will be withheld to reimburse the costs of her travel to the destination. She may not know what country she is in, she may not speak the language, and she will not know whom to contact for help. If she has arrived with fake travel documents, even her own country's embassy cannot (or will not) repatriate her. She is thus completely reliant on her employer. There have been at least four recognised waves of trafficking in women: the first from Asia (mostly Thai and Filipina women); the second from South America (particularly Dominicans and Colombians); the third from Africa (predominantly Ghanaians and Nigerians); and the fourth, the most recent, from Central and Eastern Europe (Migration Information Programme 1995: 7).

One large artists' talent agency, Stage International from Rotterdam, managed 12 clubs in Holland, Belgium, and Spain, and imported over 3,000 women between 1986 and 1992: 'Stage used the method which was applied in the whole of Europe: the alien ladies were receiving legal work permits as "artists", the same documents that Prince and Madonna have to obtain to perform' (de Stoop 1994: 7). In fact, in Switzerland, gogo-dancing is 'the only profession for women from the Third World' that qualifies for a visa application (ibid.: 52). In Japan, Filipinas (the most common ethnic group represented among the trafficked dancers) require a valid 'artist's record book' (ARB), for which they must demonstrate dance training (*Philippine Daily Inquirer* 1997: 13).

In most countries around the world, the laws pertaining to trafficked women are extremely inadequate to protect women who escape from the system, to prosecute the traffickers, and to prevent other women from being trafficked. The International Organisation for Migration report on Trafficking and Prostitution (May 1995) acknowledges that the full scale of the problem is difficult to ascertain because very few women report their situation to police. When they are brought to the attention of the authorities, few women are willing to press charges for fear of reprisals against their families. Furthermore, '[s]entences against traffickers are light, and there are few successful convictions. Partly this is because many countries deport victims immediately, thereby losing valuable witnesses' (Migration Information Programme 1995: 2). Trafficking in humans is generally seen as a low priority by law enforcement agencies.[5] An exception is Belgium, which amended its laws so that women on artists' visas were required to collect their visas in person and were given a booklet outlining the conditions of the visa as well as their rights. This amendment alone virtually stopped the requests for artists' visas in Belgium (ibid.: 23), and The Netherlands and Switzerland have since attempted to follow suit.

Culture and cultural difference also play a significant part in the explicit body performances that trafficked women are forced to enact. While club dancers may, to some extent, control their representations when they perform in their own nation state, they lose that agency – and indeed agency over their very lives – when they are trafficked to another country and forced to play the role of the cultural other. Their performing bodies that are on display to their audiences as culturally exotic are no longer their own. The intercultural exchange of women who are perceived to be 'exotic' continues to attract the attention of traffickers (the women's naïvety and poverty notwithstanding) because cultural exoticism – whatever its particular signifier may be – is consumed at a high rate in Europe, other western nations, and Japan.[6] The international trade in women recruited as dancers represents the worst-case scenario for commodification in performance: *humans* can become reified into units of culturally exotic commodity value only. They are 'expendable' commodities and are easily replaced (often by a compatriot). The farthest-reaching commodification of culture thus takes place under the guise of cultural exchange, and Kopytoff's caution concerning the trafficking in humans that we have used as an epigraph to this chapter is ignored. There seems to be little concern for any of the opprobrium associated with the trafficking in humans when the economic return is so favourable. In fact, some traffickers rationalise their activities in humanitarian terms: the manager of a Dutch club told de Stoop 'I have ten Dominican girls. I consider this as development aid' (de Stoop 1994: 50). A Dominican trafficker in women maintained 'Thanks to me, hundreds of girls presently have a better life and I will continue to send them over there [to Europe] as long as the government maintains its policy of hunger and misery' (ibid.: 50).

If we look at the widespread silence associated with trafficking in women's bodies, as contrasted to the media outrage associated with women artists employing 'explicit body' practices in their

'High Art' performances, it would appear that the work of Sprinkle and Ilotopie is seen as far more threatening to the social fabric than the widespread trafficking of women under the guise of performance. If women control and use these practices within the arena of Culture, they are censored. If they are instructed to use these practices within the designated 'red light' districts, then the display is condoned even if the commodification involves human trafficking. It is not only who owns and controls the living body of the female performer, but who also controls the female image. The next section returns to the arts festival, and to an image of a woman – possibly the most famous female image in the western world – which provoked a clash between Culture, the copyrighting of culture, and an international festival's cultural milieu.

## The 1998 Adelaide Festival poster

The 1998 Adelaide Festival poster was met with anti-feminism and homophobia couched in language denouncing intercultural insensitivity. Robyn Archer, a well-known Australian performer and the first female artistic director of the Adelaide Festival, featured an image of the Virgin Mary to celebrate her festival's themes which included 'spiritual' performance and 'sacred' music. The Greek Orthodox Church took exception to the use of the image, claiming that it belonged to them only. The leaders of other religions, local radio station talk-back hosts, and a variety of state and municipal politicians also used the controversy to their own advantage. Several sectors of the cultural milieu maintained a right to portray and preserve culture in a way that conflicted with the Festival and its marketing plan. Various participants in the controversy attempted to regulate and hierarchise the competing discourses surrounding the marketing of the arts, cultural diversity, and women's opportunities to portray themselves in art.

The image any festival uses to promote – and, effectively, to sell – its events is carefully chosen based on the audience, the programmed performances, and the nature of the festival itself. Archer selected a female image to which she ascribed a subject position: a seated Byzantine Virgin Mary playing a piano accordion. Almost as prevalent in western art as the nude, iconic representations of the Virgin Mary signify attempts to contain the place of women in the social order even more so than the nude. Archer's fascination with the image developed from her interest

*Plate 14* The 1998 Telstra Adelaide Festival Poster. Designed by Robyn Archer, George Mackintosh, and David Heacock. Photo reproduced with the permission of the Adelaide Festival.

in the Virgin of Guadalupe from Central and South American countries, who is associated with celebration and festivity: 'This Virgin is not dolorosa, she's not pain, [and] she's never got Jesus with her, ever' (interview 1998). Empowered with a subject position that does not necessarily foreground her role as mother, this Virgin has a presence and a place without Jesus. The vitality of the Virgin of Guadalupe epitomised the type of festival that Archer planned.

The sacred image accrued secular signification by means of the accordion, an instrument featured in numerous events at the 1998 Festival. To Archer, the integrity of the image was not challenged by this computer-generated modification: based on an understanding of postmodernism that enables the borrowing of images from different eras and cultures, she felt that her western background entitled her to claim the image as hers, without any fear of charges of appropriation.[7] The image was carefully layered with references to Adelaide and Australia and ghosted figures from other religions in the background.[8]

After the image's launch and in the midst of a closely fought state election, the poster drew the ire of the Greek Orthodox Church on the grounds that it desecrated an icon invested with holy status, or at the very least took it out of its context. The conflict focused on the sacred nature of icons: prayers are said over each brush stroke as icons are painted, making them literally divine images and therefore not just decorative images. The Greek Orthodox Church also took exception to the removal of the Christ child from the picture, particularly since the child was replaced by a musical instrument. It was felt that this substitution of the child for a musical instrument – and this instrument in particular because of its associations with populist culture – mocked the Church. The Festival office was inundated with letters (including many from school children, copied from a form letter) and the media pursued the issue for weeks. Church officials from other denominations also joined the fray.[9] Some offended parties threatened violence against Festival staff (5AN 1997b), in addition to smashing any windows in which the image appeared (Harris 1997a: 23), although such actions did not eventuate.

Another constituency eager to discredit the poster – and, by implication, the Festival, Archer, and the state Liberal Government's record on multiculturalism – was the Labor Party, particularly Labor politicians in marginal seats with large populations of

Greek-Australians. The poster quickly became an election issue. In a radio talk-back appearance, the Shadow Attorney-General and Opposition Spokesperson for Multicultural and Ethnic Affairs, Michael Atkinson, urged South Australians to boycott the Festival to register their displeasure (5AA 1997). The Arts Minister, Di Laidlaw, refused to bow to pressures within her own party to have the image revoked.

Talk-back radio hosts also used the controversy to discredit Archer and the other women who were associated with the poster. One station ran an alternative poster contest with repeated suggestions for posters including humiliating pictures of Archer and Laidlaw, the Arts Minister. The poster launch coincided with the televising of Archer's overtly lesbian performance on television, *The One That Got Away*; this prompted several radio stations to capitalise on homophobia among their audiences. Archer's sexual preference was raised as a further reason for attacking the poster, prompting one radio host's suggestion of a lesbian on a lance as an alternative poster (5DN 1997b).

A compromise was eventually reached with the sector most aggrieved. The Archbishop of the Greek Orthodox Church met with the Festival's general manager, Nicholas Heyward, and the chair of the Adelaide Festival Board, Dr Ed Tweddell, to reach a consensus. Because of the patriarchal nature of the Church, the Festival organisation (with Archer's approval, under the circumstances) decided that it would be in the best interests of a settlement for Archer not to attend the meeting set to arrange a compromise. The Festival refused the Church's demand of a complete withdrawal of the poster but consented neither to post it around the city, nor to use it to promote the Festival, even on the brochure. It was agreed that the image would still be available for purchase (and not distributed for free) in the form of posters or T-shirts. The Festival's programme continued, otherwise generally unaffected.

Given the number of participants in this debate, it is not surprising that there were multiple arguments competing against each other, including feminism, cultural diversity, and postmodernity. Perhaps the most basic of these opposing arguments was the place of postmodernism in discussions with the traditional Greek Orthodox Church. Unlike the creation of icons, there were no rituals performed on the secular representation that became the poster; the absence of sacredness should thus have made the poster acceptable in the eyes of the Greek Orthodox Church, but this argument was rejected. The Greek Orthodox Church also refused to accept Archer's argument that postmodernism entitled her to take the images of her choice from the western cultural tradition. For some, Archer acted in the worst tradition of postmodernism and western feminism, ignoring any cultural copyright that may exist on the particular image of Mary chosen. This clash between postmodernity and an enduring pre-modern ethos could hardly find an easy compromise.[10]

The differing perspectives on cultural diversity and how to ensure cultural sensitivity in a multicultural environment might suggest the importance of consultation between ethnic groups, including seeking permission to use an image from another group. Yet must a cultural pedigree be acknowledged this way in every instance? Archer did not consult with the Greek Orthodox Church in the poster's planning stages because, she explains,

> For a start, I chose the image from a book of Bulgarian icons. I hadn't a clue that I should talk to the Greek Orthodox Church. Even if I had, I probably would have talked to the wrong ones. This is a church divided in Australia. One side had no problem whatsoever with it. I could ask a thousand questions . . . and I still might offend somebody or some group, because in such a diverse society, *it is impossible to know* [who might take offence].
> (personal correspondence to authors, 19 January 1999)[11]

Archer preferred to take a retroactive approach in the clashes that inevitably characterise a multicultural society: 'People will eventually make mistakes. . . . So what I keep focusing on is how do you resolve inevitable conflict' (interview 1998).

The poster controversy raises larger issues about whether culture itself can be copyrighted. While Archer maintained a retroactive conflict-resolution position, others insisted that culture is 'owned' by its constituents. Numerous respondents to the poster controversy cited the *fatwah* declared against Salman Rushdie as an example of what could have happened to Archer had she used an Islamic image. The underlying threat in this example referred to conservative versions of the Islamic religion but was directed towards Archer, her art, her politics, her gender, and her sexual preference. Many more discussants chose to compare the controversy over Archer's poster to what would have transpired had she used Aboriginal spirituality instead of the image of the Virgin Mary. Even though Aboriginality continues to be used to sell Australia and Australian tourism, many people objecting to the image argued that had it been Aboriginal in origin, the image would have been withdrawn. This misleadingly assumes that the cultural sensitivities associated with Aboriginality and Christianity are interchangeable. The connections between cultural systems, spirituality, and mechanisms of access and control are fraught with difficulty. The questions which arise include whether any one person or group can control the exclusive rights to a culture, how much knowledge associated with a culture remains in the public domain, and how much is private?

Various indigenous cultures around the world, anxious to preserve control over their religion, secret knowledges, etc., are increasingly turning to copyright laws to ensure that what remains of their cultures is sequestered from the public domain. While sympathetic to their aims, Michael F. Brown notes the problems with this response:

> Although this rationale for cultural protection seems reason-able at first glance, upon reflection one begins to wonder where the legal prohibition of religious 'trivialization' or sacrilege might lead. Would citizens therefore be subject to civil and criminal penalty if they trivialized *any* religious symbols? Would indigenous peoples themselves be subject to reciprocal fine or arrest if they manipulated Christian imagery for their own purposes?
>
> (Brown 1998: 199)

The Greek Orthodox Church did object to precisely this sort of manipulation of their Christian religious symbols. The Greek Orthodox Church is not, however, in the same position as Aboriginal cultures: its symbols are not at risk of commodification in quite the same way as Aboriginal symbols that appear on T-shirts and in the promotion of Australia overseas. The Greek Orthodox Church is part of a western cultural model, but it has minority status in Australia. Does it then qualify as a culture that ought to be 'protected' in the same way that attempts are made to protect Aboriginal cultures? Brown insists that the multiple agendas operating in this discussion continue to obscure – rather than clarify – the issues. Further, these different discourses of culture and aesthetics are unequal, yet the political election campaign deployed 'cultural diversity' in such a moral way that it out-maneouvred the place of aesthetics. Cultural diversity adopted a regulatory function in this debate because politicians, Church leaders, and artists feared being labelled culturally insensitive or discriminatory because of the possibility of the social and financial implications. They were not celebrating cultural diversity because it was perceived to be a worthwhile social goal.

The cultural diversity arguments continued to collide with others, including feminist arguments – which risked being disregarded even though the poster depicted a woman's image. Some of the difficulty arose from conflicting views about the various roles assigned to the Virgin Mary, and by implication, women generally. Many members of the Greek Orthodox Church were upset that the Christ child had been removed from Mary's arms. For them, Mary is only the Mother of God: she is not a 'woman' in her own right. The removal of the child from the image imparts subjectivity to the woman, suggesting that she is creative in her own right, and that she exists independently of the child (as opposed to the image of Our Lady of Perpetual Succour). It shifts the focus from mother to independent woman, as well as refusing her subordination to the Christ child. The alteration of the image from maternal fulfilment in the child to the pleasure of self-expression through a populist instrument suggests a different order of desire emerging.

The instrument that the Virgin is playing also offers a different association of sexual desire, and an ambivalent desire at that. The use of the accordion sets up a different dynamic than the saxophone and other wind instruments which are read as phallic and the stringed instruments which are immediately associated with the female body. The accordion is more difficult to read as gendered, increasing the opportunity to read the desire in the poster as sexual ambivalence. If one were to ascribe a gender to the accordion, it would likely be female, because the instrument works on enclosed space that is constantly opening and closing. The accordion could, then, be seen to resemble female genitals more than male.

This image, which expresses women's autonomy, subjectivity, and desire, was taken out of Archer's control once the controversy occurred. The poster was detached from its festival referent, particularly when church officials of different denominations took it upon themselves to 'assess' the image to determine whether or not the image breached both religious laws and laws of good taste. The senior Adelaide male Church leaders condemned it as an inappropriate image (personal correspondence to authors, 19 January 1999). Archer found it confronting that what could be construed as 'women's business was entirely in the hands of men. And it's a great shock to the system that that can still happen. We know that it's happening in Afghanistan and an enormous number of other places but *we* feel safe' (interview 1998). The poster controversy effectively censored the feminist nature of the image. For the agents in control of the debate, cultural sensitivity (associated closely with politicians' desire to appease the patriarchal representatives of minority cultures during the election campaign) submerged feminism as well as aesthetics. The regulatory force of culture (in its reductive form of cultural diversity) replaced the complicated combination of identity politics, multiple subject positions, and intercultural exchange.

In each of our examples, the autonomy of women's subjectivity is subordinated to the clashes of the cultural context within the workings of the international arts and entertainment market. In an attempt to circumvent these facets of the market that intrude upon aesthetics and feminist subjectivity, many women have turned to international women's organisations that offer a less overtly consumption-based arena for the production and distribution of theatrical work.

There are several other kinds of meeting places outside the network of international arts markets and arts festivals, including the International Women Playwrights' Conference (IWPC) and the Magdalena Project. This separatist approach may seem a radical step, yet participants tend to find them productive fora for women's intercultural performance. The IWPC has met every three years since 1988 to perform, discuss, and witness women's international performance. Since it began in Buffalo, New York, it has met in Toronto, Adelaide, and Galway, and incorporated contemporary performance with more traditional methods. Forging a strong network of women theatre workers, the IWPC presents opportunities for women performers to watch, learn from, and interact with performers from growing numbers of other countries. The Magdalena Project began in 1986 in Wales, when 38 female theatre practitioners from 15 countries met to create a structure that would continue to generate new work and foster their skills. There have been annual Magdalena festivals and workshops in Wales, Italy, Denmark, Germany, England, Poland, Peru, Colombia, Uruguay, Norway, Belgium, and, in 1999, New Zealand. Susan Bassnett describes the Magdalena Project as 'a forum for debate among women, and although participants may share a common belief in the value of women's work in theatre, they often share very little else' (Bassnett 1989: 6). The Magdalena Project initiates cross-cultural and intercultural collaborative projects in the hope that it will influence the international theatre community. The influence is, however, likely to be the other way: the Magdalena Project's funding has been cut, and, without corporate sponsorship, it is unlikely to be able to continue supporting its international festival programme.

Those performers who play the international arts market may have more access to funding than the Magdalena Project, but there are drawbacks: these include the effects of the significations relating to culture, performance, and feminist subjectivity, in addition to the effects of contesting such significations. The performers throughout this study have attempted to manage their own representations of feminist and cultural subjectivity. However, when they perform in the intercultural world, they are frequently confronted by a variety of regulations in the international performance market which stipulate limited and homogeneous cultural, gender, and aesthetic norms. Explicit body performance, in particular, attempts to subvert the homogeneity of the subjectivity that patriarchal social orders reserve for women on and off the stage, but its complex representation of the possibilities available to the performing female body, and women generally, frequently meet with some form of sanction. While men performing in the international market also face many of the challenges to cultural diversity and autonomy, women performing in the intercultural market continue to find their work refashioned to accord with assumptions regarding the framing, marketing, and distribution of the female performing body.

# Conclusion

This study of women's intercultural performance has traversed the twentieth century from the first Japanese translation of *A Doll's House* in 1901 to the 1998 Adelaide Festival of Arts. Reflected in these intercultural performances are the lived realities of women as they are refracted through diverse political ideologies and belief systems. We have moved across six continents to report inter-cultural encounters in Africa, North and South America, Europe, Asia, the Middle East, and Australia. To conclude, we will tease out the major threads that have been running through this study, including: the emphasis on the political as well as the aesthetic; the transmission through performance of culturally specific iden-tity spaces; the sexually differentiated female body in performance; and commodification of this body within the global arts market-place.

## THE POLITICAL

Ultimately, the future of women's intercultural performance is as much a political as an aesthetic issue. This study has repeatedly returned to political questions that reflect not only our subject positions as western feminist academics/practitioners, but also the nature of the intercultural work that underpins our analysis. Through these productions we have touched upon some of the major political conflicts of the twentieth century: the emancipa-tory women's movements in the early years of the twentieth century, the Chinese Revolution, the position of women in the Iranian Islamic Republic, the struggle of women in Argentina during the Dirty War of the 1970s and 1980s, the rights of indigenous peoples to self-determination and their ancestral domain, postcolonial turmoil in Africa, and the trade in the bodies of women. In the Introduction we suggested that aesthetics have dominated the analyses of western-based intercultural theatre projects, whereas political imperatives underpin analyses of western feminist performance. Although this study has focused on women's, rather than specifically feminist, intercultural performance, we have found it impossible to separate the political content of this work from the aesthetic dimensions. Many of the productions we have considered fit within the paradigm of 'theatre for social change'. For the artists who created them, the primary motivation appears to be the disruption of established power relations. However fashionable it may be to ignore the intentions of artists in current performance analysis, this study is intimately tied to the motivations of the women who have created these intercultural performances. They have used their power as artists to challenge patriarchal family structures and struggle for equality in the eyes of the state, and to assert the rights of women (whether colonised, dispossessed, or 'free') stifled by the yoke of tradition. Even in their intercultural activities within the global performing arts markets, these artists have claimed the right for all women to control their sexuality and their representations of the female body.

We have tried to avoid the universalising tendencies of western feminism, but our investigations suggest that the very act of creating a performance work explicitly focusing on the lived realities of women involves an awareness that gender difference is almost always organised into systems of power that privilege men. Every system is culturally specific, but the intercultural performances that we have considered appear to offer women artists, and women in the audience, the opportunity of moving beyond the hegemony of their cultural frameworks to question and disrupt the gender constructions that bind them. An important mechanism in this process is the creation of new identity spaces.

## IDENTITY SPACES

We have argued that culture is not an isolated concept or empty sign; rather it is the way in which we construct our sense of self and others. Intercultural performance, therefore, constantly re-negotiates this relationship. A continuum exists in this process: one extreme sees the concretisation of fixed positions through the triggering of an ethnographic or taxonomic gaze, and the other sees the intermingling of diverse elements creating new identity spaces. The precise nature of these negotiations depends on the social context of the performance, the mix of cultural elements within the production, and the underlying power relationship between the cultures engaging in the encounter.

In Chapter 1 we suggested that intercultural performances of imported texts enabled audiences to add new identity spaces to the repertoire of multiple identities from which subjectivity is forged. We considered this dynamic with regard to *A Doll's House* and *Antigone* and demonstrated the attraction these texts had for artists and audiences encountering the social upheaval of modernity or the political turmoil associated with opposition to totalitarian states. We distinguished between the functions these texts served for their host cultures in both the public and private spheres and explored the composition of the identity spaces created and exchanged through these textual translations. The theme of subjectivity flowed into the analysis of ritual translocation in Chapter 2. We argued that these intercultural rituals have been sold in a post-industrial capitalist society as a commodity to fill an imaginary lack of spirituality, and as a symbol on which to build a corporate national identity. The power relationships underlying these exchanges were weighted in favour of the consumers, and the performances tended to concretise audience subject positions and imaginary constructions of supremacy rather than to act as a catalyst for changing perceptions.

Identity spaces were also the focus in the intercultural encounters that dominated our next two chapters, but the exchanges were structurally more complex. The spatial loss experienced by the postcolonial subject underpinned our analysis of performance texts by African playwrights. These intercultural encounters existed as much within the imaginary of the playwrights as the perceptions of the audiences, and were conceptualised spatially through the staging of the exile, the émigré, and the dispossessed returning home. In each case, these plays involve a doubling – or layering and overlaying – of cultural realities. The postcolonial nature of this cultural intermingling resulted in the enactment of complex subject positions, reflecting the ambivalence of the dramatists and their audiences to their complex cultural heritage. From the meetings of cultures in space, we moved to the meetings in the flesh; through taxonomies, which re-affirmed the audience by reifying cultural difference, to the exploration of new hybrid cultural identities, and finally to the nomadic performing bodies that begin to undermine fixed racial and sexual identities.

Thus our theme of subjectivity began with the acquisition by women of a rational subjectivity tied to modernity and defined as subjective freedom, as it was played out in a variety of cultural contexts and political systems. It then moved to an imaginary lack in this same rational subject of modernity, and the attempts of the postmodern marketplace to satisfy this void by packaging and marketing ritual performances. We considered the spatial loss of the postcolonial subject in symbolic, metaphoric, and literal terms; and finally, through the body of the performer, this study embraced a nomadic subject who 'never takes on fully the limits of one national, fixed identity' (Braidotti 1994: 36). By emphasising the intersubjective relationship underpinning intercultural performance, we have tried to privilege a dynamic model of culture that envisages the sense of self as constantly shifting and always provisional, while never denying the sexually differentiated body.

## THE FEMALE BODY

The corporeal reality of the female performing body lies at the very centre of this study and has triggered many of its interrogations: Can this body cross cultures? How is it bought and sold? Who controls its representation? What rights to cultural inheritance does it hold? At an aesthetic level, the corporeal reality of the female body influences symbolic constructions. In many of the productions we have discussed, this sexually differentiated body is translated into a 'female image or symbol' that Jessica Benjamin (1986: 83) suggests can 'counterbalance the monopoly of the phallus in representing desire'. In her analysis of female desire, she outlines that '[t]he closest we have come to an image of feminine activity is motherhood and fertility. But the mother is not culturally articulated as a sexual subject, one who actively desires something for herself – quite the contrary' (ibid.: 83). Yet in this study we have repeatedly encountered a maternal figure actively desiring 'something for herself'. She was present in the final scene of all the translations and adaptations of *A Doll's House*; and she was present in Gambaro's *Antígona Furiosa* through the associative link between the character of Antígona and the Mothers of the Plaza de Mayo. Maternal passivity is anathema to these Argentinian Mothers: they operate on the edge of legality, deploying acceptable feminine sensitivities while overtly challenging the political hierarchy by their subversive actions.

The Mothers of the Plaza de Mayo create their desiring maternal subject in a culture saturated with the cult of the Virgin, and, like Robyn Archer's poster, they no longer hold their children in their arms. In their place, the Mothers carry traces symbolising hope and sorrow; in contrast Archer's Virgin holds a piano accordion to signify pleasure, creativity, and the self-worth of the female artist. In Archer's poster the possibility of maternal desire is so explicit that it was censored.

Yet the symbolism in this study is not tied to 'just' the maternal. It is equally prevalent in the variety of symbols associated with the empty space inside the female body, as is demonstrated on the one hand by Annie Sprinkle's 'Public Cervix Announcement' and on the other by the grandmother's suitcase in *Have You Seen Zandile?* If we follow Jessica Benjamin's assertion that female desire is 'a force imbued with the authenticity of inner desire', and 'that what is experientially female is the association of desire with a space, a place within the self, from which this force can emerge' (ibid.: 97), then this linking of desire to inner space creates more overt and powerful reverberations in our discussions of *chora* as creative and regenerative space in Chapter 3, and in our discussions of ritual performance in Chapter 2. The role of shaman or *mudang* in Korea is seen as an alternative to the subordinate position of women in the traditional patriarchal family structure, and it is the female inner space with its capacity to hold the human spirit that attracts the deities: by entering this void the deities possess the human body. Hence it can be argued that the force and power of the *mudang* emanates from the inner space within the female body.

Benjamin (ibid.: 96) asserts that '[t]his experience of inner space is in turn associated with the space between self and other: the holding environment and transitional experience'. By linking the notion of female desire both to perceptions of inner space and to questions of alterity, Benjamin's theory turns a symbolic element that we have found to be significant to women's intercultural performance into a representation not only of female desire but also of intersubjectivity. However tempting it may be to tie up loose ends in a conclusion, it is not our intention to reduce the variety and range of the work we have analysed to a single paradigm; to do so would be reductionist. But it may be the case that symbolic constructions in women's intercultural theatre reflect the sexually differentiated body of the artist and a fascination with questions of alterity, even if the precise nature of these symbolic constructions will always be culturally determined.

## COMMODIFICATION

A tension exists between a dynamic model of culture embodied in an intersubjective relationship and the reification that occurs when cultures are commodified within performance. The communication between artists and their audiences is never free of the social context and production histories, and we have paid particular attention to the distribution, marketing, and commodification of culture as it pertains to contemporary intercultural performances. In many ways, our final chapter has proved the most provocative aspect of this study, because it deals with the realities of international distribution networks for the performing arts, but these processes of commodification have been present throughout the entire study. The operations of the postmodern marketplace were crucial to the discussion of ritual translocation, which demonstrated that publicists, news reporters, and art reviewers colluded in the commodifying of the Korean shaman as an exoticised spectacle. Our critique of intercultural bodies documented the impact of international arts festivals on the distribution of a specific genre, Ankoku Butoh, and the importance of these festivals on the development of taxonomic performances that reify difference for a culturally homogeneous audience.

The late twentieth-century festival circuit has impacted directly on the production and consumption of intercultural performance; yet despite the employment of increasing numbers of women as administrators and programmers in this network, there is still manifest censorship imposed on women artists. While our investigation of intercultural bodies ends with a glimpse of theatrical desiring machines created by female performing bodies, these same bodies are subjected to censorship and control in the marketplace. It is not just the representation itself at issue, but who determines the nature of the representation and controls its commodification.

Alternative distribution networks do exist, but if they are working outside the major flows of international or state capital they operate with voluntary labour and lurch from one funding crisis to another, as the history of Magdalena demonstrates.

## GLOBALISM

As the economic forces of globalisation shrink and stratify the world, the creation of intercultural performance is an increasingly complex affair. Even the concept of cultural identity is fraught with the complications of migration, cultural authenticity, and 'ethnic cleansing'. The questions concerning cultural appropriation and assimilation that used to preoccupy rehearsal rooms are being replaced with a search for a methodology that can shift representations of cultural difference from superficial descriptions to 'thick descriptions'. We cannot offer easy solutions to these problems, but we have tried to explore a number of possibilities and paradoxes that may be of use to both artists and theorists.

Ultimately the future of intercultural work is more likely to be tied to patterns of consumption than to idealistic notions of cultural exchange. The global arts market already traverses national boundaries to access wealthy citizens prepared to buy cultural bricolage. In the realm of contemporary performance, international links are a necessary stimulus to artists working in the area of performance, but they can unduly influence and drain valuable resources from local cultural production.

The impact of globalisation on the performing arts is still being assessed, but the process of transformation is extremely rapid. This book is still predicated on the existence of cultural and sexual borders, but these borders are shifting. Medical technology is undermining the sexually differentiated body, while cultural borders are constantly being redrawn and redefined. What has been fixed and impermeable is becoming fluid and permeable. In the realm of women's performance the focus is moving to experiments where cultures are no longer represented as fixed essences embodied by performers and placed side by side. They now move fluidly through the performing bodies. We have briefly touched on this art of metamorphosis in relation to the nomadic performing body, but this is still a tentative study and fraught with the problems presented by a visceral experience dependent on highly subjective perceptions. It does, however, offer a new way of reading 'thick descriptions' of culture in the body through an examination of performance energy flows. This kinaesthetic approach may be of assistance to artists grappling with the complexities of multiple cultural inheritances, and artists whose corporeal realities have been shaped by diverse geo-political spaces. For a younger generation of female artists with no passports, or too many, signing culture through costume or traditional performance forms is no longer an option. The effects of culturally heterogeneous frameworks on the creation of new performance works have to be explored at a more profound level to reveal the deep cultural elements that inform, amongst other things, performance time, dramaturgical structures, emotional expression, and the contract between the performer and the audience. This process may involve as much clashing as synthesising of culturally divergent matter. For artists working in this realm, embracing a nomadic identity space could be both an aesthetic and a political choice. If there is to be a second wave of women's intercultural performance which manages to negotiate the vagaries of the marketplace, we believe it will emerge from artists whose performance practice shapes a *chora* from the indeterminant, transitional spaces that lie in between cultural certainties.

# Notes

## Introduction: culture, feminism, theatre

1 The nineteenth-century concept of nationalism is certainly not superseded by globalism, postmodernism, or other contemporary discourses. It has, however, receded in importance in global contexts. This is not to suggest that globalism has demonstrated a superior power, but rather because globalism tends to oppose itself more to the localism of cultural or ethnic identities. Through the last 200 years, national parameters have frequently been constructed for political or economic reasons, often regardless of cultural boundaries. Nevertheless it is possible for globalism and nationalism to continue to co-exist. Appadurai (1986a: 296) makes an argument for this in the development of his five 'scapes'. It does seem, though, that Appadurai's constructions are in part an attempt to bridge too easily the cavern between the two approaches.

2 While Geertz's concept is ethnographic in origin, it is very useful to our discussion in that it situates analysis within culture: 'As interworked systems of construable signs . . . culture is not a power, something to which social events, behaviors, institutions, or processes can be causally attributed; it is a context, something within which they can be intelligibly – that is, thickly – described' (Geertz 1973: 14).

3 Interculturalism has been compared with (and occasionally mistaken for) theatre anthropology, most likely because Eugenio Barba engages in both. Rustom Bharucha is particularly scathing about theatre anthropology which all too frequently becomes a form of 'cultural tourism' (1993: 35), or an opportunity for western practitioners and/or academics to visit 'exotic' locations and publish their often decontextualised observations.

4 For more information on Artaud's predilection for incorporating material from a variety of cultures, see Bharucha (1993: 14–17). For Brecht's interest in Chinese performance, based on seeing Mei Lan-fang's company in Moscow in 1935, see 'Alienation Effects in Chinese Acting', collected in Willett (1978: 91–9).

5 Carlson's model is based in part on a three-stage version developed by Michael Gissenwehrer.
6 Pavis's conclusion regarding the efficacy of the hourglass reveals a salient warning for interculturalism:

> Unfortunately, we seem to be heading toward a two-tiered culture and interculturalism: a consumable culture for a large audience or even for a targeted group from the conservative middle class, a culture of easy access that is neither controversial nor radical, which provides ready-made answers to big questions, cavalier views on history (Cixous) or pleasing embellishments (Mnouchkine), preaching an end to cultural differentiation under the cover of 'an all-purpose culture'; or, on the contrary, an elite culture that is radical and irreducible, that abandons spectacular performance to work at the microscopic level, almost in secret, and whose results are never immediate and often obscure.
>
> (Pavis 1992: 212)

7 See Williams (1991) for the most complete account of *The Mahabharata*.
8 Noh originates from early religious celebratory dances. Formalised in the fourteenth century by Kan'ami and his son, Zeami, Noh prizes the Zen artistic ideals of restraint, minimalism, and *yugen* (mysterious or suggestive beauty). Noh's comic counterpart, Kyogen, is thought to be as old as Noh, but its scripts were not recorded until the sixteenth and seventeenth centuries. Kyogen, loud, exaggerated, and farcical, is commonly associated with the short comic performances that occur between Noh plays. Kabuki, the theatre of the people, originated from the dances of a woman named Okuni in the early seventeenth century. Spectacular and bawdy, Kabuki reflected contemporary urban life. Kabuki adapts to its times, unlike Noh. For more on these and other Japanese theatre forms, see Ortolani (1990).
9 Bharucha is quick to acknowledge that non-western cultures have themselves been guilty of pandering to this western exoticism of the 'orient': 'the "Orient" can be manufactured in India itself and then transported abroad to validate earlier modes of "orientalism" which are in the process of being dismantled elsewhere' (Bharucha 1996: 210).
10 See Bharucha (1993) for a detailed analysis of how commodification underpinned Brook's *The Mahabharata*.
11 See Chapter 2 for a sustained argument regarding the reception of ritual in western cultures. Chapter 5 also explores in greater depth the commodification of performance and culture. It is important to remember, however, that, as Hinsley points out, many cultures are complicit in their own commodification: in his analysis of the World Exhibition in Chicago in 1893, Hinsley observes that: 'wherever we traffic in the world, there are those market informants who understand the commodity premise and are prepared to authenticate their cultures accordingly' (Hinsley 1991: 363).

12  A brief (and general) exploration of the nature of alterity illuminates the ways in which interculturalism – founded on the construction of identity, identity formation, and subject position – operates. A major criticism of recent intercultural theatre can be traced back to an underlying distrust of the subject–object duality of western thinking, what Adorno and Horkheimer called 'instrumental rationality' (cited in Gardiner 1996: 125) and Martin Buber described as the I–It relation:

> I–It denotes a situation where the self confronts an external object-world, and proceeds to give this world shape, meaning, and pragmatic 'use-value'. . . . Hence, the world only has significance from the perspective of the intentional, self-contained ego, and is manipulated according to a pre-established conceptual schema.
>
> (ibid.)

In contrast to this relationship which objectifies, shapes, and controls the other as object, Buber suggests a radically different relation of the I–Thou, in which the 'self comes to the realization that it cannot be a self-constituting, autonomous ego, but part of the category "in between", or what Buber sometimes calls the "ontology of the inter-human"' (ibid.). Artists who venture across cultural borders would do well to remember the perceptual difference between the I–It and the I–Thou relations. Luckily, as Emmanuel Levinas points out, Buber's model comes to the rescue of the integrity of artists, by citing the creative impulse as an example of the I–Thou relation:

> The thing which is merely given and which I can dominate belongs to the sphere of the It. But the specific way in which the artist, for example, confronts the thing in creating a work of art, may be construed as a response to an appeal, and therefore, as a meeting.
>
> (Levinas 1989: 70)

Despite Buber's generosity, it would be difficult to argue that the I–It relation has not found a presence within intercultural theatre. One of the main criticisms levelled at western practitioners has been the ease with which they have manipulated other cultures into a 'pre-established conceptual schema'.

Buber's pursuit of an ethics of intersubjectivity and the exploration of the 'ontology of the interhuman' lie at the heart of the paradox facing the theatre artist. In the continuum of intercultural performance, the extremes are marked on the one hand by the total commodification of the other as 'It' through the reification of cultural traces and, on the other, by the illusion of an encounter with the 'Thou' based on a false sense of identification in which the fixed subject merely engages with what is familiar to reinforce a sense of self. This theoretical model can be applied to the theatre experience through the various relationships of artist to other culture, artist to artist, artist to audience, and audience and artist to the cultural 'artefact' of the other.

13  See note 12 for more on the subjective experience of artists.

# 1 Narrative trajectories: *A Doll's House* and *Antigone*

1 Eleanor Marx organised a reading of the play in London in 1886; Alexandra Kollontai spoke of the inspiration of Nora in Oslo in 1928 (Templeton 1997).

2 See Johannes Fabian (1983).

3 *Seito* was the major publication in the struggle for women's emancipation. It operated from 1911–16 and on six occasions issues were banned by government censors on the basis that they were 'an offense against public decency' and had the intention of the 'destruction of the family system'. These issues included articles and short stories that advocated free love, equality in the home, and raised the subject of abortion (Sato 1981: 286).

4 This conflation reflected the emergence of the arts as an attractive arena for middle-class women looking for new roles outside the home; actresses had also recently reappeared on the Japanese stage after an absence of 300 years (Rodd 1991: 175).

5 The first spoken drama was *The New Village Head*, written and directed by Zhang Penchun. See Yan (1992: 56).

6 The issue of arranged marriages was as topical in China as it had been in Japan several years earlier. In the journals edited by women, the tenets of Confucianism were once again under attack: articles were written on how to select a husband, claiming that now 'western civilisation had come to China – parents no longer have right to interfere' (Croll 1978: 89).

7 Women's associations and unions were accused of communist sympathies and closed down. The Guomindang disbanded all people's organisations and massacred their leaders. The girl agitators were easily recognised because of their cropped hair: during the next three years, literally thousands of women activists were killed (Croll 1978: 151).

8 Our accounts of Jiang Qing's performance of Nora are drawn from the available English language sources, and in the case of Roxane Witke's biography, the information is of questionable accuracy (Ly Singko 1979). Attempts by Li Jiaojiao, our Chinese research assistant in Shanghai, to recover important commentaries on the production by critics Cui Wanqui and Tang Na proved unsuccessful. These documents are held in the Shanghai Library in archive collections that are still not open to the public.

9 It is interesting to note that 30 years later when Jiang Qing began to exert control on the arts, particularly the Model Beijing Opera, the heroines she demanded on the stage were not rebels, but figures who conformed to the views of the political establishment (see Terrill 1984).

10 The Shah persecuted anyone who attempted to oppose him. Five thousand people died and 50,000 were forced into exile. Savak had 60,000 people working as informers and was known for its brutality. Over US$2,000 million was exported annually from Iran during 1973–8; half of this amount belonged to Pahlavi extended family members (Hiro 1985: 95).

11 In the early 1990s, women were still barred from 97 areas of academic study in universities in Iran (Afshar 1996: 203).

12 The *hejab* comes from the root word, '*hajaba*', meaning to conceal a space, to mark it off with a curtain, or a symbolic boundary. For a fascinating discussion linking the imposition of the veil and terrorism in Muslim capitals during the 1980s, see Mernessi (1996).

13 In a private correspondence with the authors (2.12.99) regarding the reception of *Sara* in Iran, Dariush Mehrjui points out:

> The women audiences in Iran were divided: there were those who were feminists and deplored the first half of the movie and applauded Sara's rebellion. And then there were those more traditional women who could not believe that an Iranian woman would make such a sacrifice for her husband, and still approved of her rebellion. In general most of the audiences were women, a lot of them crying during the projection, many of them identifying with the heroine.

14 Steiner notes that Hegel 'uses Sophocles' *Antigone* to test and to exemplify successive models of religious-civic conflict and of historical coming-into-being [while] Kierkegaard's use is desperate in its needful arbitrariness. . . . Kierkegaard makes of *Antigone* an open-ended precedent. . . . The unknown retains a greater measure of healing authority' (Steiner 1984: 104). Kierkegaard also uses the figure of Antigone to explore subjectivity and subjective truth, and the problems of Hegelian objectivity. We are indebted to Dimitri Poulos for this observation.

15 Sarumpaet's *Antigone*, performed in Jakarta in March 1991, foregrounds the extreme subservience of women in the Batak culture. For a description of the production, see Sarumpaet (1995). The writer has herself been arrested in 1998 for crimes against the state (Eisenstein 1998).

16 Subasinghe's *Antigone* was performed in Colombo in 1993. She writes exclusively in her native Sinhala language and is committed to the revival of traditional forms of folk theatre to reflect the concerns of contemporary Sri Lankan society. Subasinghe highlights Creon's familial relationship to Antigone instead of presenting Creon in terms of a particular faction (such as secular law) and Antigone representing another (such as religious law). For more information on this production, see Subasinghe (1997).

17 The original performance, on 24 September 1986 at the Goethe Institute in Buenos Aires, was directed by Laura Yusem and designed by Graciela Galán and Juan Carlos Distéfano. Antígona was played by Bettina Muraña, a *mestiza* dancer (Feitlowitz 1990: 9). Gambaro's version of *Antigone* borrows from other traditions as well, including lines from Ophelia in *Hamlet*, references to Rubén Darío, William Faulkner, and Søren Kierkegaard (Gambaro 1995: 57).

18 The phenomenon of 'disappearance', or *desaparición*, has become a particularly popular abuse of human rights. It has entered the language in several ways: one can speak of the disappeared (singular or plural)

and the word can become a verb as well (to have been disappeared). The Mothers never refer to their children as killed, murdered, dead, corpses, etc. They always use 'disappeared' because the government has never admitted to killing them.

19  While President Carter stopped all aid and loans when he learned of the disappearances, Ronald Reagan reversed this decision when he took office. Most of the higher-ranked military officers were trained in the US or by US trainers. American multinational companies also invested heavily in Argentina at this time (see Taylor 1997: 110–11).

20  The government ignored the Mothers for six months, assuming that they were mad, claiming that they were only old women and therefore incapable of harm. Then, on 15 October 1977, after they presented a petition with 24,000 names of people willing to demand investigation into the disappearances, the police fired tear-gas into the 300-strong crowd of Mothers, arresting many. As Schirmer explains, 'the Madres' immunity had come to an end, and they, too, like their relatives, became subject to the state's definition of subversion' (1989: 7). At least one of the mothers, Azucena Villaflor, was herself disappeared (Femenía 1987: 14). On an ostensibly more humanitarian front, '[s]ome of the Mothers were promised the return of their children if they would stop demonstrating in the plaza' (ibid.: 14). This seemingly helpful tactic of the return of the children was later revealed to be particularly grotesque: the relatives had long since been murdered.

21  See Taylor (1997) for a full description of the methods of murder during the Dirty War years in Argentina.

# 2  Ritual translocations: Kim Kum hwa and Warlpiri women

1  For a fuller discussion of the strands of ritual, see Gilbert and Tompkins (1996: 53–61).

2  This wholesale attack on the purposive rationality of the modern subject is taken up by Georges Bataille, who furthers Nietzsche's project by concentrating on the power of the abject. See Botting and Wilson (1997).

3  Victor Turner makes the distinction between this definition by Gurvitch and his own, more familiar, term of *communitas* (Turner 1982).

4  In the South, the role of shaman is hereditary, but in order to become a charismatic shaman, it is necessary to undergo a *sinbyoing*, or illness, which is interpreted as a calling from the deities. The following is an account of Kim Kum hwa's initiation as a shaman:

I was born quite sickly. I was always ill with one disease after another. When I was eleven, my health was extremely weakened by malaria, stomach aches and so on. When I was fourteen I was married by way of an arranged marriage. The Japanese were involved in a war [Second World War]. The Japanese occupied Korea from 1919 to

1945 so they were recruiting young men in the villages and sending them off to fight. Girls were also recruited and sent off to nearby cities to work in factories. Parents and daughter were therefore anxious to get them married. So I married.

My married life was an anxiety in itself. My mother-in-law hated me because I was always ill. She was quite mean to me as a result. My health began to deteriorate further and I felt I was losing my mind quite often. I began then to talk to spirits in gibberish. My mother-in-law thought that I was caught by an evil spirit and sent me back home.

One night, when I was seventeen, I went to a brook to admire the full moon. When I tried to leap over the stream, I fell backwards, and as I did, I rolled backward into a ball. After that incident, I became severely ill for about three months. One morning, at dawn, I dashed out of my bed and ran like a mad woman to one of the houses of a shaman in the village.

(Kim Kum hwa cited in Kim 1988: 160)

5   If a man is to practise as a shaman he must dress as a woman during the *Kut*. There are a number of explanations for the predominance of women practising charismatic shamanism in Korea. Women are seen as the receptacles for human spirits through the womb and it is believed that the deities possess the shaman by entering the inner void of the womb. 'According to the shamanic world view, the universe is born out of the Void. Because all entities are part of the universe, each entity observes the macrocosmic rule and each entity possesses a Void within itself' (Kim 1988: 169). Alternative explanations for the high numbers of female shaman emphasise the importance of the role as a possible alternative to patriarchal family structures and the lack of opportunities for women in the workforce. In 1980, the male–female wage gap was greater in Korea than in any other country for which data was available from the International Labour Organisation. See Amsden (1989).

6   Even at the public demonstration held in 1990 to mark the tenth anniversary of the infamous Kwang Ju massacre, a performer dressed as a traditional shaman could be seen – amidst the tear-gas, truncheons, armed vehicles, and police in their 'kurosawa' riot helmets – dancing a funeral rite. Behind her were the rows and rows of mothers who carried the portraits of their dead and disappeared children in protest through the streets.

7   Planning for the Third International Women Playwrights' Conference began in 1991, two months after the Council for Aboriginal Reconciliation was established by the Federal government. The Conference theme – the relationship between traditional women's ritual or storytelling and contemporary women's performance – grew out of this Australian experience. The programme highlighted the work of artists in postcolonial societies who were creating new hybrid art out of their traditional performance forms and the theatres of colonisation. Some 450 delegates from 37 countries attended the

seven-day conference and witnessed the two major ritual performances: the *Inma*, or women's ritual business, performed by the
Ngaanyatjarra, Pitjantjatjara, and Yankunytjarjara women from Central
Australia, and the *Taedong Kut* performed by Kim Kum hwa and her
company of shaman.

8 The performance included the *Shin Chong U-lim*, inviting the General
God; *Il Wall Maji*, inviting the sun, moon, star gods, and the gods
of nature; *Chil Sung Je Seok Kut*, prayers on behalf of the people; *Ta
Sal Kut*, the offering of the pig to cleanse the community of sin; *Soo
Wang Cheon*, leading wandering souls to Heavenly Paradise; *Chak Doo
Ta Ki*, the appearance of the Knife Riding General; *Tae Keum No
Ri*, community celebration, when the evil spirits have been driven
away. Madame Kim and her company took great care to reproduce
accurately the environment of the *Kut* within their Australian venues.
An altar, or god table, was set up along the back wall of the theatre
and behind the table a backdrop was created with paintings of the
various deities. Korean shaman honour 273 deities: Buddha and
*bodhisattvas*, Chinese and Korean folk heroes have all found their way
into the songs and chants. The god table is laden with food intended
to appeal to the tastes of the various deities invited to the ritual:
the Sun and Moon deities are vegetarian, the Great Warrior is carni-
vorous. The dishes on display include rice cakes, fruits, vegetables,
cooked rice, and dried fish. When the Great Ritual is performed as
an annual celebration for the well-being of the village, the god table
is laid out in one of the large farm buildings and, on completion of
the rites, the food is consumed by the participants. In theatre venues,
the god table defines the performance area, whilst the musicians who
accompany the shaman are seated on stage left. Percussion instruments dominate the sound-scape and feature a variety of drums and
cymbals; the rhythms are overlaid with traditional wind instruments
and the wailing sound of the farmer's trumpet.

9 Kim Kum hwa is protected from the pain of the blades, which she
tests on her arms and tongue. On the last night of the Adelaide season,
the company felt that ritual pollution had affected the *Kut*, and Kim
Kum hwa was forced to go into a very deep trance.

10 These interviews – in addition to the pre-publicity and performance
reviews cited in this section – are collected in the press clippings
file of the Third International Women Playwrights' Conference,
housed in the Third International Women Playwrights' Conference
Collection at the Mortlock Library in South Australia (Third
International Women Playwrights' Conference 1994b).

11 In the post-Conference documentation, Madame Kim's image dominates. For instance, a full-page photograph appeared in *Theatre Journal*,
two large format photographs in *TDR*, the photograph that accompanied the report in the NZADIE (New Zealand Association for Drama
in Education), her image was on the front cover of the special issue of
*Australasian Drama Studies*, and two full-page portraits appeared in the
special issue of *Australian Feminist Studies*. There were 65 speakers from
30 countries at the Conference. All of these speakers were leading artists,

and the press was provided with information and photographs of at least 20 of them: the closest competition for visual representation came from Joan Littlewood, whose image appeared four times.

12  Freud put forward this theory in *Totem and Taboo* while writing about Australian Aborigines:

> their psychic life assumes a peculiar interest for us, for we can recognise in their psychic life the well-preserved, early stage of our own development. . . . I am choosing for comparison those tribes which have been described by ethnologists as being the most backward and wretched: the aborigines of the youngest continent, namely Australia.
>
> (Freud 1938: 15–16)

13  The most relevant theorising of the pre-Oedipal to our investigation lies in the parallels that have been drawn between the retrieval of this state and the perception of the sublime in art. The sublime – which is as much a reworking of a classical concept by nineteenth-century Romanticism as the representations of Dionysus – is characterised by psychoanalytic theorist Thomas Weiskel as the 'primordial desire to bond or fuse with the other' (Weiskel 1976: 104). Fear and ambivalence accompany this desire for inundation: the manner in which this ambivalence is negotiated determines the nature of the sublime experience. If we accept this definition of the sublime, then an aesthetic experience should be capable of triggering a trace memory of the intersubjective bliss of the mother–child dyad.

14  See Chodorow (1978), Grosz (1989), and Conley (1984).

15  This section is based on an interview conducted on 21 August 1998 in Seoul between Kim Kum hwa and Hyun Chang on behalf of the authors. Quotations are taken from transcripts of this interview.

16  This comment was translated for the authors by Sabina Chang.

17  Shim Jung Soon, academic and major Korean theatre critic, provided the following response to Kim Kum hwa's Adelaide performance:

> To my eyes, it looked as if Kim Kum hwa and the other performers on stage had learned about the ways of Western audiences and Western performances, and in that moment, I saw a *Kut* commodified according to a Western capitalist logic. . . . I came to see her performance in a more comprehensive or global way: if we are to represent/present our authentic Korean tradition/identity to the Western audiences, we may have to appropriate their cultural/ performing paradigms. I realize that it is a necessity to accommodate the audience, but I still feel sorry that part of our authentic tradition/identity has to be moderated and disappear.
>
> (personal correspondence with the authors, 14 September 1998)

18  The Warlpiri were one of the last indigenous groups to be affected by colonisation and it was not until the late 1920s that they were forced into a dependent relationship with the Northern Territory white settlers. The deciding moment in the history of the

relationship between the Warlpiri and the colonial administration occurred in 1928, when an incident between an Aboriginal woman and a white settler culminated in the death of the latter. In response to this incident, the colonial administration organised a punitive raid near Coniston, which is in the centre of Warlpiri country. Over 100 bush people were massacred, 40 of whom were Warlpiri. Fear of further violence, starvation, drought, and the destruction of the native vegetation by cattle drew the Warlpiri out of the bush and into the orbit of the station communities. Increasingly, Warlpiri took jobs at the gold and wolfram mines and on the cattle stations, but it was not until the Second World War that they were guaranteed a wage for their labour. After a brief period as wage earners, the Warlpiri were forced out of the workforce by falling mineral prices and the post-war demobilisation. The Native Affairs branch of the Australian Government, in an attempt to keep unemployed indigenous people away from major towns like Alice Springs, established new large-scale Aboriginal settlements. Under this scheme Yuendumu was established in 1946 and Lajamanu in 1949.

19  See M. Bachelard (1997) for further discussion of this issue and its complex effect on 1990s politics in Australia.

20  All the interviews were conducted in Warlpiri, rather than English, and subsequently translated by Lee Cataldi.

21  Jeannie Herbert Nungarrayi shares certain ceremonies with Nungarrayis from different parts of Warlpiri country, but as she points out, her entitlement is extremely specific:

> All those Nungarrayis, like myself, will have our own *Jukurrpa* designs from our grandfathers and identify with different country. But I can't paint any other Nungarrayi's designs. I don't have that right. Those designs don't belong to me; it's not my country. People aren't allowed to sing songs, tell *Jukurrpa* stories or paint designs belonging to other people. In fact, when this occasionally happens, people can be punished – even physically reprimanded. Warlpiri people view the wrongful use of other people's body designs very seriously.
>
> (Herbert Nungarrayi 1995)

22  The remarks made by the Warlpiri women relating to *Yawulyu* perfor-mances are taken from transcripts of interviews conducted by the authors from 2 to 12 August 1998 in Lajamanu and Yuendumu, NT, Australia.

23  This may in part be attributable to the fact that the Warlpiri *Yawulyu* are frequently based on track dreamings (as opposed to site-based dreamings) and are therefore mimetic of journeys covering vast areas of land. See Bell (1993: 138).

## 3 Layering space: staging and remembering 'home'

1 Africa does share this legacy with a number of locations including Bali, Papua New Guinea, Japan, China, and various parts of India. Bali and Africa have been especially well mined by European inter-culturalists – not to mention other types of speculators – since the beginning of the twentieth century.

2 Indeed, Gregory and Urry comment that at the end of the twentieth century, 'spatial structure is now seen not merely as an arena in which social life unfolds, but rather as a medium through which social relations are produced and reproduced' (Gregory and Urry 1985: 3). Space does, then, have a degree of autonomy in commenting on the world and experiences in that world. Soja comments that 'spatiality, as socially produced space, must thus be distinguished from the physical space of material nature and the mental space of cognition and representation, each of which is used and incorporated into the social construction of spatiality but cannot be conceptualised as its equivalent' (Soja 1989: 92–3). The socially produced nature of space, then, makes even the most ethereal of spaces virtually tangible.

3 For a fuller explanation, see Scolnicov (1994) and Best (1995).

4 Of course, different cultures teach their members different methods of 'reading' any social structures. We hope that the methods we describe here will be useful in a variety of contexts, even though they emanate from a broadly western approach to theatre.

5 In his description of space in the postcolonial context, Young recognises the necessary layering of the types of space when he applies Deleuze and Guattari's concept of territorialisation to postcolonial spatialisation in 'a form of palimpsestual inscription and reinscription, an historical paradigm that will acknowledge the extent to which cultures were not simply destroyed but rather layered on top of each other' (Young 1995: 173–4).

6 It is important to realise that merely recognising the presence of the workings of space as reflecting or even determining dominant ideology does not necessarily reduce their impact, as Tejumola Olaniyan explains:

What the dramatic practices of Wole Soyinka, Amiri Baraka, Derek Walcott, and Ntozake Shange together show us is an empowering post-Afrocentric space, a space that calls to account and radically revises the colonialist, triumphalist narrative of European modernity. The dramatists show us that the space, though possible, is a thoroughly embattled space, a guerrilla space that is constantly forced to shift and improvise terrains because it is still a dominated space. In showing us that the space and its attendant performative conception of cultural identity are possible, the question they ask, I think, is whether the space can really flourish without its own supporting structures, that is, within still Eurocentric *institutions* . . . in the current global political economy of the production and circulation of subjectivities.

(Olaniyan 1995: 139)

Recognising the nature of these spatial structures is, however, the first step towards any type of dismantling or reorganising project.

7 It is important to acknowledge, however, that early attempts to theorise and empower postcolonial Africa were based in pan-African movements and negritude, both of which aimed to destabilise the Manichean Europe/Africa or white/black binaries by constructing theoretical and political movements that operated well beyond political borders.

8 The Mother Africa figure has endured in writing by African men, even after the end of the colonial era. While no longer necessarily imbued with racist assumptions, these figures in literature tend to be governed by sexist boundaries ostensibly determining women's subject positions.

9 Algeria won independence from France in 1962, after an eight-year war. During most of the 1990s, Algerians have lived through a civil war that has pitted various ruling regimes (usually characterised by militarism and a willingness to suspend elections when the opposition appeared to be gaining power) against an Islamic party (the Islamic Salvation Front, or FIS, now banned). Since the mid-1980s, the influence of Islam on Algeria has been profound, coinciding with the fall of oil prices and domestic economic hardship (Out There News 1997; ArabNet 1997; Marlowe 1997). One of the effects of the unrest since the mid-1980s is that thousands of people, particularly artists and writers, have been killed. Some such murders have resulted from terrorist acts by opposition forces, while others have been caused by government intervention. Many of the dead were educated people considered to be threats to one side or the other.

10 This does raise a question regarding the objectification of women and women's bodies. Hanna Scolnicov (1994: 8) argues that from the time of modernism, leaving the house is the sign of women's emancipation – A Doll's House is the obvious example. Bachelard's construction suggests the importance of the return to the home, which, for Scolnicov, could be read as a sign of man's return to dominate the house, and thereby, its female inhabitants (Bachelard 1964: 8). This does not, however, seem to be a necessarily logical outcome of memory space, particularly since the desire to return to a memory space obviously applies to women as well as to men.

11 Grosz (1995) reads chora through Plato, Jacques Derrida, and Luce Irigaray.

12 It is useful to introduce a fourth play here, Djanet Sears's Afrika Solo. This is another play that explores the African imaginary in terms of homecoming as it stages a journey to Africa through space, time, and history for the eponymous character to 'find herself'. Her adventures include reclaiming African histories and various cultural practices specific to the countries she visits and culminate in her decision to

return to Canada, but not to abandon Africa. She carries Africa 'with' her in her body: the spatial location of Africa (as well as all the other significations of 'Africa') becomes coded within and upon the body of Djanet. In other words, Djanet's body, which she comes to recognise as beautiful 'despite' its blackness, with its renewed sense of self-worth, becomes the site of *chora*.

13  Suitcases also represent the state of the vast majority of blacks in South Africa during apartheid who were forced to live and work away from their families, returning 'home' for just a short, annual visit.

14  The mother figure is, of course, not solely associated with Africa. It is also present in India and in cultures with a strong Roman Catholic religious base where the worship of Mary is important. Mary and/or the idealised woman then becomes conflated with nationality and patriotism, as we have seen in Argentina.

15  For a full discussion, see Best (1995: 183–92).

16  Of course, any number of other considerations may also play a part, including the size of the theatre (a theatre seating 3,000 people necessarily deploys different kinesics to an actor performing in a small studio theatre seating 30), the differences between indoor and outdoor performance, and discrete cultural differences in the coding of performance.

17  Formerly a food market for approximately 60 years (Fuchs 1990: 35–6), the Market's main space is in an octagonal building once known as the Indian Citrus Market. Located in Newtown, near central Johannesburg, 'on the edge of an Indian residential neighbourhood' and 'the white city of Johannesburg' (Fuchs 1990: 36), the Market Theatre complex has grown to include other performance spaces: Upstairs at the Market, the Laager, and the Rehearsal Room. In 1995 Mhlope became the first black woman to be artistic director of the Market Theatre.

## 4  Intercultural bodies: meetings in the flesh

1  In tracing the origins of this racial discourse, we are indebted to the ground-breaking analysis by Colette Guillaumin (1995): she distinguishes between the European aristocracy, who claimed their status through systems of lineage and divine right, and the bourgeoisie, who claimed power through the definition of what they were not.

2  We use this term ironically, in the same way that it was used by Rustom Bharucha in his address to the Australasian Drama Studies Association annual conference at Hamilton, New Zealand in 1998. 'We don't need any more intercultural masterpieces', Bharucha stated, referring to the extravagant productions that have been commissioned by international festivals in recent years.

3  The performing bodies may have existed in the same theatrical place and time, and frequently performed a designated classic with so-called universal themes (Shakespeare was a popular choice), but

the narrative and discourse allowed cultures to be located in a system that established hierarchical positions and values. The premise for each of these works was identical. The host country provided the creative team, the production was financed through Government arts bureaux and international agencies, and the actors were cast either according to the amount of sponsorship provided by their governments, or by their ability physically to denote racial and cultural differences. *King Lear*, performed at the Theatre of Nations Festival in Seoul in September 1997, was a marvellous illustration of this genre of inter-cultural theatre. The production was funded through the United Nations, the International Theatre Institute, and the American, Korean, German, and Japanese Governments. Lear and Cordelia were Korean, Kent was an American, Edgar Japanese, and Gloucester German. The two actors from Sierra Leone were dressed in feathers, furs, and body paint, and were not assigned characters. Rehearsals happened to coincide with the major currency crisis of the ASEAN countries in late 1997. Eight weeks after the final performances in Tokyo, the International Monetary Fund organised a US$57 billion bail-out of the Korean economy, widely reported as the biggest financial rescue package in history. Kent was indeed a faithful servant (*King Lear* 1997).

4  The original *Akwanso* cast consisted of Rhoda Roberts, Dorinda Hafner, Jigzie Campbell, and Aku Kadogo.

5  The original members of the Top End Girls were: Joanna Barrkman, Maria Alice Casimiro Branco, Venetia Gillot, Betchay Mondragon, Lilliane Rababarisoa, Desak Putu Warti, Paia Ingram, Hortensia 'Tetchy' Masero, and Alison Mills. As we discuss below, Desak Putu Warti was forced to withdraw from the production and her place was taken by Dorothea Randall.

6  At the time of writing, Australian troops are stationed in East Timor as part of the United Nations multinational force deployed to establish security after the vote for independence on 30 August 1999. The Indonesian military were implicated in the pro-Jakarta violence perpetrated by local militias following the referendum. On assuming power in November 1999, the newly elected President of Indonesia, Abdurrahman Wahid, pledged to decentralise control of the provinces and to attack the overriding power of the army.

7  See Bhabha (1994b).

8  See Friedman (1997), Chow (1991: ch. 2), and Young (1995) for extensive arguments about problematic perceptions of hybridity.

9  This section uses the western-style order of Japanese names for reasons of consistency and in line with contemporary Japanese usage in English-speaking countries.

10  The apartment block had been built by the Government to provide accommodation for the increasing numbers of professional women entering the workforce in the 1930s. There were 150 Japanese- and western-style one-room apartments. All the tenants were the sole occupants of their rooms, all visitors were monitored, and a strict curfew was enforced. The architectural design of this building conformed to

all the practices of enclosure, partitioning, and surveillance identified by Foucault in his analyses of the spatial power mechanisms employed in factories, workshops, schools, and prisons. The new and independent women who moved into this purpose-built accommodation in Tokyo were subjected to a bodily regime that had little in common with the body-spaces inhabited by their mothers and grandmothers.

11 The 'Hybrid Committee' of the Australia Council was established to consider funding applications for new works that crossed conventional art forms. The term 'Hybrid' was later replaced by 'New Media'.

12 'The Co-Prosperity Sphere, formalised in 1940, was an integral part of Prime Minister Konoe Fumimaro's idea of a "New Order" in which the Japanese would lead a Pan-Asian effort towards Asian self-sufficiency and stability, anti-communism, and resistance to Western imperialism' (Robertson 1998: 93, n. 3).

13 In *Sayonara* (1954), the film based on the James Michener novel, the Marlon Brando character, Major Gruver, has an affair with a Takarazuka *otokoyaku*, in yet another variant on the Madame Butterfly theme. When this process of displaced sexual desire was re-directed at the Takarazuka Revue by Hollywood, the management refused to co-operate with the production (Robertson 1998: 221, n. 12).

14 Ankoku Butoh is the name given to the strain of *butoh* developed by Tatsumi Hijikata. There are numerous forms of *butoh* that have developed in the past 40 years, so much so that critics argue whether there is any consistency in the work that can legitimate the present categorisation into a single genre.

15 Ohno, the most famous of the dancers associated with the *butoh* movement, cites his major inspirations as the Christian religion, the famous flamenco dancer Antonia Merce, Monet, *Les Enfants du Paradis*, and his mother. It was through Ohno that Hijikata became aware of the work of the choreographer and initiator of Ausdruckstanz, Mary Wigman, and Harald Kreutzberg, a dancer infamous for the ambiguity of his performed sexuality. It was through Hijikata that Ohno was introduced to the works of Genet, the Marquis de Sade, Lautréamont, Aubrey Beardsley, Hemingway, and Artaud. Ironically, some of these artists, most prominently Wigman and Artaud, had themselves drawn major inspiration from 'oriental' sources; in fact, one of Wigman's most famous works was entitled *Marche Orientale* (Takai, interview 1998).

16 It was not until Ohno and Sankai Juku achieved critical success in Europe and America that it became more than a minor avant-garde phenomenon in Japan. The first major *butoh* season, the 'Reimport Festival', was held in downtown Tokyo in 1985. By this time there were over 100 *butoh* companies in Japan and another 100 overseas. It was impossible to attend an international arts festival in the late 1980s and early 1990s and not see a *butoh* performance.

17 It is arguable whether these companies comprise a consistent choreographic movement; certainly Hijikata felt that *butoh* was being commodified before reaching maturity. To many of its critics the dance form has degenerated into exoticism.

18 One of the most famous transformation exercises created by Hijikata was based on the rooster. Ojima Ichiro explains: 'The idea was to push out all of the human inside and let the bird take its place. You may start by imitating, but imitation is not your final goal; when you believe you are thinking completely like a chicken, you have succeeded' (cited in Klein 1988: 97).

19 Quotations by Pol Pelletier regarding her performance practice are taken from transcripts of an interview conducted by the authors on 3 June 1998 in Montréal, Canada.

# 5  Intercultural markets: the female body and censorship

1 Large corporations now support arts organisations (theatre, dance, opera companies, museums, as well as festivals) almost as heavily as they support sporting events. This is not, however, generally motivated by philanthropy or an interest in the arts. Rather, it is generally useful as a tax write-off, a promotional or advertising exercise, or to entertain clients: 'Australian Ballet corporate development manager Kenneth Watkins says some companies sponsor the ballet purely for its opening night parties, at which they can entertain a host of existing clients and potentially meet and woo any number of new ones' (Strickland 1998: 6). As Marie-Hélène Falcon, director of Montréal's Festival de Théâtre des Amériques, explains, 'Sponsors will not get involved because they want to support art. They will get involved because you have an audience that they're interested in. . . . That's what sponsorship is about. It's extremely naïve to think of anything else' (interview 1998).

2 There is, of course, some complicity in this commodification, and we do not assume that all cultures are powerless to change how they are represented. Neither do we lay the responsibility for the sustained commodification of culture on festivals.

3 The official definition of trafficking in women is defined by the International Organisation of Migration as the situation in which

> a woman in a country other than her own is exploited by another person against her will and for financial gain. The trafficking element may – cumulatively or separately – consist of: arranging legal or illegal migration from the country of origin to the country of destination; deceiving victims into prostitution once in the country of destination; or enforcing victims' exploitation through violence, threat of violence, or other forms of coercion.
>
> (Migration Information Programme 1995: 6)

4 Trafficked women also comply with the structural exchange of women through marriage, which Claude Lévi-Strauss observed as a means of ensuring the continuation of a social order (Lévi-Strauss 1963: 309).

5 Penalties for human smuggling remain low throughout Europe: 'In Poland, there are no specific laws governing the smuggling of aliens, whilst in the Czech Republic, smuggling aliens is considered a misdemeanour' (Migration Information Programme 1995: 10). Trafficking in women was the subject of a European Commission conference in Vienna in June 1996 that was successful in placing the issue on the EU agenda of concerns (Commission of the European Communities 1996: 26). The Circle against Sex Trafficking of The Global Fund for Women held a conference in October 1996 in Reno, Nevada, which acknowledged that trafficking is partly assisted by the nebulous laws on prostitution. In addition, questions regarding the victims' culpability remain (particularly whether or not they chose to become involved). Sentences for trafficking in the US carry a maximum of only five years (Circle against Sex Trafficking 1997: 10). Some of the key European-based men who have been heavily involved in trafficking thousands of women have been convicted of tax evasion, a crime which is more easily proven than trafficking (de Stoop 1994: 8).

6 De Stoop explains that 'exotic girls were much cheaper' but their cultural capital as 'exotic' is their chief attraction (de Stoop 1994: 105).

7 See Begg (1996: 13) for a description of the Virgin Mary as a product of cultural adaptation originating with the Egyptian goddess Isis.

8 The geographical points are the Southern Cross constellation, roman numerals to signify the twentieth festival, Mt Lofty (Adelaide's highest point) and its television antennae, the Rotunda (an image frequently used to market Adelaide as a tourist destination), the Festival Centre building, and St Peter's Cathedral in Adelaide (which is known as the City of Churches). The religions encompass Frejha from the Germanic tradition, a Buddha, the Egyptian gods Horus and Seti, an Aboriginal Mimi or spirit person, a Siberian Shaman, Athena, and the Hindu god Ganesha (Harris 1997b: 7).

9 The grounds of condemnation were at times extremely tenuous: Father John Fleming, a Catholic priest who also hosts a radio talk-back programme, argued that the two large Xs which signified the twentieth festival in roman numerals were upside-down crosses, and thereby symbols of satanic worship (5AN 1997a). Indeed, the poster became 'fair game' for any and all attacks: even the representation of St Peter's Cathedral was condemned by Reverend Peter Osborn, the honorary Chaplain for the Arts, who said 'Its spires are better than that' (The Advertiser 1997: 7).

10 Noris Iannou, a cultural historian of Greek heritage, was able to find a way to read both sides of this clash in equivalent postmodern terms: he applauded the poster in terms of a postmodern hybridity, but condemned it on the grounds of interculturalism because it did not take into account the views of Greek Orthodoxy (Iannou, interview 1998). He seems to have been the exception, however. Interestingly, Iannou's position was of limited interest during the controversy: most

participants preferred to use inflammatory arguments that registered cultural pique more than rigour.

11 Some Catholic leaders subsequently demanded that Archer should have approached them for permission (5DN 1997a) to use the image of the Virgin Mary as well.

# References

3IWPC (1994a, b, c, d) See under Third International Women Playwrights' Conference.

5AA (1997) 'Sunday Night Talk hosted by John Fleming', radio broadcast, 11.45 pm, 17 August.

5AN (1997a) Radio news broadcast, 12.30 pm, 4 September.

—— (1997b) Radio news broadcast, 5 pm, 5 September.

5DN (1997a) Radio news broadcast, 6 am, 14 August.

—— (1997b) Radio broadcast hosted by Jeremy Cordeaux, 10 pm, 26 August.

*Adelaide Festival Booking Brochure: 'Ilotopie'* (1992), Adelaide, South Australia: the Festival.

Adorno, T. (1991) *The Culture Industry: Selected Essays on Mass Culture*, ed. J.M. Bernstein, London: Routledge.

*The Advertiser* (1992a) 'Festival Arrests Uproar: Angry Director Hits Out at Police Action', 11 March: 1.

—— (1992b) 'Latest Incident Just Traditional Friction', 11 March: 2.

—— (1997) 'Chaplain Condemns Director', 15 August: 7.

Afshar, H. (1989) 'Women and Reproduction in Iran', in N. Yuval-Davis and F. Anthias (eds) *Woman–Nation–State*, New York: St Martin's Press.

—— (1993) *Women in the Middle East: Perceptions, Realities, and Struggles for Liberation*, Hampshire and London: Macmillan.

—— (1996) 'Islam and Feminism: An Analysis of Political Strategies', in M. Yamani (ed.) *Feminism and Islam: Legal and Literary Perspectives*, New York: New York University Press.

*The Age* (1997) 'Play It Again, Mary', 19 August: C10.

Agosin, M. (1987) 'A Visit to the Mothers of the Plaza de Mayo', *Human Rights Quarterly* 9: 426–35.

Ahmed, L. (1992) *Women and Gender in Islam: Historical Roots of a Modern Debate*, New Haven, CT, and London: Yale University Press.

Aidoo, [C.]A.A. (1965) *The Dilemma of a Ghost*, Accra: Longman.

Amsden, A. (1989) *Asia's Next Giant: South Korea and Late Industrialisation*, New York: Oxford University Press.

Anouilh, J. (1960) *Antigone*, trans. L. Galantière, London: Methuen.

Aoki, M. (1997) Personal correspondence with M. Moore, 15 December.

Appadurai, A. (1986a) 'Introduction: Commodities and the Politics of Value', in A. Appadurai (ed.) *The Social Life of Things: Commodities in Cultural Perspective*, Cambridge: Cambridge University Press.

—— (ed.) (1986b) *The Social Life of Things: Commodities in Cultural Perspective*, New York: Cambridge University Press.

—— (1990) 'Disjuncture and Difference in the Global Cultural Economy', in M. Featherstone (ed.) *Global Culture: Nationalism, Globalization, and Modernity*, London: Sage.

ArabNet (1997) *Algeria, History, After Independence (1962–1995)*. On-line. Available HTTP: http://www.arab.net/algeria/history/aa_independence.html (30 October).

Archer, R. (1997) *The One That Got Away*. Written and performed by R. Archer, directed by D. Drew, produced by W. Barry and L. Kitching. Australian Film Commission and New South Wales Film and Television Office, Close Up Series, ABC Television, 19 August.

—— (1998) Interview with authors, 27 January, Adelaide, Australia.

—— (1999) Personal correspondence with authors, 19 January.

Avignon Festival (1998) *Brochure*, Avignon: the Festival.

Awasthi, S. (1993) 'The Intercultural Experience and the Kathakali *King Lear*', *New Theatre Quarterly* 9, 34: 172–8.

Bachelard, G. (1964) *The Poetics of Space: The Classic Look at How We Experience Intimate Places*, Boston, MA: Beacon.

Bachelard, M. (1997) *The Great Land Grab: What Every Australian Should Know about Wik, Mabo, and the Ten-Point Plan*, Melbourne: Hyland House.

Barba, E. (1982) 'Theatre Anthropology', *TDR* 26, 2 (T94): 5–32.

Bassnett, S. (1989) *Magdalena: International Women's Experimental Theatre*, Oxford: Berg.

Batty, P. (1997) 'Saluting the Dot-spangled Banner: Aboriginal Culture, National Identity, and the Australian Republic', *Art Link* 17, 3. Online. Available HTTP: http://www.lib.latrobe.edu.au/AHR (17 September 1998).

Baudrillard, J. (1988) *Selected Writings*, Cambridge: Polity Press.

—— (1990) *Seduction*, trans. B. Singer, London: Macmillan.

Begg, E. (1996) *The Cult of the Black Virgin*, London: Penguin.

Bell, D. (1993) *Daughter of the Dreaming*, Minneapolis, MN: University of Minnesota Press.

Benjamin, J. (1986) 'A Desire of One's Own: Psychoanalytic Feminism and Intersubjective Space', in T. de Lauretis (ed.) *Feminist Studies/Critical Studies*, Bloomington, IN: Indiana University Press.

Benjamin, W. (1978) *Reflections: Essays, Aphorisms, Autobiographical Writings*, New York: Schocken Books.

Bennett, T. (1995) *The Birth of the Museum: History, Theory, Politics*, New York and London: Routledge.

Berlin, Z. (1988) 'Takarazuka: A History and Descriptive Analysis of the All-female Japanese Performance Company', unpublished PhD Thesis, New York University.

Best, S. (1995) 'Sexualizing Space', in E. Grosz and E. Probyn (eds) *Sexy Bodies: The Strange Carnalities of Feminism*, London and New York: Routledge.

Bhabha, H.K. (1994a) *The Location of Culture*, London: Routledge.

—— (1994b) 'Signs Taken for Wonders: Questions of Ambivalence and Authority under a Tree outside Delhi, May 1817', in H.K. Bhabha, *The Location of Culture*, London and New York: Routledge.

Bharucha, R. (1993) *Theatre and the World: Performance and the Politics of Culture*, London: Routledge.

—— (1996) 'Somebody's Other: Disorientations in the Cultural Politics of Our Times', in P. Pavis (ed.) *The Intercultural Performance Reader*, London: Routledge.

Blunt, A. and Rose, G. (1994) 'Introduction: Women's Colonial and Postcolonial Geographies', in A. Blunt and G. Rose (eds) *Writing Women and Space: Colonial and Postcolonial Geographies*, London: Guildford Press.

Bocock, R. (1993) *Consumption*, London: Routledge.

Botting, F. and Wilson, S. (eds) (1997) *The Bataille Reader*, Oxford: Blackwell.

Braidotti, R. (1991) *Patterns of Dissonance: A Study of Women in Contemporary Philosophy*, Cambridge: Polity Press.

—— (1994) *Nomadic Subjects: Embodiment and Sexual Difference in Contemporary Feminist Theory*, New York: Columbia University Press.

Brau, L. (1990) 'The Women's Theatre of Takarazuka', *TDR* 34, 4 (T128): 79–95.

Brown, M.F. (1998) 'Can Culture Be Copyrighted?', *Current Anthropology* 19, 2: 193–222.

Brysk, A. (1994) 'The Politics of Measurement: The Contested Count of the Disappeared in Argentina', *Human Rights Quarterly* 16, 4: 676–92.

Butler, J. (1993) *Bodies that Matter: On the Discursive Limits of 'Sex'*, London: Routledge.

*Butoh: Body on the Edge of Crisis* (1993) Videorecording, directed and produced M. Blackwood, Sydney: SBS.

Carlson, M. (1990) 'Peter Brook's *The Mahabharata* and Ariane Mnouchkine's *L'Indiade* as Examples of Contemporary Cross-Cultural Theatre', in E. Fischer-Lichte, J. Riley, and M. Gissenwehrer (eds) *The Dramatic Touch of Difference: Theatre, Own and Foreign*, Tübingen: Gunter Narr.

Cataldi, L. (1998) 'A Chance to Speak', *Southerly* 58, 2: 5–19.

Chang, C. (1988) 'An Introduction to Korean Shamanism', in C. Yu and R. Guisso (eds) *Shamanism*, Berkeley, CA: Asian Humanities Press.

Chang, H. (1999) Personal correspondence with authors, 14 May.

Chaudhuri, U. (1991) 'The Future of the Hyphen: Interculturalism, Textuality, and the Difference Within', in B. Marranca and G. Dasgupta (eds) *Interculturalism and Performance: Writings from PAJ*, New York: PAJ.

—— (1995) *Staging Place: The Geography of Modern Drama*, Ann Arbor, MI: University of Michigan Press.

Cheshire, G. (1998) 'Revealing an Iran where the Chadors Are Most Chic', *New York Times*, 8 November: Arts and Leisure 28.

Chin, D. (1991) 'Interculturalism, Postmodernism, Pluralism', in B. Marranca and G. Dasgupta (eds) *Interculturalism and Performance: Writings from PAJ*, New York: PAJ.

Chodorow, N. (1978) *The Reproduction of Mothering: Psychoanalysis and the Sociology of Gender,* Berkeley, CA: University of California Press.

Chow, R. (1991) *Women and Chinese Modernity: The Politics of Reading between East and West*, Minneapolis, MN: Minnesota University Press.

—— (1995) *Primitive Passions: Visuality, Sexuality, Ethnography, and Contemporary Chinese Cinema*, New York: Columbia University Press.

Christ, C. (1989) 'Rethinking Theology and Nature', in J. Plaskow and C.P. Christ (eds) *Weaving the Visions: New Patterns in Feminist Spirituality*, San Francisco, CA: HarperCollins.

Chun, A. (1996) 'Discourses of Identity in the Changing Spaces of Public Culture in Taiwan, Hong Kong, and Singapore', *Theory Culture Society* 13, 1: 51–75.

Circle against Sex Trafficking of the Global Fund for Women (1997) *Sisters and Daughters Betrayed: The Sex Trade of Women and Girls.* Proceedings of 'An International Conference on the Dynamics of Sexual Coercion', held 17–18 October 1996, Reno, Nevada. Palo Alto, CA: The Global Fund for Women.

Cohen, R. (1986) *Face to Face with Levinas*, New York: State University of New York Press.

Commission of the European Communities (1996) *Communication from the Commission to the Council and the European Parliament: On Trafficking in Women for the Purpose of Sexual Exploitation*, Brussels: Ellis.

Conley, V.A. (1984) *Hélène Cixous: Writing the Feminine*, Lincoln, NE, and London: University of Nebraska Press.

Croll, E. (1978) *Feminism and Socialism in China*, London: Routledge & Kegan Paul.

Crossley, N. (1996) 'Body-Subject/Body-Power: Agency, Inscription, and Control in Foucault and Merleau-Ponty', *Body and Society* 2, 2: 99–116.

Crouch, B. (1997) 'Poster Sacrilege to Sell Festival', *Sunday Mail*, 14 September: 55.

Daniels Nampijinpa, D. (1998) Interview with authors in Warlpiri with Lee Cataldi translating, 12 August, Yuendumu, NT, Australia.

de Certeau, M. (1984) *The Practice of Everyday Life*, trans. S.F. Rendall, Berkeley, CA: University of California Press.

de Lauretis, T. (1987) *Technologies of Gender: Essays on Theory, Film, and Fiction*, Bloomington, IN: Indiana University Press.

de Stoop, C. (1994) *They Are So Sweet, Sir: The Cruel Traffickers in Filippinas and Other Women*, n.p.: Limitless Asia.

Deleuze, G. and Guattari, F. (1983) *Anti-Oedipus: Capitalism and Schizophrenia*, trans. R. Hurley, M. Seem, and H.R. Lane, Minneapolis, MN: University of Minnesota Press.

—— (1987) *A Thousand Plateaus: Capitalism and Schizophrenia*, trans. B. Massumi, Minneapolis, MN: University of Minnesota Press.

Diprose, R. (1994) *The Bodies of Women: Ethics, Embodiment, and Sexual Difference*, London: Routledge.

Doggart, S. (1996) *Latin American Plays: New Drama from Argentina, Cuba, Mexico, and Peru*, London: Nick Hern.

Dussart, F. (1989) 'Warlpiri Women's *Yawulyu* Ceremonies: A Forum for Socialisation and Innovation', unpublished PhD thesis, Australian National University.

*Eddie Mabo v. the State of Queensland* (1992) 175, *Commonwealth Law Report* 1.

Edinburgh Festival Theatre (1999) '. . . about the theatre'. Online. Available HTTP: http://www.eft.co.uk/about/index.html (19 January).

Eisenstein, L. (1998) 'Ratna Sarumpaet: Urgent Action Needed'. Online. Available HTTP: http://www.en.com/users/herone/Ratna.html (21 August).

Eliade, M. (1964) *Shamanism: Archaic Techniques of Ecstasy*, trans. W.R. Trasik, London: Routledge & Kegan Paul.

Fabian, J. (1983) *Time and the Other: How Anthropology Makes Its Object*, New York: Columbia University Press.

Falcon, M. (1998) Interview with authors, 6 March, Adelaide, Australia.

Featherstone, M. (1991) *Consumer Culture and Postmodernism*, London: Sage.

Featherstone, M., Lash, S., and Robertson, R. (eds) (1995) *Global Modernities*, London: Sage.

Feitlowitz, M. (1990) 'Crisis, Terror, Disappearance: The Theatre of Griselda Gambaro', *Theater* 21, 3: 34–8.

—— (1992) Translator's note, in G. Gambaro, *Information for Foreigners: Three Plays of Griselda Gambaro*, Evanston, IL: Northwestern University Press.

Femenía, N.A. (1987) 'Argentina's Mothers of Plaza de Mayo: The Mourning Process from Junta to Democracy', *Feminist Studies* 13, 1: 9–18.

Fischer-Lichte, E. (1990a) 'Staging the Foreign as Cultural Transformation', in E. Fischer-Lichte, J. Riley, and M. Gissenwehrer (eds) *The Dramatic Touch of Difference: Theatre, Own and Foreign*, Tübingen: Gunter Narr.

—— (1990b) 'Theatre Own and Foreign: The Intercultural Trend in Contemporary Theatre', in E. Fischer-Lichte, J. Riley, and M. Gissenwehrer (eds) *The Dramatic Touch of Difference: Theatre, Own and Foreign*, Tübingen: Gunter Narr.

Fischer-Lichte, E., Riley, J., and Gissenwehrer, M. (1990) *The Dramatic Touch of Difference: Theatre, Own and Foreign*, Tübingen: Gunter Narr.

Foucault, M. (1977) *Discipline and Punish: The Birth of the Prison*, trans. A. Sheridan, London: Penguin.

Freud, S. (1938) *Totem and Taboo: Resemblances between the Psychic Lives of Savages and Neurotics*, trans. A.A. Brill, Harmondsworth: Penguin.

—— (1960) *Jokes and their Relation to the Unconscious*, trans. J. Strachey, London: Routledge & Kegan Paul.

Friedman, J. (1994a) *Cultural Identity and Global Process*, London: Sage.

—— (1994b) Introduction, in J. Friedman (ed.) *Consumption and Identity*, Chur, Switzerland: Harwood Academic.

—— (1997) 'Global Crises, the Struggle for Cultural Identity, and Intellectual Porkbarrelling: Cosmopolitans Versus Locals, Ethnics, and Nationals in an Era of De-Hegemonisation', in P. Werbner and R. Modood (eds) *Debating Cultural Hybridity: Multi-Cultural Identities and the Politics of Anti-Racism*, London: Zed Books.

Frow, J. (1997) *Time and Commodity Culture: Essays in Cultural Theory and Postmodernity*, Oxford: Clarendon Press.

Fuchs, A. (1990) *Playing the Market: The Market Theatre Johannesburg, 1976–1986*, Chur, Switzerland: Harwood Academic.

Gallaire-Bourega, F. (1988) *You Have Come Back. Plays By Women: An International Anthology*, ed. and trans. J. MacDougall, New York: Ubu Repertory Theatre.

Gambaro, G. (1992) *Antígona Furiosa*, in G. Gambaro, *Information for Foreigners*, ed., trans., and intro. M. Feitlowitz, Evanston, IL: Northwestern University Press.

—— (1995) 'New Stories from Old', *Australian Feminist Studies* 21: 55–8.

Gardiner, M. (1996) 'Alterity and Ethics: A Dialogical Perspective', *Theory Culture Society* 13, 2: 121–43.

Geertz, C. (1973) *The Interpretation of Cultures*, New York: Basic Books.

George, J. (1994) 'The Arrest and Trial of Malayali Indians in the United Arab Emirates: When Performance, (Inter)Culture, and Human Rights Collide', *TDR* 38, 2 (T142): 138–49.

Gibson, M. (1996) 'Sprinkle More a Dirty Spray', *The Advertiser*, 14 March: 15.

Gilbert, H. and Lo, J. (1997) 'Performing Hybridity in Post-colonial Monodrama', *Journal of Commonwealth Literature* 32, 1: 5–19.

Gilbert, H. and Tompkins, J. (1996) *Post-colonial Drama: Theory, Practice, Politics*, London: Routledge.

Gillot, V. (1995) 'Identity and Displacement', *Australian Feminist Studies* 21: 108–13.

—— (1997) Interview with authors, 18 May, Brisbane, Australia.

Gissenwehrer, M. (1990) 'To Weave a Silk Road Away: Thoughts on an Approach towards the Unfamiliar: Chinese Theatre and Our Own', in E. Fischer-Lichte, J. Riley, and M. Gissenwehrer (eds) *The Dramatic Touch of Difference: Theatre, Own and Foreign*, Tübingen: Gunter Narr.

Goto, M. (1999) 'Tokyo International Festival of Performing Arts'. Online. Email: gomiki@mxc.meshnet.or.jp (9 February).

Granites Nampijinpa, J. (1998) Interview with authors in Warlpiri with Lee Cataldi translating, 2 and 10 August, Yuendumu, NT, Australia.

Gregory, D. and Urry, J. (1985) Introduction, in D. Gregory and J. Urry (eds) *Social Relations and Spatial Structures*, Basingstoke: Macmillan.

Grimes, R.L. (1982) 'Defining Nascent Ritual', *Journal of the American Academy of Religion* 50, 4: 539–55.

Grosz, E. (1989) *Sexual Subversions: Three French Feminists*, Sydney: Allen & Unwin.

—— (1994) *Volatile Bodies: Towards a Corporeal Feminism*, St Leonards, NSW: Allen & Unwin.

—— (1995) *Space, Time, and Perversion: Essays on the Politics of Bodies*, New York: Routledge.

Grosz, E. and Probyn, E. (eds) (1995) *Sexy Bodies: The Strange Carnalities of Feminism*, London and New York: Routledge.

Guillaumin, C. (1995) *Racism, Sexism, Power, and Ideology*, London and New York: Routledge.

'H' (1912) 'A Letter to Nora', *Seito*, January: 133–41.

Habermas, J. (1987) *The Philosophical Discourse of Modernity*, trans. F. Lawrence, Cambridge: Polity Press.

Hahm, P. (1988) 'Shamanism and the Korean World-View, Family Life-Cycle, Society, and Social Life', in C. Yu and R. Guisso (eds) *Shamanism*, Berkeley, CA: Asian Humanities Press.

Hall, S. (1991a) 'The Local and the Global: Globalization and Ethnicity', in A. King (ed.) *Culture, Globalization, and the World-System: Contemporary Conditions for the Representation of Identity*, Binghamton, NY: Dept. of Art and Art History, State University of New York at Binghamton.

—— (1991b) 'Old and New Identities, Old and New Ethnicities', in A. King (ed.) *Culture, Globalization, and the World-System: Contemporary Conditions for the Representation of Identity*, Binghamton, NY: Dept. of Art and Art History, State University of New York at Binghamton.

Harris, S. (1997a) 'Madonna and the Myth', *The Advertiser*, 30 August: 23.

Harris, S. (1997b) 'Mother of All Icons', *The Advertiser*, 22 August: 13.

—— (1997c) '"No Offence Intended": Robyn Archer Defends Madonna Poster', *The Advertiser*, 15 August: 7.

Hata, K. (1997) 'Notes on *Butoh*', trans. Kasait and M. Martin, *Programme: 'Cry of Asia 3'*, the Asian Council for People's Culture in the Philippines, 2 November.

Hélie-Lucas, M. (1993) 'Women's Struggles in the Rise of Fundamentalism in the Muslim World: From Entryism to Internationalism', in H. Afshar (ed.) *Women in the Middle East*, London: Macmillan.

Herbert Nungarrayi, J. (1994) 'Ritual', presentation at the Third International Women Playwrights' Conference, 4 July, Adelaide, Australia.

—— (1995) 'Ritual and the Body', *Australian Feminist Studies* 21: 13–18.

Herrnstein Smith, B. (1984) 'Contingencies of Value', in R. von Hallberg (ed.) *Canons*, Chicago, IL: University of Chicago Press.

Hinden, M. (1995) 'Drama and Ritual Once Again: Notes towards a Revival of Tragic Theory', *Comparative Drama* 29, 2: 183–202.

Hinsley, C.M. (1991) 'The World as Marketplace: Commodification of the Exotic at the World's Columbian Exposition, Chicago, 1893', in I. Karp and S.D. Lavine (eds) *Exhibiting Culture: The Poetics and Politics of Museum Display*, Washington, DC: Smithsonian Institute Press.

Hiro, D. (1985) *Iran under the Ayatollahs*, London: Routledge.

Hollander, N.C. (1996) 'The Gendering of Human Rights: Women and the Latin American Terrorist State', *Feminist Studies* 22, 1: 41–80.

Holledge, J. (1981) *Innocent Flowers: Women in Edwardian Theatre*, London: Virago.

Hong Kong Arts Festival (1998) *Brochure*, Wanchai, Hong Kong: the Festival Society.

Hwa, Y.J. (1996) 'Phenomenology and Body Politics', *Body and Society* 2, 2: 1–22.

Iannou, N. (1998) Interview with Adele Chynoweth on behalf of the authors, 8 April, Adelaide, Australia.

Ibsen, H. (1997) *Ibsen Plays Two: A Doll's House, An Enemy of the People, Hedda Gabler*, trans. M. Meyer, London: Methuen.

Janelli, R.L. and Janelli, D.Y. (1982) *Ancestor Worship and Korean Society*, Palo Alto, CA: Stanford University Press.

Jelin, E. (1994) 'The Politics of Memory: The Human Rights Movement and the Construction of Democracy in Argentina', *Latin American Perspectives* 21, 2: 38–58.

Jenks, C. (1993) *Culture*, London: Routledge.

Jones, L. (1994) 'The Emergence of the Druid as Celtic Shaman', *Folklore in Use* 2: 131–42.

Kahn, J.S. (1995) *Culture, Multiculture, Postculture*, London: Sage.

Karmi, G. (1996) 'Women, Islam, and Patriarchalism', in M. Yamani (ed.) *Feminism and Islam: Legal and Literary Perspectives*, New York: New York University Press.

Karp, I. (1991a) 'Festivals', in I. Karp and S.D. Lavine (eds) *Exhibiting Cultures: The Poetics and Politics of Museum Display*, Washington, DC: Smithsonian Institute Press.

—— (1991b) 'Other Cultures in Museum Perspective', in I. Karp and S.D. Lavine (eds) *Exhibiting Cultures: The Poetics and Politics of Museum Display*, Washington, DC: Smithsonian Institute Press.

Karp, I. and Lavine, S.D. (eds) (1991) *Exhibiting Cultures: The Poetics and Politics of Museum Display*, Washington, DC: Smithsonian Institute Press.

Kendall, L. (1985) *Shamans, Housewives, and Other Restless Spirits: Women in Korean Ritual Life*, Honolulu, HI: University of Hawaii Press.

—— (1988) *The Life and Hard Times of a Korean Shaman: Of Tales and the Telling of Tales*, Honolulu, HI: University of Hawaii Press.

Kendall, L. and Dix, G. (eds) (1985) *Religion and Ritual in Korean Society*, Korea Research Monograph, University of California, Berkeley: Instititute of East Asian Studies.

Kennedy Napaljarri, L. (1998) Interview with authors in Warlpiri with Lee Cataldi translating, 4 August, Yuendumu, NT, Australia.

Kim Kum hwa (1995) 'Ritual and the Body', *Australian Feminist Studies* 21: 18–20.

—— (1997) *Boken Nanugo Haneun Pushige* [Share your Fortune and Resolve Resentment], Seoul: Pureunsoop.

—— (1998) Interview with Hyun Chang on behalf of the authors, 21 August, Seoul, South Korea.

Kim, T.K. (1988) 'The Relationship between Shamanic Ritual and the Korean Masked Dance-Drama: The Journey Motif to Chaos/Darkness/Void', unpublished PhD thesis, New York University.

*King Lear* (1997) by W. Shakespeare, Produced by International Theatre Institute, Theatre of Nations Festival. Seoul, Korea, 9–14 September.

King, Y. (1990) 'Healing the Wounds: Feminism, Ecology, and the Nature/Culture Dualism', in I. Diamond and G. Orenstein (eds) *Reweaving the World: The Emergence of Ecofeminism*, San Francisco, CA: Sierra.

Kirshenblatt-Gimblett, B. (1991) 'Objects of Ethnography', in I. Karp and S.D. Lavine (eds) *Exhibiting Cultures: The Poetics and Politics of Museum Display*, Washington, DC: Smithsonian Institute Press.

Kister, D.A. (1995) 'Dramatic Characteristics of Korean Shaman Ritual', *Shaman* 3, 1: 15–40.

Klein, S.B. (1988) *Ankoku Butoh: The Premodern and Postmodern Influences on the Dance of Utter Darkness*, Ithaca, NY: Cornell University Press.

Kopytoff, I. (1986) 'The Cultural Biography of Things: Commoditization as Process', in A. Appadurai (ed.) *The Social Life of Things: Commodities in Cultural Perspective*, Cambridge: Cambridge University Press.

Kuniyoshi, K. (1997) *Butoh in the Late 1980's*, trans. R. Hart. Online. Available HTTP: http://www.geocities.com/Tokyo/3642/end_2.html (7 June 1999).

Lampe, E. (1993) 'Collaboration and Cultural Clashing: Anne Bogart and Tadashi Suzuki's Saratoga International Theatre Institute', *TDR* 37, 1 (T137): 147–56.

Lash, S. and Friedman, J. (eds) (1992) *Modernity and Identity*, Oxford: Blackwell.

Lattas, A. (1990) 'Aborigines and Contemporary Australian Nationalism: Primordiality and the Cultural Politics of Otherness', *Social Analysis* 27: 50–69.

—— (1991) 'Nationalism, Aesthetic Redemption, and Aboriginality', *The Australian Journal of Anthropology* 2, 3: 307–24.

Laughren, M., Hale, K.L., and Hoogenraad, R. (1999) *Warlpiri–English Encyclopaedic Dictionary*, electronic files 9,500 k., St Lucia, Qld: University of Queensland.

Lawson, A.J. (1987) 'The Recognition of National Literatures: The Canadian and Australian Examples', unpublished PhD thesis, University of Queensland.

Lee, J.Y. (1981) *Korean Shamanistic Rituals*, New York: Mouton.

Levinas, E. (1989) 'Martin Buber and the Theory of Knowledge', in S. Hand (ed.) *The Levinas Reader*, Oxford: Blackwell.

Lévi-Strauss, C. (1963) *Structural Anthropology*, trans. C. Jacobson and B. Grundfest Schoepf, New York: Basic Books.

Lim, A. (1998) 'Road Far-travelled Is Now an Essential', *The Australian*, 9 January: 18.

Lingis, A. (1994) *Foreign Bodies*, New York: Routledge.

Ly Singko (1979) *The Fall of Madame Mao*, New York: Vantage.

MacAloon, J.J. (1984) 'Olympic Games and the Theory of Spectacle in Modern Societies', in J.J. MacAloon (ed.) *Rite, Drama, Festival, Spectacle: Rehearsals toward a Theory of Cultural Performance*, Philadelphia, PA: Institute for the Study of Human Issues.

McClintock, A. (1995) *Imperial Leather: Race, Gender and Sexuality in the Colonial Contest*, London and New York: Routledge.

Malin, A. (1994) 'Mother Who Won't Disappear', *Human Rights Quarterly* 16, 1: 187–213.

Market Equity SA and Economic Research Consultants (1996) *1996 Adelaide Festival: An Economic Impact Study*, Adelaide: Market Equity SA and Economic Research Consultants.

Marlowe, L. (1997) 'Police Seize Lawyer for the "Disappeared" in Algeria', *The Irish Times on the Web*, 21 October. Online. Available HTTP: http://www.irish-times.com/irish-times/paper/1997/1021/fro2.html (21 October).

Marranca, B. (1996) *Ecologies of Theater: Essays at the Century Turning*, Baltimore, MD, and London: Johns Hopkins University Press.

*Masterkey* (1998) Directed by M. Moore, Perth and Adelaide Festivals, February and March.

Matsui Sumako (1912) 'Problems on Stage', trans. J. McGrory, *Seito*, January: 162–3.

Meggitt, M.J. (1965) *Desert People: A Study of the Walbiri Aborigines of Central Australia*, Chicago, IL, and London: University of Chicago Press.

Merleau-Ponty, M. (1968) *The Visible and the Invisible*, trans. A. Lingis, Evanston, IL: Northwestern University Press.

—— (1986) *Phenomenology of Perception*, trans. C. Smith, London: Routledge.

Mernessi, F. (1996) *Women's Rebellion and Islamic Memory*, London: Zed Books.

Mhlope, G., Vanrenen, M., and Mtshali, T. (1988) *Have You Seen Zandile?*, Braamfontein: Skotaville.

'Midori' (1912) 'A Doll's House', *Seito*, January: 118–25.

Migration Information Programme (1995) *Trafficking and Prostitution: The Growing Exploitation of Migrant Women from Central and Eastern Europe*, Budapest: Migration Information Programme. Online. Available HTTP: http://www.iom.ch/doc/MIP_TRAFWMN (4 February 1997).

Mills, J. (1994) Presentation, New Storytellers Panel, International Women Playwrights' Conference, Adelaide, Australia.

Min, X. (1962) 'The Stage Performance of *Nora* and Others', *Wen Hui Bao*, 16 February: n.p.

Mir-Hosseini, Z. (1993) 'Women, Marriage, and the Law in Post-Revolutionary Iran', in H. Afshar (ed.) *Women in the Middle East*, Hampshire and London: Macmillan.

Mohanty, C.T. (1991a) 'Cartographies of Struggle: Third World Women and the Politics of Feminism', in C.T. Mohanty, A. Russo, and L. Torres (eds) *Third World Women and the Politics of Feminism*, Bloomington, IN: Indiana University Press.

—— (1991b) 'Under Western Eyes: Feminist Scholarship and Colonial Discourses', in C.T. Mohanty, A. Russo, and L. Torres (eds) *Third World Women and the Politics of Feminism*, Bloomington, IN: Indiana University Press.

Moore, M. (1997) Personal correspondence with M. Aoki, 15 December.

Myerhoff, B.G. (1984) 'A Death in Time: Construction of Self and Culture in Ritual Drama', in J.J. MacAloon (ed.) *Rite, Drama, Festival, Spectacle: Rehearsals toward a Theory of Cultural Performance*, Philadelphia, PA: Institute for the Study of Human Issues.

Nakamura, T. (1985) 'Three *A Doll's House* in Japan', *Edda: Scandinavian Journal of Literary Research* 73, 3: 163–71.

Napangardi, M. (1998) Interview with authors in Warlpiri with Elizabeth Ross Nungarrayi translating, 2 August, Lajamanu, NT, Australia.

Nead, L. (1992) *The Female Nude: Art, Obscenity, and Sexuality*, London and New York: Routledge.

Nelson Nakamarra, L. (1998) Interview with authors in Warlpiri with Elizabeth Ross Nungarrayi translating, 2 August, Lajamanu, NT, Australia.

Nelson Napurrurla, J. (1998) Interview with authors in Warlpiri with Lee Cataldi translating, 3 August, Lajamanu and Yuendumu, NT, Australia.

Niranjana, T., Sudhir, P., and Dhareshwar, V. (1993) Introduction, in T. Niranjana, P. Sudhir, and V. Dhareshwar (eds) *Interrogating Modernity: Cultural and Colonialism in India*, Calcutta: Seagull.

Nolte, S.H. and Hastings, S.A. (1991) 'The Meiji State's Policy toward Women, 1890–1910', in G.L. Berstein (ed.) *Recreating Japanese Women, 1600–1945*, Los Angeles, CA: University of California Press.

Olaniyan, T. (1995) *Scars of Conquest/Masks of Resistance: The Invention of Cultural Identities in African, African-American, and Caribbean Drama*, New York and Oxford: Oxford University Press.

Oldfield Napaljarri, R. (1998) Interview with authors in Warlpiri with Lee Cataldi translating, 2 and 6 August, Yuendumu, NT, Australia.

Organisation for Human Rights and Fundamental Freedoms for Iran (1997) 'Hope Betrayed: Women of Iran'. Online. Available HTTP: http://www.iranffo.org/women.html (7 August).

Ortiz, A.D. (1995) 'The Mothers of the Plaza de Mayo', *UNESCO Courier*, September: 22–4.

Ortolani, B. (1990) *The Japanese Theatre: From Shamanistic Ritual to Contemporary Pluralism*, New Haven, NJ: Princeton University Press.

Out There News (1997) *Political Islam World Guide: Algeria*. Online. Available HTTP: http://www.megastories.com/islam/world/algeria.htm (30 October).

Pavis, P. (1992) *Theatre at the Crossroads of Culture,* London: Routledge.

—— (ed.) (1996a) *The Intercultural Performance Reader,* London: Routledge.

—— (1996b) 'Introduction: Towards a Theory of Interculturalism in Theatre?', in P. Pavis (ed.) *The Intercultural Performance Reader*, London: Routledge.

Pelletier, P. (1998) Interview with authors, 3 June, Montréal, Canada.

*Philippine Daily Inquirer* (1997) 'Drop noted in Number of Filippino "Japayuki"', 16 February: 13.

Philp, R. (1986) 'Kazuo Ohno: Out of Darkness – Butoh, Part 1', *Dancemagazine*, April: 60–3.

Plane, T. (1997) 'Arts Bullies Bulldoze the True Believers', *The Australian*, 15 September: 13.

Porter, K. (1996) 'Titillated and Teased for Shock Value', *The Advertiser*, 13 March: 5.

Poulson Napurrurla, P. (1998) Interview with authors in Warlpiri with Lee Cataldi translating, 2 August, Lajamanu and Yuendumu, NT, Australia. Wendy Nungarrayi and Jorna Nelson Napurrurla joined the end of the interview.

Pratt, M.B. (1984) 'Identity: Skin, Blood, Heart', in E. Bulkin, M.B. Pratt, and B. Smith, *Yours in Struggle: Three Feminist Perspectives on Anti-Semitism and Racism*, New York: Long Haul.

Reinelt, J.G. (1992) Introduction, in J.G. Reinelt and J.R. Roach (eds) *Critical Theory and Performance*, Ann Arbor, MI: University of Michigan Press.

Robertson, J. (1998) *Takarazuka: Sexual Politics and Popular Culture in Modern Japan*, Los Angeles, CA: University of California Press.

Rockman Napaljarri, P. and Cataldi, L. (1994) *Yimikirli: Warlpiri Dreamings and Histories*, San Francisco, CA: HarperCollins.

Rodd, L.R. (1991) 'Yosana Akiko and the Taisho Debate over the "New Woman"', in G.L. Bernstein (ed.) *Recreating Japanese Women, 1600–1945*, Los Angeles, CA: University of California Press.

Ross Napaljarri, K. (1998) Interview with authors in Warlpiri with Lee Cataldi translating, 7 August, Yuendumu, NT, Australia.

Rubin, D. (1997) *The World Encyclopedia of Contemporary Theatre*, vol. 3, New York and London: Routledge.

*Salt Fire Water* (1994) By Top End Girls. Directed by V. Gillot, Adelaide, 7 July.

*Sara* (1993) Video recording, directed D. Mehrjui, produced H. Seifi and D. Mehrjui. Tehran, Iran: Farabi Cinema Foundation.

Sarumpaet, R. (1995) 'New Stories from Old', *Australian Feminist Studies* 21: 58–61.

Sato, T. (1981) 'Ibsen's Drama and the Japanese Bluestockings', *Edda: Scandinavian Journal of Literary Research* 5: 265–93.

Schirmer, J.G. (1989) '"Those Who Die for Life Cannot Be Called Dead": Women and Human Rights Protest in Latin America', *Feminist Review* 32: 3–29.

Schneider, R. (1997) *The Explicit Body in Performance*, London and New York: Routledge.

Scobie, I. (1998) Interview with authors, 9 January, Adelaide, Australia.

Scolnicov, H. (1994) *Women's Theatrical Space*, New York: Cambridge University Press.

Sears, D. (1990) *Afrika Solo*, Toronto: Sister Vision.

*Seito* (1912) 'What We as Women Can Learn from *A Doll's House*', editorial, January: 62–114.

Shaaban, B. (1988) *Both Right and Left Handed: Arab Women Talk about Their Lives*, London: Women's Press.

Shahidian, H. (1997) 'Women and Clandestine Politics in Iran, 1970–1985', *Feminist Studies* 23, 1: 7–42.

Soja, E. (1989) *Postmodern Geographies: The Reassertion of Space in Critical Social Theory*, London and New York: Verso.

Sophocles (1947) *The Theban Plays: King Oedipus, Oedipus at Colonus, Antigone*, trans. E.F. Watling, London: Penguin.

Starick, P. (1996) 'Annie's Sex Show-and-Tell', *The Advertiser*, 11 March: 3.

Steiner, G. (1984) *Antigones*, Oxford: Clarendon Press.

Strickland, K. (1998) 'Sponsors Perfect the Fine Arts of Schmooze', *The Australian*, 14 April: 6.

Subasinghe, S. (1997) 'Antigone in Sri Lanka: An Interview with Phyllis Jane Rose', in J. Tompkins and J. Holledge (eds) *Performing Women/ Performing Feminisms: Interviews with International Women Playwrights*, St Lucia, Qld.: Australasian Drama Studies Association Academic Publications.

Suh Kwang Seok (1997) Interview with authors, 14 September, Seoul, South Korea.

Sunder Rajan, R. (1993) *Real and Imagined Women: Gender, Culture, and Postcolonialism*, London and New York: Routledge.

Swain, T. (1993) *A Place for Strangers: Towards a History of Australian Aboriginal Being*, Melbourne: Cambridge University Press.

Takai, T. (1998) Interview with authors, 25 September, Adelaide, Australia.

Taussig, M. (1987) *Shamanism, Colonialism, and the Wild Man: A Study in Terror and Healing*, Chicago, IL: Chicago University Press.

Taylor, D. (1992) 'Violent Displays: Griselda Gambaro and Argentina's Drama of Disappearance', in M. Feitlowitz (ed.) *Information for Foreigners: Three Plays by Griselda Gambaro*, Evanston, IL: Northwestern University Press.

—— (1997) *Disappearing Acts: Spectacles of Gender and Nationalism in Argentina's 'Dirty War'*, Durham, NC: Duke University Press.

Templeton, J. (1997) *Ibsen's Women*, Cambridge: Cambridge University Press.

Terrill, R. (1984) *The White Boned Demon: A Biography of Madame Mao Zedong*, London: Heinemann.

Therborn, G. (1995) 'Routes To/Through Modernity', in M. Featherstone, S. Lash, and R. Robertson (eds) *Global Modernities*, London: Sage.

Third Australian Performing Arts Market (1998) *The Australia Council's Third Australian Performing Arts Market: The Guide*, Adelaide: the Market.

Third International Women Playwrights' Conference (3IWPC) (1994a) *Conference Programme*, Adelaide: the Conference.

—— (1994b) *International Women Playwrights' Conference*, archival material, no. SRG 530, Mortlock Library, State Library of South Australia, Australia.

—— (1994c) 'New Stories from Old: Transcript of Proceedings of Third International Women Playwrights' Conference, 7 July 1994', Adelaide: Auscript.

Third International Women Playwrights' Conference (3IWPC) (1994d) 'Storytelling: Transcript of Proceedings of Third International Women Playwrights' Conference, 5 July 1994', Adelaide: Auscript.

Tierney-Tello, M. (1996) *Allegories of Transgression and Transformation: Experimental Fiction by Women Writing under Dictatorship*, Albany, NY: State University of New York Press.

Tohidi, N. (1991) 'Gender and Islamic Fundamentalism: Feminist Politics in Iran', in C. Talpade Mohanty, A. Russo, and L. Torres (eds) *Third World Women and the Politics of Feminism*, Bloomington and Indianapolis, IN: Indiana University Press.

Tolentino, R. (1996) 'Bodies, Letters, Catalogs: Filippinas in Transnational Space', *Social Text* 14, 3: 49–76.

Tung, C. (1995) 'Why Doesn't the Chinese Nora Leave Her Husband?: Women's Emancipation in Post-1949 Chinese Drama', *Modern Drama* 38: 298–307.

Turner, V. (1982) *From Ritual to Theatre: The Human Seriousness of Play*, New York: PAJ Publications.

Vasseleu, C. (1998) *Textures of Light: Vision and Touch in Irigaray, Levinas, and Merleau-Ponty*, London and New York: Routledge.

Viala, J. and Masson-Sekine, N. (1988) *Butoh – Shades of Darkness*, Tokyo: Shufunotomo Co.

Villeneuve, R. (1992) 'The Concordance of Body and Meaning', *Assaph: Studies in Theatre* 8: 113–26.

Vitebsky, P. (1995) 'From Cosmology to Environmentalism: Shamanism as Local Knowledge in a Global Setting', in R. Fardon (ed.) *Counterworks: Managing the Diversity of Knowledge*, London and New York: Routledge.

Waterstradt, J.A. (1979) 'Making the World a Home: The Family Portrait in Drama', *Brigham Young University Studies* 19: 501–21.

Weiskel, T. (1976) *The Romantic Sublime: Studies in the Structure and Psychology of Transcendence*, Baltimore, MD: Johns Hopkins University Press.

Wilentz, G. (1992) *Binding Cultures: Black Women Writers in Africa and the Diaspora*, Bloomington and Indianapolis, IN: Indiana University Press.

Willett, J. (ed.) (1978) *Brecht on Theatre*, New York: Hill & Wang.

Williams, D. (1991) 'Theatre of Innocence and of Experience: Peter Brook's International Centre: An Introduction', in D. Williams (ed.) *Peter Brook and The Mahabharata: Critical Perspectives*, London and New York: Routledge.

—— (1996) '"Remembering the Others That Are Us": Transculturalism and Myth in the Theatre of Peter Brook', in P. Pavis (ed.) *The Intercultural Performance Reader*, London and New York: Routledge.

Williams, N. (1996) 'What Women Think of Annie's Antics', *The Advertiser*, 13 March: 5.

Williams, N. and Fox, C. (1996) 'Sprinkle Sex Show in Theatre Booking Row', *The Advertiser*, 15 March: 15.

Witke, R. (1977) *Comrade Chiang Ching*, Toronto: Little, Brown.

Wu, X. (1956) 'Before the Performance of *Nora*', *People's Daily*, 28 July: n.p.

Yan, H. (1992) 'Modern Chinese Drama and Its Western Models: A Critical Reconstruction of Chinese Subjectivity', *Modern Drama* 35: 54–64.

Young, R. (1995) *Colonial Desire: Hybridity in Theory, Culture, and Race*, London: Routledge.

Yu, C. and Guisso, R. (eds) (1988) *Shamanism*, Berkeley, CA: Asian Humanities Press.

Zarrilli, P. (1992) 'For Whom is the King a King? Issues of Intercultural Production, Perception, and Reception in a Kathakali *King Lear*', in J.G. Reinelt and J.R. Roach (eds) *Critical Theory and Performance*, Ann Arbor, MI: University of Michigan Press.

Zhao Dan (1980) *Diyu Zhi Men* [Gate of Hell], Shanghai: Literature and Art Publishing House.

# Index